Halting the Hacker

A Practical Guide to Computer Security

Second Edition

ISBN 0-13-046416-3

90000

9 790130 464162

Hewlett-Packard® Professional Books

HP-UX

Fernandez	Configuring CDE: The Common Desktop Environment
Madell	Disk and File Management Tasks on HP-UX
Olker	Optimizing NFS Performance: Tuning and Troubleshooting NFS on HP-UX Systems
Poniatowski	HP-UX 10.X System Administration "How To" Book
Poniatowski	HP-UX 11i Virtual Partitions
Poniatowski	HP-UX 11i System Administration Handbook and Toolkit
Poniatowski	The HP-UX 11.x System Administration Handbook and Toolkit
Poniatowski	HP-UX 11.x System Administration "How To" Book
Poniatowski	HP-UX System Administration Handbook and Toolkit
Poniatowski	Learning the HP-UX Operating System
Rehman	HP Certified: HP-UX System Administration
Sauers/Weygant	HP-UX Tuning and Performance: Concepts, Tools, and Methods
Weygant	Clusters for High Availability: A Primer of HP-UX Solutions, Second Edition
Wong	HP-UX 11i Security

UNIX, LINUX, WINDOWS, AND MPE I/X

Diercks	MPE i/X System Administration Handbook
Mosberger	IA-64 Linux Kernel
Poniatowski	UNIX User's Handbook
Poniatowski	UNIX User's Handbook, Second Edition
Roberts	UNIX and Windows 2000 Interoperability Guide
Stone/Symons	UNIX Fault Management

COMPUTER ARCHITECTURE

Kane	PA-RISC 2.0 Architecture
Markstein	IA-64 and Elementary Functions

NETWORKING/COMMUNICATIONS

Blommers	Architecting Enterprise Solutions with UNIX Networking
Blommers	OpenView Network Node Manager
Blommers	Practical Planning for Network Growth
Brans	Mobilize Your Enterprise
Cook	Building Enterprise Information Architecture: Reengineering Information Systems
Lucke	Designing and Implementing Computer Workgroups
Lund	Integrating UNIX and PC Network Operating Systems

SECURITY

Bruce	Security in Distributed Computing: Did You Lock the Door?
Pearson et al.	Trusted Computing Platforms: TCPA Technology in Context
Pipkin	Halting the Hacker, Second Edition
Pipkin	Information Security

Halting the Hacker

A Practical Guide to Computer Security
Second Edition

Donald L. Pipkin

Hewlett-Packard Company

www.hp.com/hpbooks

Prentice Hall PTR
Upper Saddle River, New Jersey 07458
www.phptr.com

Library of Congress Cataloging-in-Publication Data

Pipkin, Donald L.
    Halting the hacker : a practical guide to computer security / Donald L. Pipkin.--2nd ed.
       p. cm. -- (Hewlett-Packard professional books)
    Includes index.
    ISBN 0-13-046416-3
     1. Computer security. 2. UNIX (Computer file) I. Title. II. Series.
    QA76.9.A25 P56 2002
    005.8--dc21   2002029250

Editorial/production supervision: *Patti Guerrieri*
Composition: *Donald L. Pipkin*
Cover design director: *Jerry Votta*
Cover design: *Nina Scuderi*
Manufacturing buyer: *Maura Zaldivar*
Acquisitions editor: *Jill Harry*
Editorial assistant: *Kate Wolf*
Marketing manager: *Dan DePasquale*
Publisher, Hewlett-Packard Books: *Patricia Pekary*

Published by Pearson Education
Publishing as Prentice Hall PTR
Upper Saddle River, New Jersey 07458

Prentice Hall books are widely used by corporations and government agencies for training, marketing, and resale. For information regarding corporate and government bulk discounts, please contact: Corporate and Government Sales (800) 382-3419 or corpsales@pearsontechgroup.com.

Printed in the United States of America

10 9 8 7 6 5 4 3 2

ISBN   0-13-046416-3

Pearson Education LTD.
Pearson Education Australia PTY, Limited
Pearson Education Singapore, Pte. Ltd.
Pearson Education North Asia Ltd.
Pearson Education Canada, Ltd.
Pearson Educación de Mexico, S.A. de C.V.
Pearson Education — Japan
Pearson Education Malaysia, Pte. Ltd.

For my children.

May your love of learning last a lifetime.

Contents

Foreword

Just a few short years ago few people cared about computer security. This topic was only relevant to academics, financial institutions, and secret government agencies. Today, around the world, the general public is familiar with computer security. They are especially cognizant of computer viruses, privacy of personal information available online, and trust associated with interactions conducted over the Internet.

The global economy has become increasingly reliant on computers and the Internet. Hence, the security, trust, and privacy of these systems are paramount. Attacks, whether from teenaged hackers or determined terrorists, can lead to disclosure of sensitive information, major system disruptions, and chaos on the Internet. It is, therefore, more important than ever that people understand, from both a business and technical perspective, how to minimize risk and protect critical infrastructure, systems, applications, and data.

Organizations must perform an assessment to understand the threats that they face, the probability of the threat occurring, and the degree of damage that would result if the threat were exploited. Risk is rarely eliminated; rather it must be managed such that an acceptable level of risk is achieved. Connectivity to the Internet provides individuals and businesses a great deal of benefit. It also exposes them to a substantial amount of risk. Some threats are overlooked because they are not obvious. However, in the mistaken belief that they will not be affected people often ignore clearly identified, serious threats.

Don Pipkin's many years of hands-on experience in the field of computer security allows him to explore computing environments through the "eyes of the hackers." This perspective helps the reader to understand the threats they face from hackers and what constitutes a "good target" for a hacker. *Halting the Hacker* is interspersed with examples of true hacker exploits, which serve as both interesting reading and proof that these threats are not just theoretical. While this information is entertaining and informative, it is the author's description of how to counteract these threats that is of greatest importance. Putting this knowledge into practice can significantly reduce your risk of being a target. Further, this book provides valuable guidance to prepare you in the event that a hacker attacks your systems.

This second edition has been expanded to include many exploits that have occurred over the past few years. It is a valuable resource for audiences ranging from the novice to the experienced security professional. Likewise, *Halting the Hacker* delivers useful information for both technical and non-technical audiences.

The public's awareness of security has been greatly heightened by the tragic events of September 11, 2001. The dependence of our society on technology makes it clear that we must improve our computing infrastructure and reduce many risks that have been ignored to this point. Failure to do so could result in significant disruption of business, and would not even require a perpetrator to step on the soil of the country that is being attacked. It is more important than ever that the appropriate level of due diligence be performed to secure the worlds computing infrastructure. Following the guidance that is provided in *Halting the Hacker* is a significant step toward achieving this goal.

Craig Rubin
Information Security Architect
Internet Security Solutions Lab
Hewlett-Packard Company

Foreword

Information is today's most important commodity. Protecting that information from unauthorized access and/or modification is what information security professionals constantly try to do. The objective: Keep your information protected as long as it has value!

Have you ever wondered about the vulnerability of your information systems to hackers? Knowing the enemy is the best way to defeat him! *Halting the Hacker* looks at information systems from the perspective of hackers. It describes how they gain access to information, with many excellent examples of how information has been compromised, and what can be done to prevent similar losses.

An ounce of prevention is still worth a pound of cure. Viewing information systems from a hacker's perspective exposes the motives behind the threats and allows the information security professional to protect his systems before he becomes a victim. What actions to take, and how and when to take them, are key components of the ounce of prevention.

Halting the Hacker describes what actions to take to protect information systems, from access control and authentication to detecting break-ins — and what to do if a break-in does occur.

This book describes how to implement strong security mechanisms to protect your information systems. It outlines the hacker's objectives and then gives details on how to counter those objectives.

The book describes when to implement security mechanisms. It takes you from installation and security education through security policy reviews within an organization.

Halting the Hacker is written by a security professional who's made his career in security consulting and helping to prevent hackers from gaining unauthorized access to valuable information. The author has seen all types of hackers — young, old, insiders, outsiders, professionals, and amateurs from home and abroad. We can now learn from those experiences and gain the advantage in protecting valuable information by "halting the hacker!"

Jim Schindler
Information Security Program Manager
Hewlett-Packard

Preface

Never in the history of computing has there been such a great opportunity for hackers. Falling prices and the increasing performance of computer equipment have made it possible for any hacker to afford a powerful computer system of his own. Inexpensive high-speed Internet access is available almost everywhere. Hacker tools have become widely available and easy to use, making anyone able to be a hacker.

At the same time, business are making dramatic changes in the way they use their information systems. Companies are downsizing from proprietary mainframes to open systems, there is a tremendous demand for the information on office PCs to be shared around the globe, and businesses are flocking to the Internet to provide new avenues for customers, enable remote mobile or work-from-home employees, and replace dedicated private networks with cheap virtual private networks. International networking, with the increasing number of computers and growing connectivity, has provided an ease of access to computers heretofore unknown.

Financial pressures are pushing companies to explore new opportunities. Companies are outsourcing operations. They are entering into new business arrangements with partners that require greater sharing of information with remote individuals who are not employees. These new environments are uncharted territories for many of the companies who are leaping online. Companies, administrators, and users are all having to change their understanding of their computational environment. There are new rules for using, managing, and evaluating this new environment. Reduction in staff has been made to contain costs, and has led to many systems with inexperienced managers, responsible for a greater number of systems with operating systems with which they are unfamiliar. The combination of ease of access with overworked and inexperienced system managers is a potentially explosive one.

Many companies are moving to UNIX® system-based operating systems — some because of mainframe downsizing, others because Linux is free, and others because they are tired of the alternatives. The more widespread an operating system, the more attractive it will be for hackers to attack. UNIX systems have traditionally been used by universities and research facilities. Since it is common in research and scientific areas, there is an abundance of information about the operating system. Also, universities and scientific research institutes are often more lax with security, providing a fruitful playground for hackers to learn and hack. UNIX operating systems are some of the most documented operating systems, and versions of the source code are widely available, making it a common target of hackers today.

In the computer industry, security has mostly been an afterthought. It is often thought that putting security into programs that don't demand it will only get in the way. Most software systems have evolved from older systems and quite often large software systems actually incorporate code from many sources, written by many authors. When you have software that does not have a single design, it is almost impossible to design security into it after the fact.

Computer security is part of the larger field of corporate information security and has a significant effect on system availability. Data security encompasses all aspects of management of proprietary information, including information classification, ownership, appropriate access, use, handling, and storage.

Vendors in the computer industry have spent a good deal of time and money addressing the other areas of data security and system availability. Most corporations have a disaster plan in place that has detailed contingency plans that cover fire, flood, and earthquake, but rarely do they cover security-based disasters. Even though only a small percentage of corporate losses is from this threat, a tremendous amount of money and resources is spent each year to reduce the losses from physical disasters. However, few company disaster plans cover contingencies for the losses due to computer security incidents, which are often the result of malicious activities, with the greatest share of these being the actions of disgruntled or dishonest employees, the rest being the result of outside threats. These outside threats account for only a tiny percentage of corporate losses. However, this tiny percentage gets the lion's share of the publicity. It can be much more damaging to the company's reputation than the actual damage it may cause to the data it compromises.

The tragic events of September 11th have changed forever the way the world looks at security. Companies are putting security at the top of their lists — as a concern, as an issue needing to be addressed, and as a budget item. The question "What about security?" is being asked at the beginning of a project with the requirement that it be addressed. Security is no longer an afterthought — it is now being seen as the fundamental foundation for every project.

When the first edition of this book was originally conceived in the mid-nineties, it was very difficult to get information on how information systems were compromised. It was equally difficult to get a book published that described the process by which systems were compromised. Even though it was written to raise the awareness of system administrators that there were security issues which had to be addressed to avoid being attacked, there was fear that such a book would be used by hackers to attack systems. There is a thin line between informing system managers and providing a guidebook for hackers. It is unavoidable that some will utilize this book to attempt to hack into systems. Today, security information is a much more open topic. Everyone is aware of hackers. The headlines are full of hacker stories.

This book is designed to give system and security managers insight into the mind of a hacker and to provide tools to fight both existing and yet-to-come system attacks. You will see that even seemingly harmless services can become valuable tools in the hands of a skilled hacker who uses them to search for weak points in a system. The information here is broadly available to those who know where to look for it. Unfortunately, all too often it is the hacker who knows where to look and those responsible for computer security who do not. System managers generally do not have the time or inclination to peruse the dark corners of the Internet for hacking information and tools, and certainly they are not going to cruise the bulletin boards that are frequented by hackers.

This book is written with a dual viewpoint. We look through the eyes of a potential intruder and expose cracks in systems that can be widened to gain access or privileges, and we also take the system manager's viewpoint and explore methods of sealing those cracks. This dual viewpoint allows you to understand how a hacker thinks so you can block the intruder. It is organized by the processes hackers use to gain access, privileges, and control of a computer system, instead of simply illustrating how to secure each software subsystem. This helps you understand how the different subsystems can be used in harmony to attack a computer, and how the changes you make in one system can affect another and leave you without a secure computer system. This book explains why and how a problem can be leveraged into a security breach and discusses how to fix it. Understanding the *why* of a problem is a skill you can use throughout your career.

This edition of the book details building and securing a UNIX system, with specifics for HP-UX® and Red Hat® Linux® systems.

This book puts the hacker under the microscope to bring to light the common motives and basic methods that are used. In so doing it gives you, the system manager, the knowledge to apply security effort efficiently and effectively to secure systems now and into the future.

About the Author

Donald L. Pipkin, CISSP, is an Information Security Architect for the Internet Security Division of Hewlett-Packard. He is an internationally renowned security expert with fifteen-plus years of experience in the industry. He is a frequent speaker on security and is the author of the new book *Information Security: Protecting the Global Enterprise.* He is versed in all aspects of security, including policy and procedures, and has hands-on experience with computer intrusions. He has made presentations on security at various conferences from a regional to the international level. His years of experience have allowed him to bring his understanding of security issues and his experiences with computer crime to bear when consulting with Fortune 500 companies on issues of policies and procedures addressing specific security issues.

Acknowledgments

I would like to thank everyone who supplied feedback on the first edition and the educators who have used my book in their classrooms and provided direction for this edition. I would especially like to thank those who have assisted me in the creation of this book, in particular, Chris Cooper, Gary LaBeau, Ken Privette, and Craig Rubin, whose reviews provided invaluable suggestions for improvement.

Most of all I would like to thank my wife and children, who sacrificed their time with me so I could produce this book.

Donald L. Pipkin, CISSP

## PART I

Understanding Hackers

It is important to understand your adversary. With understanding comes the ability to anticipate behavior and motivation, which is required to be able effectively detour attacks. People who compromise information systems cover a broad range of people with diverse motives and varied skill levels. To understand the hacker who is likely to attack your systems, you need to understand what it is that makes you a target. The systems might be targeted because of the information that they contain or some specific resources to which they have access, or their ability to be compromised. The reason for an attack can be financial, political, personal, or merely convenience due to location or ease of access. The attacks can be simple scripted attacks or they can be well-thought-out and orchestrated. They can be hit-and-run or ongoing. This extreme diversity in attacks and attackers increases the need for system administrators to have a general understanding of the hacking environment.

The Hacking Environment

A serious hacker must have a computer, network connectivity, and time to hack. The hacker will generally use a Linux computer, high-speed networking, and be a student or someone with plenty of discretionary time at work. This describes the environment at universities, which have been a popular location of hackers. Students have access to powerful computers which are attached to high-speed networks and they have plenty of time on their hands. However, each of these attributes is becoming more available at home every day, home computers are now very fast and very cheap, and always-on high-speed networking has reached the home via DSL and cable networks.

Linux is the operating system of choice among hackers. It has the ability to run the greatest variety of tools and the flexibility to control all aspects of the system. Having his own computer allows the hacker to be a peer to the system that he is attacking, not just a client. With a system of his own, he is in control of the permissions and privileges, so he can appear as anyone he wants to on an outside system. This also gives him experience at managing and securing a system, and therefore insight into his opponent, the system manager. He will need to manage his system and secure it from outside attack so he will know if someone is probing his system. If he is found out, it is likely that a system manager will be trying to identify his system's attacker.

The more network bandwidth the hacker has, the more scans, probes, and attacks he can perform. Bandwidth is generally the limiting factor to accessing remote systems.

Historic Perspective

There have been hackers for as long as there have been computer systems. Early on, hackers were students wanting access to more computer resources than they were allocated. So they would find ways to get those unauthorized resources. They might "find" another account to use to run programs or store file, or they might hack the accounting software so it didn't charge them for the resources they used. Computers were new to everyone, including instructors, so the inventiveness and ingenuity of these hacks received more focus than the infractions of misappropriation of resources. These hacks, even though they may be viewed as minor infractions, are still theft.

Over time, with the proliferation of computers, the number, variety, and severity of computer crimes have increased. Today, the diversity of computer criminals who are identified as hackers is astounding. When hacking was new, hackers were mostly students who had access to systems. This group of hackers is still a large demographic, but it has been joined by professionals with criminal motives.

Today the term "hacking" is used routinely to mean intruding into computer systems by stealth and without permission or any crime committed with, by, through, or against a computer. Computer crime dates back to the early 1970s, when employees discovered ways to use the computer to embezzle from their employers by falsifying sales records. The losses due to these hackers ran into the millions of dollars.

This book does not differentiate based on the intent of the hacker. The actual intent of the hacker is not the issue. Anyone who enters an information system without permission is committing a crime which has the possibility of causing damage. He or she will cost the owners of the systems time and money as they investigate the incident and determine what has been done and if there has been any damage. Damage, whether accidental or intentional, will have to be repaired and the impact to the business evaluated. The method of intrusion will have to be determined and repaired to eliminate recurrence.

Hacker or Cracker

Today, there is a debate about the term hacker. Those who oppose the use of the word to describe computer criminals indicate that its original use was to describe someone who could rapidly hack out a piece of code that will do what is necessary. The code was written quickly, without benefit of design and concern for maintainability. The hacker's ability to understand the system seemed to come intuitively. Hacking signified the unfettered exploration of computer systems for the sake of the intellectual challenge. The term hacker changed to a more mystical meaning: one who is a computer wizard, able to make systems do anything he wished, while the popular use of the word continues to focus on those who had started exploring the ARPAnet — the predecessor of today's Internet. These hackers were often accessing systems and information on systems which were far away from where they were and without permission. Those who have idolized the hacker as the elite computer enthusiast are offended by the popular use of the term and have invented the term *cracker* to indicate one who cracks into systems or is in any way criminal in his or her hacking activities.

Emmanuel Goldstein, the editor of *2600* magazine, had this to say on the subject: "Now, we have a small but vocal group who insist on calling anyone they deem unacceptable in the hacker world a "cracker." This is an attempt to solve the problem of the misuse of the word "hacker" by simply misusing a new word. It's a very misguided, though well-intentioned, effort." [1]

However, much of what is known about early hacks are stories which have been handed down through the hacker community, which would have a tendency to glorify the hacker and vilify any organization which wanted to stop him or her. This small but vocal group which wants to "preserve" the term hacker has had little support. The popular media continue to use the term hacker to identify computer criminals, as do the criminals themselves.

Self-Identification

Possibly the most important input to the debate on use of the term hacker comes from those who access systems and information without permission. They identify themselves as hackers. They use the term to identify the skill and prowess which they display. Nobody who hacks into systems willingly describes himself as a "computer intruder," "cracker," or "computer vandal." These terms have been invented by people who consider themselves hackers in the classic sense, and who fiercely and publicly resist any besmirching of the "noble" title of hacker. Naturally and understandably, they deeply resent the attack on their values implicit in using the word "hacker" as a synonym for computer criminal. But none of the terms has caught on. The only term that has received some acceptance is "cyberpunk" — although not in the mainstream media.

---

[1] "Q&A with Emmanuel Goldstein of 2600: The Hacker's Quarterly," *CNN Online*, April 1999.

## CHAPTER 1

Who Hackers Are

The popular image of a hacker is reflective of the movie *WarGames*: a young boy sitting in front of his TRS-80®, illuminated only by the glow of the screen. His computer has dialed every number in a phone exchange during the day while he was at school, and now he is exploring the treasures that have been collected. Trying simple passwords on system after system, dialing and dialing....

Of course, this description of a hacker is too narrow. Today, hackers are much more likely to be adults, with sophisticated tools and specific goals. Their backgrounds are diverse and their computer skills range from being a novice to an expert.

Internal Hackers

Attacks from the inside are the most common attack which causes financial loss. The internal hacker is someone who has valid access to a system but decides for whatever reason to perform unauthorized acts. This is often a disgruntled or dishonest employee. This is the type of hacker who can cause the most damage to a company's computers and data.

Internal hackers should be the information security officer's number one concern. They have both access to and knowledge of the organization's computing resources. The motives of in-house hackers will vary, but generally they are either trying to profit from their actions or seeking revenge on the company or an individual. The methods used to gain profit from hacking can range from directly manipulating financial information to selling information to competitors or convincing the company to pay the hacker as a consultant to repair the system he has destroyed. Attacks to seek revenge can take almost any form, depending on what the hacker thinks will damage the company or individual the most.

Disgruntled Employee

Disgruntled employees are the most dangerous type of hacker. This person may be anyone from an end user, who has access to the company's data, to a system programmer, who knows the system inside and out and has the ability to turn the system upside down. Disgruntled employees will not be stopped because the effort outweighs the value of the information. Often their goal is much more personal than financial.

Their intimate knowledge of the inner workings of the organization will be used to cause the most damage possible. They may understand how to go unnoticed and avoid being caught. Often internal hackers already have been given privileges which they will abuse to attack the system.

> Patrick McKenna hacked into his former employer's computer server on two occasions over the Internet. On these occasions he deleted approximately 675 computer files, modified computer user accounts, altered billing records and transmitted e-mails, which purported to have originated from an authorized representative of the victim corporation, to over one hundred clients. Those e-mails contained false statements about business activities of the corporation.
>
> McKenna was convicted for "unauthorized computer intrusion" and sentenced to serve six months in federal prison and ordered to pay $13,614.11 in restitution for the damage he caused. [2]

Contracted Employee

Today, many positions within a company are outsourced to contractors or consultants. These people have a different relationship with the company from its employees and therefore need different controls.

Definitions of appropriate behavior and the scope of their duties should be made contractually. Contractors are not bound by employee policies and procedures. The contract with the contractor defines what he/she can and cannot do.

Contracted employees are often granted access to systems like regular employees, but they often lack the commitment to the employer. They may find that hacking a system is a way to make a fast buck, or they may be unhappy with their job and just want to cause trouble. They are also targets of competitors who want to gather internal company information. Sometimes, just being refused a raise is enough to set them off.

> A former subcontractor named Robert M. Abarbanel had worked for several years as an instructor for Dan Keller Technical Ser-

---

[2]   "Major Investigations: Patrick McKenna," *National Infrastructure Protection Center*.

vices, a technical training business. In the spring of 1998, he asked for an increase in his billing rate, which was refused.

Abarbanel attempted to hack his way into the company network and bombarded it with literally hundreds of e-mails, many containing threats. Other activities by Abarbanel included supplying Dan Keller's e-mail address to a variety of Internet sign-up lists for e-mail from retailers, alumni associations, etc., the purpose being, presumably, to cause a flood of junk e-mail. He also forged an e-mail message in which Keller "confessed" to owing him a lot of money.

Abarbanel's six-month rampage finally ended when the court granted a restraining order. He seems finally to have gotten the message and hasn't contacted Keller since. [3]

Indirectly Contracted Employee

Most companies are located in a building which is shared by other tenants. The building will often provide certain shared services such as building security, office cleaning, business equipment repair, and utilities maintenance. Building owners will contract out these services to companies with which your company has no association.

Your company has very little control over these indirect contractors. There is a legal, contractual relationship with the facilities owner who in turn has a contract with them, but any actions have to follow this indirect path.

However, these indirectly contracted employees will require access to your facilities to provide their services, usually outside of regular business hours. In fact, these people may come and go so regularly that their presence is not noticed and without going through the normal security process.

These type of services companies often express their trustworthiness by being bonded and insured. This may offer some financial relief, but rarely is it useful in response to a computer crime. Their employees are often low-paid workers, who are targeted by computer criminals.

A U.S. defense contractor, subcontracted with a foreign firm for on-site contractors. These foreign contractors were allowed access only to the areas of the premises that were necessary to their duties. However, they used their knowledge of the company's computer system to access other areas of the company's computer

---

[3]   Keller, Dan, "Hackers on the Internet: The Threat Is Real!, " *www.keller.com/attack/*, September 1999.

> network, which were off limits to non-U.S. employees. The foreign contractors were able to access proprietary and potentially classified information regarding the U.S. company's government contracts. Their activities jeopardized the competitiveness of the company and posed a potential threat to U.S. national security. [4]

External Hackers

The rapid growth of computer use and the proliferation of the Internet have contributed to a phenomenal growth in computer crime and a significant diversity in computer criminals. Even though most attacks which cause financial loss come from within, crime studies continuously show that most attacks come from outside the organization.

Recreational Hacker

The recreational hacker is the closest thing today to the classic hacker of old — the hacker who hacks just to learn and for the enjoyment of manipulating technology. This is also the group that most closely resembles the average perception of hackers. The term recreational does not imply that they are not serious about hacking; for most of them, hacking is their life. Rather, it indicates that they do not make money from their hacking activities.

Recreational hackers are mostly male; however, ten to fifteen percent are female. They are usually between twelve and twenty-eight, highly intelligent, but not high achievers in school. They often come from dysfunctional families and find refuge in the computer systems as the only place where they are in control.

They may not be socially adept, but they do have social bonds within the hacker community. Hackers with the most information gain the highest prestige. Hacking involves the accumulation of knowledge, which is accompanied by greater status and power.

Many enjoy the challenge of developing new hacking techniques:

> *The Register* magazine expressed skepticism over claims that the famous HTML bug — an invisible one-pixel image embedded in an HTML document or e-mail message referencing another image on a remote server — could be used for more than verifying e-mail addresses and garnering IPs. They asked their readers to suggest more malicious uses.

---

[4] "Statement of Louis J. Freeh, Director Federal Bureau of Investigation," *Senate Select Committee on Intelligence*, 28 January 1998.

> A number of respondents illustrated the ability to create detailed tracking methods which could collect a variety of client-side information. Others suggested that the included image could be used to create entries in the log files which could be incriminating to the unknowing user. Finally, one reader suggested using the bug to capture the client's IP address and then scan that host for open SMB shares to attack. [5]

Professional Hacker

The professional hacker is a "new breed" of hacker. He is professionally trained to gather information from any means available. He has the social skills to get people to give him information and the technical skills to attack systems successfully. Many professional hackers have gotten their training from government intelligence agencies around the globe. What differentiates them from other hackers is that they hack for very specific targets with the value of the information in mind. Their information gathering may be for government intelligence or more often corporate espionage. They are often a hacker-for-hire. Organized crime has moved into hacking.

> Some entrepreneurs from Chicago have started a new service called "Be A Hacker." It is basically hacking for hire. They say they can break into school, government and corporate computers and alter records for a fee.
>
> Even though they guarantee the service is legitimate, there are some who remain skeptical. First, because it is not guaranteed that they will succeed in the requested break-in and, also, because everybody knows that breaking into others' systems is a serious violation. [6]

The key to outsmarting a hacker lies in understanding why someone would want to become a hacker. Many people who are interested in computer technology want to be a hacker to some degree. The challenge of outsmarting the system and the thrill of discovering the forbidden hold an appeal even for the most honest person. Computer crime has attracted all types of people with all levels of skill and all types of motives.

---

[5]   Greene, Thomas, "Fun with Internet Bugs," *The Register*, 13 December 2000.
[6]   Sigvartsen, Ana Letícia, "Hackers for Hire," *InfoSatellite.com*, 5 April 2002.

Categorizing Hackers

There have been numerous studies and surveys trying to understand the type of people who use computers to commit crimes. Some studies have focused on the juvenile hacker while others have examined those who perform specific types of attacks. Some of these studies report similarities while other illustrate only the diversity in both the crimes and the criminals.

It may be a stereotype to describe computer hackers as anti-social geeks, but it is an accurate one — at least for the best-known type of hacker, says Marc Rogers, a University of Manitoba psychologist and former Winnipeg police officer. He reports that the average "cyberpunk," a hacker whose hobby has put him before the criminal courts, is a white, middle-class male, aged 12 to 28, who lacks social skills and comes from a dysfunctional family. They tend to be loners. They feel more comfortable behind a computer system than in face-to-face interaction. [7]

Sarah Gordon, who profiles cyber-criminals for IBM's Thomas J. Watson Research Center, performed a study of virus writers which indicated a different picture of these cyber-criminals.

The virus writers in Gordon's study range from teenagers to college students to professionally employed grown-ups. Most virus writers have normal social lives, get along just fine with family and friends, and generally mean no harm.

Most lose interest in virus writing as they get older. However, adults who remain in the "virus underground" do tend to have a few social problems.

Otherwise, the only evident pattern she has found among virus writers is that they tend to be intelligent, educated, and male. Given the tools required for their trade, common sense also suggests that most probably live in households with middle-class or higher incomes. [8]

Demographics

The wide variety of people who identify themselves as hackers makes it is difficult or even dangerous to assume that all hackers fit some specific profile. However, there are demographics of hackers which warrant specific consideration, due to the difficulties which they bring to the process of identification, capture, and conviction of these attackers.

Age

The usual hacker starts when he is a minor and is no longer dedicated to hacking by the time he is thirty. Many hackers are minors and are not held to the same level of responsibility as adults. The criminal justice system in the U.S. and other countries makes a clear distinction between adults and minors. There are separate courts, separate detention centers, and separate views of how the laws should be applied and the punishment implemented. Punishment for juveniles, even if convicted, is often little more than a slap on the wrist.

---

[7]   Bell, Stewart, "Computer Hackers Really Are Anti-social Geeks," *National Post Online*, 13 April 1999.

[8]   Beiser, Vince, "Inside the Virus Writer's Mind," 8 July 1999.

> A 15-year-old hacker chose to launch an attack on the Television Corporation of Singapore's (TCS) Internet site after seeing an advertisement for it on television. He replaced all the pages on the news channel's site with a variety of obscene and abusive messages for about 10 hours for no discernible reason.
>
> The judge passing sentence requested that the boy be home before 6 pm every night for a year, and demanded that he write a formal apology, to be posted on the news channel's web site. [9]

Sympathetic

Computer crime, like other white-collar crime, is not violent. It generally does not cause bodily injury. It is often difficult to explain the crime to a jury. The theft of information does not deny the victim the information; it is a copy which is stolen. Some people have sympathy for hackers who have been caught.

Many people are enamored of hackers. Much like Robin Hood, who committed crimes against the rich and became a hero of the poor, the victims of computer crimes are generally big businesses. Some people believe that it is acceptable to steal information from companies if their systems are not secure enough to keep them out. This makes it difficult to enlist a sympathetic jury. In computer crime cases, the defense will capitalize on the David and Goliath syndrome. They will paint the hacker as the little guy and the company as evil. This is true throughout the world.

> Israeli Prime Minister Benjamin Netanyahu praised a teenage hacker, known as the "Analyzer," who intruded upon hundreds of government computers in the U.S. and Israel. After the incident, the hacker was drafted into the Israeli army to serve in an information warfare division, an assignment which will utilize his computer talents.
>
> Before his induction, he celebrated with friends at a disco near his hometown of Hod Hasharon, north of Tel Aviv, where the disc jockey told the crowd "The Analyzer" had done their town proud. [10]

---

[9] Knight, Will, "Hacker Grounded for World's Easiest Crack," *ZDNet UK (www.zdnet.co.uk)*, 30 September 1999.

[10] "Israeli Teen Hacker Details Prowess," *Associated Press*, April 1998, Reprinted with permission of The Associated Press.

Location

The global environment of the Internet makes it possible to access systems anywhere in the world. This also allows hackers to attack systems from anywhere in the world. There are no political boundaries on the Internet. There are no border checkpoints or customs inspectors.

Tracking attacks across a world-wide network is a difficult task, especially when the hacker is trying to obscure his tracks. This problem is compounded when there is a need for search warrants or other participation from investigative organizations. Inconsistencies in international laws make what is legal in one place illegal in another. This makes it difficult to get support for investigating someone for committing an offense which is legal in the location where he is. However, sometimes agencies in different countries do work together.

> A computer hacker using the name "Curador" allegedly compromised multiple E-commerce websites in the U.S., Canada, Thailand, Japan and the United Kingdom, and apparently stole as many as 28,000 credit card numbers with losses estimated to be at least $3.5 million. Thousands of credit card numbers and expiration dates were posted to various Internet websites. After an extensive investigation, the American FBI assisted the Welsh Dyfed Powys Police Service in a search at the residence of "Curador," an 18-year-old whose real name is Raphael Gray. Gray was arrested in Wales along with a co-conspirator under the UK's Computer Misuse Act of 1990.
>
> This case was predicated on the investigative work by the FBI, the Dyfed Powys Police Service in the United Kingdom, Internet security consultants, the RCMP in Canada, and the international banking and credit card industry. This case illustrates the benefits of law enforcement and private industry around the world working together in partnership on computer crime investigations. [11]

Classified by Skill Level

Among hackers, skill level is the key differentiator. There are those skilled hackers who can write code in their sleep and know UNIX software inside and out. Then there are those "wannabes" who know how to run tools which crack passwords or sniff networks, but are unable to create a new or unique attack.

---

[11]   "Major Investigations: Curador," *National Infrastructure Protection Center*.

A skilled hacker must have the knowledge of a good system manager, a good network manager, and a good security manager and must understand various aspects of computer technologies, including networking and operating systems. The hacker must understand what a system manager and a security manager look for to see if someone has been prowling. He must be able to tell immediately if a system is well-maintained or not in order to evaluate if the system is a good candidate to attack. He must be able to manage his own system so that when he is discovered, the system manager's task of tracking him down will be as difficult and time-consuming as possible.

The hacker must also be a good networker; that is, he must be able to seek out other hackers and interact with them, feeding their egos and absorbing their knowledge. He will want to learn from their experiences and make profitable trades of information with them. Most hackers also desire the company of others with whom to share their exploits.

The hacker will need a good set of hacker tools. He will either need to create these tools or have access to already existing tools. To be a good hacker, he will need to understand and modify these tools to meet his specific needs.

There are a variety of categories of the hacker skill levels which can be useful in discussing and classification.

Script Kiddy

A script kiddy is someone with very little technical skill who uses scripts of programs which have been written by someone else to exploit known vulnerabilities. This hacker will often blindly follow an attack script, entering commands that may be inappropriate for the specific system that is under attack. These hackers usually compromise systems for bragging rights among their peers as to how many systems they have compromised and what well-known sites they have hacked. They may deface websites or otherwise mark their conquests, and their inexperience can also lead to inadvertent damage.

> Four Israeli secondary-school students have admitted to creating the "Goner" e-mail worm as part of a competition with a rival group of hackers. The virus arrives as an e-mail attachment disguised as a screen saver. Researchers have said the economic damage was minimal; the students intent was to launch a denial-of-service attack against a rival gang of script kiddies over Internet Relay Chat. [12]

---

[12] Perera, Rick, "Israeli Teens Arrested for 'Goner' Worm," *PC World,* 10 December 2001, reprinted with permission of the IDG News Service.

Script Kiddies will usually select their target by their ability to compromise it. They will sweep IPs looking for a system which has the known vulnerability which their tool of the day attacks. Once found, the tool will be launched against the system to gain privileged access. Often the entire process will be automated, so the script kiddy will start the program and come back in a day or two to see what he has succeeded in compromising.

Dedicated Hacker

A dedicated hacker will do research. He will know the ins and outs of the operating system, know what auditing and security tools there are, and how to use them to help him get in and out of systems. He will be able to write C code and shell scripts to modify tools for his needs and automate attack procedures. He reads the latest security bulletins from the Computer Emergency Response Team (CERT), the National Institute of Standards and Technology (NIST), and the vendors and the information from the underground about security holes. He will also read the security news groups and mail lists. Sometimes, a dedicated hacker will stay in a system for months or even years, until he achieves his goal.

> Over a period of two years, a band of Russian hackers siphoned off an enormous amount of research and development secrets from U.S. corporate and government entities in an operation codenamed Moonlight Maze by American intelligence. The value of this stolen information is in the tens of millions — perhaps hundreds of millions — of dollars; there's really no way to tell. The information was shipped over the Internet to Moscow for sale to the highest bidder.
>
> Fortunately, this threat was detected by a U.S. government agency. Unfortunately, that information was not passed on to the private institutions that it might have helped. [13]

Skilled Hacker

The skilled hacker realizes that to really understand the system he's going to be attacking, he has to know it inside and out and understand concepts and details. This means being able to read the operating system code. For UNIX systems, this is C. So he will get Linux or the UNIX source code and see what makes it tick. He will pay attention to the interaction between systems,

---

[13]   "Testimony of James Adams Chief Executive Officer, Infrastructure Defense, Inc.," *Committee on Governmental Affairs, United States Senate,* 2 March 2000.

such as all the networking tools. It is also very helpful for him to understand the network protocols.

It is almost a given that a successful hacker will know more about the internals of the operating system than you do. However, you will know more about what your system does and how it behaves: that is, when you have peak times, what kind of users you have, and what they do on the system. This is your advantage. This is why you must be vigilant in monitoring logs and system utilization, with a lookout for suspicious activity. You will need to know how to configure your system so when something occurs it will notify you.

We often see that the hacker has an exceptional ability to write code an manipulate systems, as in this example:

Korean officers apprehended a super hacker who turned out to be a fifteen-year-old high school boy named Kim. To date, 152 people have filed complaints about the 15 super viruses Kim created and e-mailed, but police expect the final figure to be over 2,000.

Kim told police that he mailed the viruses to demonstrate his talents and to find out if anyone could develop a "vaccine" for them. The viruses were so complex that they were virtually impossible to kill. The spokesman said that Kim was known as a computer genius from the 7th grade, when he learned to handle the machine code language "assembly 3" — one of just forty to fifty people in Korea with such a talent.

Yang Keun-won, head of the National Police Office's computer crime team, commented that a virus creator and hacker like Kim could become a "national treasure" in the information society of the future. He added that he will guide Kim along the legal path of computer work. [14]

Superhacker

The superhacker is a hacker who does not brag and does not post information on the bulletin boards; rather, he watches what others are doing and absorbs the information about new and different ways to compromise a system. He moves freely throughout computer systems taking what he wants without leaving a trace. If he decides that he wants to get on your system, he will eventually get there, and if he decides to crash your system, it will crash without explanation. Many consider the superhacker a myth because there is no evidence of his existence.

---

[14] "Super Hacker Apprehended," *The Digital Chosun*, 27 March 1999.

This is the goal of many hackers. The number of hackers who fall into this category is a microscopic percent, far fewer than those who claim to be superhackers.

Max Butler, who is know to the computer underground as the incredibly skilled hacker, "Max Vision," boasted that he'd never met a computer system he couldn't crack. He was also known as "The Equalizer," a security expert. It was with this identity he was an FBI informant, reporting on the activities of other hackers. As Max Butler, he was a family man in Santa Clara, California who ran a Silicon Valley security firm. He specialized in running "penetration tests," attempting to break into corporate networks to prove that their security wasn't as good as it could be.

Max was charged with 15 counts of hacking-related crimes, including computer intrusion, possession of stolen passwords, and interception of communications.

For five years, Max passed on information about several major cracks to the FBI, including the identities of phone hackers who penetrated 3Com's PBX system in 1996 and made free long-distance calls. According to court documents, Max tracked the hackers, engaged in IRC chats with them, and gave the transcripts of those chats to the FBI. He also attended hacker convention DefCon 6 in July 1998 with specific instructions from the FBI to "collect PGP encryption keys from conference attendees and try to match people's real names to their keys." [15]

---

[15]   Greene, Thomas, C., "FBI Computer Security Consultant Busted," *The Register*, 27 March 2000.

## CHAPTER 2

Hacker Motives

The hacker's motives are as diverse as the hackers themselves. Many hackers started as kids, swept up in the online culture of hackers. Hacking can be very exciting for a teenager who can be considered a hero by others. For some people, it gives them power and control which they lack in the real world. It provides a feeling of belonging for those who are otherwise outcast.

Some hackers are anarchists wanting to perform random acts of violence, or wanting to become famous; others have a personal score to settle with someone or some company, while others plan to get rich stealing information on the electronic frontier and hack only for the financial rewards. Still others are classic hackers who just want to learn how systems work and hack for the thrill and excitement.

The more criminal or personal the hackers' motives, the more dangerous he will be. Often computer security is like home security. If your system is harder to break into than your neighbor's, then the hacker is likely to go down the street and leave your system alone. However, if your system is being attacked because it contains information the hacker wants, or the hacker has specific reasons to attack your system, then he won't go away. In this case, you will have a battle on your hands.

To understand what kind of hackers your system and your company in general will attract, you need to perform a threat assessment. If your system contains information that would be valuable to others or damaging to the company if the information became public, or if the loss of the integrity of the data would cause financial hardship, it is likely that your system will be targeted by corporate hackers looking for specific information.

If your system contains financial information, then your system will be a target of a very wide variety of hackers. If the system contains only company information that would be damaging only to the company or of benefit to its competitors, then its attackers will be much more likely to be disgruntled employees or corporate spies. In any case, the amount of security should be appropriate to the amount of loss if the system is compromised. You must understand that no computer is an island, and the security level is also dependent on the other systems with which your system has contact.

Intellectually Motivated

Early on, most system intrusions were characterized as side-effects of intellectual curiosity, the curiosity of how things work, including security and how far it will bend before it breaks. Computers were a thing of science fiction. Using one was touching the future. Their abilities seemed miraculous and their potential had barely been touched. Many early hackers would not be content to have limited access to systems, and would venture across the early computer networks to find other systems they could explore. Very little thought was given to where the systems were, who owned them, or what they were supposed to be doing. They felt that cyberspace had to be explored.

Educational Experimentation

Hackers often take the position that they were using systems without permission "for educational purposes." There was a time when computers were expensive and found only at universities and large corporations, so this is where hackers experimented with systems without the knowledge or consent of the owners of the systems. In these early cases of computer trespassing, this excuse may have had some merit. However, today computers are so inexpensive, there is no excuse that one can not have systems to experiment with for educational purposes. Even so, computer criminals continue to harness the power of large systems.

> A 28-year-old computer expert allegedly diverted 2,585 US West computers to assist him in his effort to solve a 350-year-old math problem — the search for a new prime number. Investigators estimate that during a very short period he used 10.63 years worth of computer processing time — lengthening lookup time for customers' telephone numbers from five seconds to five minutes and causing calls to be rerouted to other states. At one point, the delays threatened to shut down the Phoenix Service Delivery Center. The man, a contract computer consultant working for a vendor for US West, told investigators that he had been working on the math problem for a long time, and that all that computational power at US West was just too tempting. [16]

---

[16]   Copyright 1998 EDUCAUSE. "Hacker Diverts US West Computers in Search of Prime," published in "Edupage," 17 September 1998.

Harmless Fun

Hackers often do not see their actions as malicious. They feel that painting a mustache on a website does not cause any *real* damage. The lack of physical interaction with the target and the association of computer games leads some hackers to view their activities as just harmless fun. The relationship between computers and video games has led to the view by some hackers that everything on the computer is just a game. Their addiction to the game creates a desire for inside information, so they can be the best, even to the extent of being the first to get the game, no matter what the cost.

> In an interview, a 14-year-old member of the hacker community explained that they hack systems just for fun. These hackers do not intend to hurt anyone. Most invasions are never documented or even discovered.
>
> To them it is much more interesting than "playing video games."
>
> They spend most of their time communicating using mail or ICQ as they listen to rock bands from Napster. They know other hackers by nicknames, so they do not have any idea of who is who. The trick is to exchange the maximum amount of information around well-known operating system bugs. Even when documented, most people do not apply the fixes. Most shops still use, as he put it, "stupid passwords" or have bad protection policies. [17]

As a Wake-up Call

Some attackers will say that their attack was meant to illustrate a flaw in the system or software which was exploited, so that the developer or administrator can repair the problem. They may feel that they were performing a service and should be rewarded for illustrating the problem.

Within the hacker community, hackers are often viewed as being persecuted "just because they know too much." They believe that they know more than the systems administrators and the security professionals and when they attempt to show these people their errors, the hackers are called criminals. The hackers may defend their actions by saying that they were "just trying to show the flaw" which they exploited, or that the system administrator thought he was smarter than the hacker so the hacker had to prove him wrong.

---

[17]   "A Visit with a Hacker," *Ignite/400 Newsletter.*

An Oklahoma man who claimed he accidentally found a security flaw in the website of the Poteau (Oklahoma) *Daily News and Sun* newspaper pled guilty to intentionally accessing and obtaining information from a protected computer without authorization. Using MS Front Page and a web browser, Brian West discovered a security flaw which allowed him to access proprietary information and password files.

West then reported to the newspaper editor that he had penetrated the website, accessed the site using a username and password, and downloaded several files, terming his intrusion "accidental." The website owner reported him to law enforcement authorities. The case generated a substantial amount of e-mail to the prosecutor from the Internet community questioning why someone who appeared to be a "good Samaritan" was being punished. [18]

Personally Motivated

Personal motives run the entire gamut from hacking into systems for fun to extracting revenge on a company that the attacker feels has wronged him. Personal motives are very strong and will often make the attacker continue fruitless attacks well beyond reason.

When the resources are unique or difficult or expensive to get otherwise, the attacker may compromise a system to use the resources for personal use. Some systems are targeted because of these special resources. Systems with dial-out modems are often valued, since the attacker can use them to dial out to another ISP and thereby increase the difficulty of tracking the hacker.

The Internet has become a popular place for personally motivated attacks against companies and individuals. The anonymity of the Internet creates a sense of security which gives the personally motivated hacker the feeling of freedom and invincibility.

Disgruntled Employees

Disgruntled employees and ex-employees are the largest group of computer criminals. They are strongly motivated and are very focused on their target. They will often expend more energy and money to achieve their goal than the value of the attack.

---

[18]   Brian K. West, Employee of Oklahoma ISP, Pleads Guilty to Unauthorized Access Charge Under 18 U.S.C. § 1020(a)(2)(c)," *U.S. Department of Justice Press Release*, 24 September 2001.

An ex-employee of Tornado Development, Bret McDanel, allegedly spammed Tornado's computer system, causing a denial-of-service attack and forcing Tornado to shut down its system. McDanel accessed Tornado's system five times in about three weeks, twice gaining unauthorized access to Tornado's mail server, then spamming approximately 11,000 of Tornado's customers on three occasions.

These intrustions into Tornado's system resulted in a loss of approximately $325,000 to Tornado. [19]

Cyber-stalking

Cyber-stalking is a growing problem. With more people being connected more of the time, harassing and menacing messages and activities are increasing. The perceived anonymity of computers and the Internet has allowed some individuals to use this media to harass other individuals. Often it enables them to show off their superiority in the area of technology to someone to whom they feel inferior in real life.

At times the harassment turns violent. There are incidents where it is the individual himself who, having become obsessed, turns violent and there are incidents where the individual has convinced others to perform the violent acts for him.

In the first successful prosecution under California's new cyber-stalking law, prosecutors in the Los Angeles District Attorney's Office obtained a guilty plea from a 50-year-old former security guard who used the Internet to solicit the rape of a woman who rejected his romantic advances. The defendant terrorized his 28-year-old victim by impersonating her in various Internet chat rooms and online bulletin boards, where he posted, along with her telephone number and address, messages that she fantasized of being raped. On at least six occasions, sometimes in the middle of the night, men knocked on the woman's door saying they wanted to rape her. The former security guard pleaded guilty in April 1999 to one count of stalking and three counts of solicitation of sexual assault. He faces up to six years in prison. [20]

---

[19]   "FBI Arrrests Computer Hacker Wanted in Los Angeles," *FBI San Diego Division*, 18 July 2001.
[20]   "1999 Report on Cyber-stalking," *A Report from the Attorney General*, August 1999.

Socially Motivated

Social motives are based on rectifying the inequality of social injustices that an organization has done or is perceived to have done. Cyber-activism is growing rapidly, using the anonymity of computer networks to release information about the organizations alleged activities, to cause damage to an organization, or to disrupt the organization's activities.

Cyber-activism

Using the cyberspace to perform acts of electronic civil disobedience has become a popular method of activism. Hacktivism, as it has become popularly known, offers a level of personal anonymity to those who perform the acts and an outlet where media coverage can be widespread.

Activists use website vandalism to bring attention to their cause and denial-of-service attacks to disrupt the activities of their targets.

> An environmental campaign group has "hijacked" the URL of Treasury Holdings, after the Irish property group forgot to renew the domain name.
>
> The domain name TreasuryHoldings.com is now directed to the home page of LuskPeople.com, a group of activists which is lobbying against plans by Treasury Holdings to build a waste incinerator in Lusk, north county Dublin. The group obtained the URL by the simplest method of all: buying it for $37.
>
> LuskPeople conducted its coup against Treasury Holdings yesterday, on the day of the Irish general election. In a press release, the pressure group quotes an anonymous Treasury employee: "We didn't know the name had lapsed. We want our name back." [21]

Politically Motivated

Political motives are based on advancing a political idealism, usually focused on damaging the sites of opposing views or posting political messages on such sites. Recently there has been an explosion of attacks which are politically motivated. It seams that everyone has a cause to support. These causes cover the spectrum of ideals and beliefs. Some are well-organized, long-standing causes while others are supported by fringe groups.

The Internet has enabled more participation since the group can gather a following from around the world and since online events can be attended by anyone no matter where he or she

---

[21]   Cullen, Drew, "Campaigners 'Hijack' Treasury Holdings URL," *The Register*, 19 May 2002.

is. The anonymity provided by the Internet has allowed more participation in those groups which are not looked upon favorably. An individual's involvement is less likely to be exposed.

Cyber-terrorism

In the wake of the September 11th attacks on the World Trade Center and the Pentagon, terrorism has been on the minds of everyone. There is a real concern about cyber-terrorism — the politically motivated attacks that cause serious disruption to the infrastructure (power, water, transportation, communication). In the United States, the federal government is taking strides to mandate security for these critical infrastructures in order to ensure national security. However, info-terrorism — the politically motivated attacks causing a disruption or corruption of information systems — could have an equally devastating effect.

Info-terrorism has been a topic of discussion as well as a subject for science fiction novels for a number of years. Many people have hypothesized how much damage could be done by disrupting the flow of data. It is certain that, as we become more and more dependent on computers, the threat of this kind of terrorism grows.

The earliest report of this type of attack was in 1988 when the Israeli government and university computer systems were found to have a logic bomb planted in them that was synchronized to go off at the same time as the "Israeli Virus," a PC virus. Both the virus and the logic bomb were found and disabled before any damage occurred. No one claimed responsibility and officially it was not an act of terrorism.

Cyber-terrorism has been going on for several years.

A group calling themselves the Internet Black Tigers took responsibility for attacks in 1977 on the e-mail systems of Sri Lankan diplomatic posts around the world, including those in the United States. Italian sympathizers of the Mexican Zapatista rebels crashed web pages belonging to Mexican financial institutions. While such attacks did not result in damage to the targets, they were portrayed as successful by the terrorists and used to generate propaganda and rally supporters. [22]

Cyber-warfare

Cyber-warfare offers a great military potential for disrupting communications, disseminating misinformation, and disrupting computerized armaments and defensive systems. Any actual use of cyber-warfare has been kept quiet. There have been no official reports of govern-

---

[22]   Tenet, George J., Director of Central Intelligence, "Terrorist Use of Information Warfare Tactics," *Testimony Before the Senate Committee on Government Affairs*, 24 June 1998.

ments using offensive computer attacks as part of a military action, even though many countries have cyber-warfare departments. However, there's plenty of speculation. In an interview about his book, *The Media and the Military*, Peter Young, who has spent 50 years in defense and foreign affairs as field agent, journalist, publisher, and retired Griffith University Associate Professor recounts one theory that keeps cropping up:

> Whilst there's no evidence at all, and no one can say with any certainty, in the Iraqi Gulf War we were suddenly confronted with the whole of the Iraqi Air Force, which had performed quite well up to that stage against the Iranians. An experienced, well trained, well equipped, force with US, British and German technology, suddenly decamped overnight.
>
> One answer to this may be, may be, that we saw the first real example of cyber-warfare on a grand scale in that somebody or something got to the Iraqi command/control/communication system, which left them (the aeroplanes) blind and unable to be directed. And this may have been the first instance of the microchip being used at this level in warfare. [23]

Financially Motivated

Most crime is financially motivated. Financial motives, need or greed, are very powerful. The computer has become just one more tool available to these criminals. There has been a growing trend of attacks for financial gain accomplished by selling the information acquired or extorting the victim organization. Many hackers start with criminal intent and find computer systems an easy way to achieve their goals. Some are paid by third parties to compromise an organization's systems, or to acquire information. Others may cause damage expecting to be hired to fix the damage. A sudden financial need can cause an individual to become involved in activities in which he would not otherwise engage. The impersonal nature of computer crimes gives many criminals a sense of security that they won't be caught.

Personal Profit

Financial profit has long been a motive for computer crimes. Hackers embezzle from their employers and steal information to sell to competitors. More recently, electronic theft of credit card numbers has become common and identity theft, the process of stealing enough personal information to impersonate someone financially, is on the rise. Financial crimes of all kinds are

---

[23]   Dayton, Leigh, "Cyberwarfare — The Story," *Australian Broadcasting Corporation*, 13 March 1999.

increasing online. The computer and the computer networks have become a vehicle for common crime.

> Two Cisco Systems accountants were sentenced to 34 months in prison on charges of computer fraud for issuing almost $8 million in Cisco stock to themselves.
>
> As part of their scheme, Geoffrey Osowski and Wilson Tang exceeded their authorized access to computer systems at Cisco in order to access a system used to manage stock option disbursals. They then used that access to identify control numbers to track authorized stock option disbursals and create forged forms authorizing disbursals of stock. They faxed the forged forms to the company responsible for issuing Cisco stock, and had the stock sent to their personal brokerage accounts.
>
> They transferred a total of over 200,000 shares of stock before being caught. [24]

Damage to the Organization

Many attacks are focused on damaging the organization. This can be anything from vandalizing its website to destroying critical business data. Organizations are selected by outsiders because of their public image or perceived image or by disgruntled employees or dissatisfied customers. In most cases, these attacks have little lasting effect on the organization; occasionally, they are devastating to the victim.

> A British Internet service provider, Cloud Nine, went out of business after being hit by a crippling security attack. The denial of service attack was so bad the ISP said it would have to rebuild its network, but its CEO, Emeric Miszti, said that the disaster cover insurance it held was insufficient to cover the rebuild.
>
> Effectively, the attacks have put the company completely out of business.

---

[24] "Former Cisco Systems, Inc. Accountants Sentenced for Unauthorized Access to Computer Systems to Illegally Issue Almost $8 Million in Cisco Stock to Themselves," *U.S. Department of Justice Press Release*, 26 November 2001.

> The ISP tightened its firewalls after the initial attack. "What fol-
> lowed was first a Firewall password brute forece attack resulting in
> successful hash and destruction of the firewall," the company said
> in an online post.
>
> Speaking to the UK's *The Register*, a dejected Mr. Miszti said, "This
> is terrorism — pure and simple. I never want to relive the last
> seven days again. We still don't know who's behind it — nor do we
> know who's next." [25]

Motivated by Ego

The hacker's ego is probably the largest contributing factor to the attacks he performs. Many are looking only for their 15 minutes of fame. Virus writers, website vandals, and others leave their handles on their work so that they can receive credit for their exploits. The hacker community is built on the status of the most amazing hack in the game of one upmanship. Each hacker has a need to prove himself, his skill, daring, and ability.

Even in those attacks which are not performed merely for their visibility, the hacker's ego plays a part in the attack. The hackers believe that they are smarter and more skilled with computers than their adversary and the law enforcement who might be called in to assist. They believe that they will not be caught, so they are free to do as they please online.

It may not even be necessary to actually perform the hack to get famous for it. With a little social engineering on the news media, a hacker can be credited for nearly anything.

> MTV has been duped by a hoaxer in its much-maligned "True Life:
> I'm a Hacker" program. After the show was screened, the main
> character in the show, Shamrock, issued a statement revealing
> that he made the whole thing up.
>
> Shamrock who gave an in-depth interview with MTV explaining the
> motivation behind his hacking exploits, said the show was total
> nonsense and was designed to illustrate how gullible MTV was.
>
> In the statement, published on the Hacking News Network, Sham-
> rock explained it was MTV's cynical approach to hacking that
> prompted his scam. "We waited for months to see if they would be
> realistic and after it was obvious that they wouldn't, we figured the

[25] Richardson, Tim, "Cloud Nine Blown Away, Blames Hack Attack," *The Register*, 22 January 2002.

only option would be to discredit them with as much fiction as possible."

Shamrock adds that he and fellow hoaxers never expected MTV to swallow the absurdities they made up and argued the hoax illustrated the shallow nature of the mainstream media. "We had no intention of making hackers look bad. All I can do is reiterate to you just how fake and hollow what you see on television is. After this experience I wonder where if any truth lies in what we are told to watch. This is the obvious issue the hacker community needs to address." [26]

---

[26]   Knight, Will, "MTV Made to Look Ridiculous by Fake Hacker," *ZDNet UK (www.zdnet.co.uk)*, 19 October 1999.

## CHAPTER 3

What Hackers Do

The phenomenal growth of the Internet has been accompanied by new methods of hacking. While a user is connected to the Internet, his computer is extremely vulnerable. Some computers are always attached to the Internet. Sometimes entire local area networks keep their Internet connection open twenty-four hours a day to allow users access to the web and e-mail all the time. Hackers routinely break into networks via the Internet by spoofing the identity of computers that the network expects to be present.

Systems on the Internet without registered names, only numeric addresses, which offer no services are scanned dozens of times a day. Within minutes of publishing a new host name to Domain Name Services, the system will be profiled — the process of determining the type of system and services available.

The description of what hackers do is largely dependent on the reporter's opinion of hackers. Many of the activities can be spun to sound benign or malicious.

Modern Day Robin Hood

There are many hackers who don't consider themselves criminals because they are not stealing money, credit cards, computer hardware, or anything made of atoms. Rather, they are only making copies of software and data and utilizing computer resources, CPU, disk, and networking. They seem to believe that since they are not depriving anyone of anything and the original copy of the information is still where it was, unaltered, they are not committing a crime. Since what they are taking is composed of bits, not atoms, and thereby, less tangible, they believe the laws of the tangible world do not apply.

Some hackers do not necessarily see their activities as criminal. In fact, many see themselves as defenders of the digital frontier. Some in the hacker community view corporations as evil and hackers as the only ones who can protect the world.

They feel that they are being persecuted because they know too much and that their knowledge is somehow threatening to the companies and governments which are persecuting them.

Releasing Information

For many, the free flow of ideas and information is the definition of the Internet. It started as a research network interconnecting universities and research institutions to facilitate communications. They see the commercialization of the Internet is the crime, and belive that "information must be free." For them, anyone who is controlling this free flow of information is doing it at the expense of all people.

A Norwegian teenager, Jon Johansen, was indicted for his role in creating software that permits DVD owners to view DVDs on players that are not approved by the entertainment industry.

Johansen originally published DeCSS as part of the open source development project LiVid (Linux Video) in building a DVD player for the Linux operating system. The MPAA CSS licensing entity, named DVD-CCA, refuses to license CSS to projects such as LiVid, which is an open source project collaborating on the Web to build interoperable software tools. LiVid's independently created DVD player software would compete with the movie studio monopoly on DVD players.

Electronic freedom advocates were quick to defend his work:

"Johansen shouldn't be prosecuted for breaking into his own property," said Robin Gross, staff attorney at the Electronic Frontier Foundation (EFF). "Jon simply wanted to view his own DVDs on his Linux machine."

"Although prosecutors in Norway failed to defend the rights of their citizens against Hollywood's unprecedented demands, we are confident that neither the Norwegian people nor their justice system will allow this charge to stand," added EFF Legal Director Cindy Cohn. "The movie studios have used intellectual property rights to silence scientists, and censor journalists. Now, they are declaring war on their customers."[27]

Releasing Software

Many hackers view the nature of software licensing agreements to be unfairly restrictive. Most licenses will not allow you to have copies of the software on multiple computers even if

---

[27]   "U.S. Entertainment Industry Pressured Norwegian Prosecutors," *Electronic Frontier Foundation Press Release*, 10 January 2002.

you are the only one who uses those computers. In retaliation, hackers will crack the licensing codes so the software can be used anywhere by anyone. There is the debate that people who use cracked software cannot afford the licensed version and would not have purchased it anyway. Software companies look at the millions of dollars' worth of illegal software which is being used as lost revenue. Some users make a game of obtaining software for free.

> In a certain elite circle that includes programmers, graphic designers, and many others, not paying for software is more than just money-saving, it's a point of pride. "Everything on my computer is stolen. I haven't bought one program," says a New York special-effects artist who estimates that his Apple Macintosh is loaded with more than $15,000 worth of software for which he hasn't paid a penny. [28]

Consuming Unused Resources

It is common for the hacker to feel that if the resource is not being used, then there is nothing wrong with using it. Network bandwidth, computer cycles, telephone lines, and any resource to which a hacker can get access are likely to be used by the hacker. Of course, the consumption of these resources often leads to the company who owns them having to buy more resources when ample resources are available if they were not being used by hackers.

The consumption of unused resources is not always done with malicious intent. Often a hacker feels it is his duty to make these resources available to those who can use them, especially if it seems to be for a worthwile cause.

> David McOwen, once a systems administrator at DeKalb Technical College, was brought up on charges of computer theft and computer trespassing for connecting a number of DeKalb computers to Distributed.net so that the spare computing cycles could assist in a communal code-breaking challenge. The state claimed that McOwen had drained $815,000 worth of DeKalb computing time and bandwidth consumption since installing the software early in 1999.
>
> Under the Georgia computer trespass statute, criminal liability may only be imposed if the person uses the computer or network with

---

[28]   Rosner, Hillary, "Steal This Software," *The Industry Standard*, 21 June 2000.

knowledge that the use is unauthorized. The state would have to prove that he had fair notice that installing the Distributed.net client software was prohibited.

A deal was finally struck, in which McOwen will receive one year of probation for each criminal count, to run concurrently, make restitution of $2100, and perform 80 hours of community service unrelated to computers or technology. [29]

Discover and Document Vulnerabilities

There are types of hackers who have taken it upon themselves to disclose the vulnerabilities in systems by making the details of the vulnerabilities as widely known as possible. They will often write programs which exploit the vulnerability as proof of the vulnerability. These scripts rapidly become tools for hackers who do not have the skill to create the tools themselves.

Adrian Lamo, who has a publicized history of exploring the inner workings of corporate computer networks in search of system weaknesses, sees himself as helping companies improve their system security by reporting flaws. He does this kind of work, he said, because he enjoys solving mysteries. Lamo doesn't hold a full-time job because, he said, it would be too restrictive and time-consuming.

He has been reported to have uncovered security lapses in networks run by Worldcom, America Online Inc., Excite@Home, Yahoo Inc., Microsoft Corp., and The New York Times. Lamo, who describes himself more as a "security researcher" than as a hacker, said he neither sought nor received any payment for his information.

His claims that he has never done any damage have come into question with his altering of news stories at Yahoo and The New York Times. Yet still there are those who identify him as a misguided youth with good intentions. [30]

[29]   "Distributed Computing Prosecution Ends with Whimper Not Bang," *Electronic Frontier Foundation Media Release,* 17 January 2002.
[30]   Weiss, Todd, "Security Holes Closed after Hacker Intrusion," *Computerworld,* 27 February 2002.

Finding Fame

Fame is key to many hackers. This is obvious from the number of widespread attacks, such as viruses and website defacements, which do nothing other than draw attention to the attack. These attention-grabbing attacks are a way to prove the skill of the hacker. The more visible the target or the more widespread the victims, the greater the hack and therefore the better the hacker.

Some hackers want to gain fame from the technical ability of the hack. They want to show that they are able to do things which no other hacker has been able to do before. Others are hoping to become famous from the cunning of the attack. The selection of the target and the type of attack are key to demonstrating the courage necessary to pull off such an attack. And yet others are looking for as much publicity as possible by making the attack as widespread as possible.

> Kevin Mitnick, a computer hacker who was once among the FBI's most wanted, guest-starred as a computer expert on an episode of ABC's spy drama "Alias." Mitnick served about five years in prison for a number of computer fraud crimes, including stealing proprietary software for cell-phone systems. He was released in January 2000.
>
> "If someone else had cast him on another show, I would have been jealous," says "Alias" creator and executive producer J.J. Abrams. "I've always been a fan of Kevin's renegade spirit and sense of genius and curiosity."[31]

Digital Dillinger

For the information security professional who is attempting to keep systems available, and maintain the confidentiality and integrity of the information they contain, his or her view of these hackers is somewhat different. These are attacks against systems, networks, and information. They are attacks against the profits of the company and the productivity of its employees. There is nothing noble about it; they are criminal acts which require a judicial response.

Theft of Information

A hacker may want to steal information for himself, or to prove to someone that he can do it, or to sell the information for profit. Today, information is money. Every day more money changes hands electronically than in currency. The electronic funds transfer network is an

[31]   "Famed Hacker to Guest-star on 'Alias'," *Zap2it.com*, 8 October 2001.

inviting target but has remained very secure. Hackers will generally target easier systems. Criminals have found a variety of interesting ways to use computers to facilitate their access to financial information. They intercept bank card numbers and PIN numbers and acquire personal information, such as a Social Security number or mother's maiden name, and use this information to impersonate their victim to get access to their victim's accounts. This information can be converted directly into money.

> Suzanne Scheller, while she was a financial institution employee, accessed the financial institution computer system and searched for potential customers for a friend who was starting a real estate business. After identifying prospects, she then provided the friend with the customer account information. She admitted that she knew her unauthorized access was against the policy of the financial institution. The investigation established that some of the information provided was actually used by another individual unknown to her as part of an identity theft scheme. Imposters used the customer account information to steal the identity of the customers and conduct transactions at the financial institution.
>
> Two of the imposters in the identity theft/bank fraud scheme have previously pled guilty and have been sentenced. Scheller was sentenced to a term of thirty-six months probation, in connection with obtaining confidential customer account information and providing it to another individual outside the financial institution. [32]

Software Piracy

Theft of software, or software piracy as it is called, is a major concern for companies who are in the business of producing commercial software. However, this is only one aspect of software theft; many organizations that do not produce software commercially still produce software for internal use. The production of this software is expensive and represents a large number of jobs. Often this software offers a competitive advantage to a company by being part of the organization's processes that make it more efficient, profitable, or unique. Other companies are hindered by the costs of producing comparable software.

Many organizations' secrets are contained not only in the information they have, but are also imbedded in the software that they have created internally. Theft of an organization's

---

[32]   "Former Financial Institution Employee Sentenced for Unauthorized Computer Access to Customer Account Information in Latest Bank Fraud/Identity Theft Prosecutions," *U.S. Department of Justice Press Release*, 30 November 2001.

proprietary software can disclose some of the organization's most private secrets. This theft may also deprive the organization of the ability to use the software if the original copy is destroyed in the process of the theft, leading to an inability to continue to do business.

Chung-Yuh Soong, a software engineer who worked for Kodak for a year before resigning, was accused of transmitting several large data files containing software programs used in Kodak digital cameras and other digital devices listed as "highly confidential" to a Xerox computer in California, just days before she left Kodak. According to court documents, the alleged theft was discovered because the data being transmitted was so large that it crashed a Kodak server and alerted the company's computer-security system.

Soong, 37, was charged in federal court with wire fraud related to interstate transfer of Kodak's software and has also been sued by Kodak in civil court for misappropriation of trade secrets. Kodak said it did not know who the files were intended for and where precisely they ended up. Soong's lawyer maintains she was sending them for safekeeping to her sister, who works for Xerox, and had no intention of passing them on to the copier company or anyone else.[33]

Theft of software costs more than the cost of the software. It impacts the ability of the business to remain solvent and it affects jobs and people's lives.

Theft of Resources

Theft of resources may be difficult to prove to a court of law's satisfaction. There have been some cases where the hacker has been released because the prosecution was unable to prove the value of the lost resources. This is one of the hackers' favorite justifications. A hacker will say he is using only unused resources, and since they are spare and were not going to be used he did not actually steal anything since no one suffered any loss. There are many reasons that a hacker might have for wanting to use your resources. It is may be for personal gain, or to enable his hacking activities.

---

[33] "Kodak Sues Former Employee," *Counterintelligence News & Developments*, September 1998.

Raymond Torricelli admitted that he was a computer hacker, known as "rolex," and a member of a hacking organization known as "#conflict." Operating from his residence, he used his personal computer to run programs designed to search the Internet, and seek out computers that were vulnerable to intrusion. Once such computers were located, he obtained unauthorized access to the computers by uploading a program that allowed him to gain complete access to all of a computer's functions.

Torricelli accessed computers owned by National Aeronautics and Space Administration (NASA), Jet Propulsion Laboratory (JPL), and San Jose State University. After gaining unauthorized access to the computers and loading a hostile program, he used many of the computers to host chat-room discussions. Torricelli admitted that in these discussions, he invited other chat participants to visit a website that enabled them to view pornographic images and that he earned 18 cents for each visit a person made to that website. Torricelli earned approximately $300-400 per week from this activity. [34]

Compromising Systems

The earliest illegal conduct was gaining access to systems without permission. Often these hackers think it's harmless since they usually don't "do" anything besides go in and look around. However, they do consume resources, such as network bandwidth and computing power, and can inadvertently cause damage. Most of the time hackers will leave a back door into the system so they can return at any time without concern for security measures.

Compromised systems cost organizations even if the hacker did not cause any damage. The organizations have to spend resources determining the extent of the damage whether there is any damage or not. They have to determine how the system was compromised and repair the system to prevent further compromises. All of these activities take a great deal of time and manpower.

Today, it is rare that a compromised system has no damage. Most hackers immediately apply a "rootkit" which changes the system's software so that it does not report the presence of the hacker or his tools. Even the most benign hackers want to "own" the system (i.e., to have super user privileges so they can completely control the system). Many of these are "collectors"

---

[34]   "Hacker Sentenced for Breaking into Computer Maintained by NASA," *NASA Office of Inspector General News Release*, 18 September 2001.

wanting to "own" as many systems as possible to prove their power. These hackers may also have motives which are not as friendly.

> Jason Allen Diekman, who had already pled guilty to hacking into NASA computers and using stolen credit card numbers to purchase electronic equipment, was arrested a few months later for hacking into more computers and attempting to commit wire fraud.
>
> Diekman used his personal computer at home to gain unauthorized access to computers at Oregon State University (OSU) in Corvallis, Oregon. He hacked into the university's computers 33 times in three months. Using the account of an OSU student to gain access to the school's computer system, he stored computer programs on the school's computer to control Internet Relay Chat channels. Additionally, individuals afffiliated with him attempted to make three wire transfers to him through Western Union, but Western Union stopped the transactions. [35]

Website Vandalism

Website vandalism has become the most visible of attacks. Dozen of websites are defaced daily. Stolen passwords account for most, but software vulnerabilities are also a significant cause. Compromised websites are often used as bragging rights. Both the number of sites and the visibility of the website are important to the prestige of the compromise. Sometimes website attacks are launching points to other systems or an attempt to compromise an e-commerce site, but most times defacing the website is the goal.

Websites are generally selected because of the ability to exploit the system, but websites are also targeted because of their visibility or because of the organization whose site it is. Hactivism, which includes defacing websites of organizations with whom the hactivist has issues or posting political or social messages on compromised websites, is becoming more common. Website vandalism has been growing by leaps and bounds.

> One of the most predominant sections of the Attrition.com website has been the defacement mirror. What began as a small collection of website defacement mirrors soon turned into a near 24/7 chore of keeping it up to date. In one month, the company experienced

---

[35] "Hacker Sentenced", *NASA Office of Inspector General News Release*, 5 February 2002.

single days of mirroring over 100 defaced websites, over three times the total for 1995 and 1996 combined. With the rapid increase in web defacement activity, there are times when it requires them to take mirrors for four or five hours straight to catch up. Add to that the scripts and utilities needed to keep the mirror updated, statistics generated, and mail lists maintained, and the time required for basic functionality is immense. [36]

[36]   "ATTRITION: Evolution," *Attrition.org Press Rlease*, 21 May 2001.

## CHAPTER 4

How Hackers Do What They Do

Early on, hacking required extensive knowledge of systems, networks, and protocols. Gaining unauthorized access required using the knowledge to either manually subvert protocols or to write programs which could exploit flaws. Those days of the hands-on hacker are almost gone.

Today, the process of hacking computer systems has become automated. There are many tools which are easily available to identify and exploit vulnerabilities to compromise a system. The user of these tools does not need to understand what the tool does, only how it works.

Hackers have an amazing arsenal of weapons. Powerful software tools for breaking into networks are freely distributed. They require little knowledge to use, and they can be virtually undetectable until the damage is done. Most hackers carry their own bag of tricks. This "toolbox" will include versions of programs with back doors, programs that will help mask their activities, and programs that exploit known problems. These hacking tools will assist in all areas of hacking: gaining access and privileges, hiding hacker activities, and monitoring the system manager's activities. These tools will vary from simple to extremely sophisticated.

Malicious Code

One of the tools in the hacker's arsenal is the use of malicious code. Of course, software algorithms are not inherently either bad or good; they are only tools that can be used either constructively or destructively. However, there are some types of programs that are often utilized by hackers.

Logic Bomb

A logic bomb is a program that lies dormant until it is activated. It can be activated by anything that the computer system can detect. Often it is time-based (a time bomb), or based on the presence or absence of some data, such as when a programmer's name is no longer in the payroll file. This trigger can be almost anything. Once activated, the logic bomb will "deliver its payload." This payload is any type of destructive software, which can consume resources or delete files. This destruction can be widespread or focused at specific individuals. With computers now in control of so many physical systems, the attack could actually become a physical attack.

Logic bombs usually have to be in the system; that is, they are a running process, even if they are in a wait queue. Be aware of any process that has been running on your system for a long time but has used no CPU resources.

> Timothy Lloyd, a former computer network administrator, was sentenced to 41 months in prison for unleashing a $10 million "time bomb" that deleted all the production programs of a New Jersey-based high-tech measurement and control instruments manufacturer. He was the former chief computer network program designer for Omega Engineering. After being terminated from Omega, where he worked for approximately 11 years, he activated a "time bomb" that permanently deleted all of the company's sophisticated manufacturing software programs. [37]

Parasite

A parasite is a piece of code that is added to an existing program and draws information from the original program. It is used to gather information for which the hacker may not have privileges. By its definition it is a covert, nondestructive program. It may use a virus to spread around a system.

When a parasite is added to a piece of software, some of the attributes of that program will be changed. These attributes include the program's size, its timestamp, its permissions, ownership, and its checksum, which is an algorithmic summation of all the information in the file. If you inventory this information for all the programs on your system when you know your system is clean, you will be able to tell if any of the programs have been altered. This requires running a program to build your original inventory and periodically rerunning this program to spot any differences.

Trojan Horse

A Trojan horse is a program that looks like a useful program that has an alternate agenda. How does a hacker plant a Trojan horse? This generally requires social engineering. That is, the

---

[37]   "Former Computer Network Administrator at New Jersey High-Tech Firm Sentenced to 41 Months for Unleashing $10 Million Computer 'Time Bomb'," *U.S. Department of Justice Press Release,* 26 February 2002.

hacker will need to advertise the existence of the Trojan horse so people will run it. The best Trojan horses will do what they advertise to do as well as the covert action.

There are a number of ways Trojan horses can be introduced. They can be introduced as games, usually under development, so that anything that acts flaky is just a bug, or as utilities. Utilities are especially effective since they are more likely to be run by someone with privileges.

Beware of geeks bearing gifts. It is a cliché, but if something sounds too good to be true, it is. You should not load any unofficial software or any software from an unofficial source without minimally validating the software on a safe quarantine system. Software policy should cover acceptable software sources and validate procedures.

It has been shown that postscript files can contain Trojan horses. The postscript language has the ability to do file input/output (I/O). When all you do with postscript is send it to a printer, these commands have no value. However, if you view them online, these commands can access anything you have permission to access.

Even documentation has been targeted with Trojan horses. If the document has to be processed, either with UNIX text processing commands or in a word processor that supports macros, there is the possibility of inserting code that can have an alternate objective.

Virus

A virus is a program that infects another program by replicating itself into the host program. Considered by itself, the virus has three phases: the infection phase, where the host is infected from a previously existing virus; the activation phase, where this new copy is triggered to find another host to infect; the replication phase, where the virus finds a suitable host and copies itself to the host. Most viruses are destructive, carrying a logic bomb with them, which is separately activated to deliver its payload. However, some viruses do not; they merely replicate consuming resources. These are referred to as bacteria, or rabbits.

Historically, viruses have been primarily targeted at PCs. But, as systems become more and more standard, they will become more prevalent on larger systems as well. Viruses are transported from one system to another by being in a file that is moved from one system to another.

> The constant onslaught of high-profile viruses cost the industry over $13 billion in 2001, according to research from Computer Economics. These new viruses are combining traditional virus technology with new hacking techniques. These viruses not only propagated across computers, they left back doors or hijacked machines for later use in denial of service attacks. [38]

---

[38] Middleton, James, "Major viruses cost industry $13bn in 2001," *Computing*, 10 January 2002.

Software from unauthorized sources can lead to many security issues. The security policy should clearly state the company's position on what are appropriate sources of software and what the process is to put the software onto the system. This should include both a reference to your "approved software list" which should contain details on the process to obtain software that is on the list and software that is not, and a reference to documentation detailing any corporate license agreements that the company may have.

If you are in an environment where the use of "freeware" is prevalent, or people regularly bring software onto your system, you are at greater risk of virus infection. You may want to create a quarantine system. A quarantine system is a system on which any incoming software must live for a period of time so it can be checked for viruses and validated for proper software behavior. This can also detect Trojan horses and spoofs. Virus detection is much the same as detecting parasites. You should petition your software suppliers to supply the size and cryptographic checksum information with all of their software, so you can be sure that you have a clean system.

Worms

A worm is a program that is used as a transport mechanism for other programs. It utilizes the network to spread programs from one system to another. It will utilize a flaw in a network transport, such as network mail or remote process execution, to get its package from one system to another. The worm has three basic processes. First, it will search for a receptive system. Second, it will establish a connection to that system. Finally, it will transport its program to the remote system and execute the program. This program may contain a worm itself so it can spread further, or it may be any other type of malicious code.

> Franklin Wayne Adams, of Houston, created a computer "worm" that seeks out computers on the Internet that have certain sharing capabilities enabled, and uses them for the mass replication of the worm. The worm causes the hard drives of randomly selected computers to be erased. The computers whose hard drives are not erased actively scan the Internet for other computers to infect and force the infected computers to use their modems to dial 911. Because each infected computer can scan approximately 2,550 computers at a time, this worm had the potential to create a denial of service attack against the emergency 911 system. [39]

[39]   "Major Investigations: 911 Virus," *National Infrastructure Protection Center.*

Modified Source Code

Linux source code is freely available and widely distributed. Skilled hackers have the ability to create their own unique back doors or data capture routines. The hacker may bring compiled modules for the system, if he has executable code for your type of machine, or he might bring his own source code and compile it on your system. This requires that the hacker port the code to your specific version of the UNIX system and that he have access to the compilers on the system. Therefore, when securing a system, the editors and compilers should be removed from the systems which do not need them.

Other UNIX systems, which do not have freely available source code, are still vulnerable to source code attacks, since UNIX system code is highly transportable. However, the hacker must have access to a development environment for the specific type of system. If your system provides this environment, then it is easier to create these back doors. Systems that are not software development systems should not have a developer's environment. Compilers should be removed from nondevelopment systems and access to development systems should be restricted. All your software development should use a source code management package that has strong authentication and logging. Source code is a valuable asset and should be handled with all the controls appropriate for an asset of its value.

> Ken Thompson, one of the authors of UNIX, illustrated that examining the code may not be enough to catch a Trojan horse. He rewrote the C compiler so that when it compiles the login process, it plants a back door. The source that seemed to be infected, the login program, was checked and was clean of any tampering; however, the back door persisted until a new version of the C compiler was installed. [40]

Dynamically Loadable Modules

Dynamically loadable modules are a relatively new addition to the UNIX environment. They allow the system to load the module only when it is needed instead of integrating it into the software program. They are available in both user space, as shared libraries, and in kernel space, as dynamically loadable kernel modules (DLKM).

A **shared library** is a library of utilities that can be called from any program. Shared libraries differ from archive libraries in that they are not loaded into the executable program at program link time; instead, they are only pointed to from the executable and are executed at run time. Consequently, any modifications to the shared libraries are immediately realized by the

[40]   Thompson, Ken, "Reflections on Trusting Trust," *Communications of the ACM*, v. 27, i. 8, August 1984.

programs that use them. So if a hacker replaces a utility in a shared library, all the programs which use that utility will be compromised. Shared libraries should be given more protection than programs since a modified shared library can have a much greater effect than a single modified executable program. The development tools required to modify modules should be only on secured development systems.

Dynamically loadable kernel modules work in the same manner. They are not statically linked into the kernel; rather, they are loaded when the system that uses the module is initiated. The ability to unload and reload these modules provides the ability to update modules without having to shut down the system. It also opens the door for hackers to install kernel level code into the system with little effort and little likelihood of discovery.

Software Developers

Sometimes vulnerabilities in a system will come from software developers — not that they intentionally create them. Sometimes code is moved into production while it still contains debugging information or developer hooks.

Both these issues can be minimized if greater care is taken in the software development cycle. Regular software design reviews can help isolate design flaws that can lead to security issues. Before moving from development to production, code reviews should be performed to locate any development code that is still in the system.

Source code management is a large endeavor, and it is key, not only to the control of a software project, but also to improving the security of the software.

Exploiting Network Protocols

Today, most exploits use network services, since most systems are accessed over the network. There are hundreds of network services from which hackers can choose to attack.

The internet daemon, `inetd`, controls some of the processes that communicate over the network. The internet daemon listens to each port and when a connection is identified, it passes control of the socket to the associated program.

A hacker can add a back door into a system by adding a line in `/etc/inetd.conf` that will attach a shell with root privileges to a specific socket. The line can be like this:

```
hack  stream  tcp  nowait  root /bin/csh csh -i
```

This direct approach is probably too visible to be used by any real hacker. It is more likely that a hacker will replace one of the programs that is already configured in `inted.conf` with an alternate program or just enable programs that are normally disabled, such as `rexd`.

The `rexd` server has a serious security design flaw. User authentication is done in the client and not in the server. The `rexd` daemon relies on the `on` command for any user authentication. A simple C program can send a request to a client and supply any command and any user

ID, and `rexd` will happily execute the command. This would allow a hacker to write a program that would be a client to the `rexd` daemon and bypass all authentication. Running `rexd` is like having no passwords at all.

E-mail Spoofing

The e-mail spoof is one of the most trivial of all spoofs. SMTP, the simple mail transfer protocol, consists of simple ASCII commands. These commands can be easily input manually by using a telnet connection to the system's SMTP port. E-mail forgery does not require access or authorizations that have to be obtained improperly.

```
telnet victim.com smtp
```

Once connected, the hacker can type the mail protocol command directly to the port. Identifying someone else in the mail "From:" command will show that the mail was sent from the user identified. This technique can be used to send mail to other systems by entering a "To:" command to another system. Careful examination of the mail header will usually indicate where the spoof has come from.

If the spoofed e-mail originates from a compromised system, then even the *ident* protocol, RFC 1413, cannot be trusted to return correct information from the compromised system.

Several state legislatures began trying to regulate commercial e-mail as early as 1997. At least 18 states have enacted or are working on legislation that would impose stiff penalties on commercial e-mailers who engage in unsavory tactics. More states are writing their own legislation — complete with pricey penalties for violating the law. Many state's laws require that the sender's contact information not be falsified and allow damages to be recovered. In Rhode Island, damages can be as high as $500 per message, up to $25,000 per day and spammers can also be liable to the state, with fines of up to $5,000 and imprisonment up to five years.[41]

IP Spoofing

Internet Protocol (IP) spoofing is the act of sending packets with source addresses other than the actual address of the originating host. These "spoofed" packets can have addresses that are unassigned or addresses that belong to another host.

---

[41]   Cave, Damien, "States Outlaw Spam," *Salon.com*, 19 April 2000

The Internet Protocol (IP) was first designed when the Internet was a much smaller and friendlier place. Authentication was not a feature that was considered necessary and was not added into the protocol until the development of IPSec and it will still take many years before IPSec is widely utilized.

Currently there is no way to stop IP spoofing. The best we can do is to protect ourselves against attacks that attempt to spoof our own addresses and stop our network from being the source of such attacks.

To stop a network from being the source of such an attack, the border routers should be configured to drop any packet exiting the internal network with a source address that does not belong to the internal network.

- **Source Routing** — Source routing is a feature of IP that allows the packet to define the path that the return packet should take to find its way back to the source host. This feature is virtually never used by legitimate applications since the Internet utilizes dynamic routing protocols to optimize the traffic. However, it is often used by attackers who use IP spoofing to get packets returned, unless the attacker is either on the same network as the spoofed address or reliably along the path between the spoofed source and destination hosts. Since there is little legitimate use for source routing, it should be disabled on all hosts and routers and routers should be configured to drop any packet that contains a source route.

- **Network Flooding** — Network flooding is the process of creating more network traffic than the network is able to process, thereby making the network unavailable to legitimate traffic, and the hosts that require that network to communicate unreachable. The large number of packets received by the host often overwhelm the system resources before they overload the network. Every packet received by the system consumes memory and computational power to determine its disposition.

- **SYN Flooding** — SYN floods send a large number of spoofed TCP connection requests. These requests utilize data structures in the target machine which consume memory and kernel resources and may cause legitimate connections to be denied.

  This exploit was published, complete with source code, in two hacker publications. Shortly thereafter, numerous SYN flooding attacks ensued, including an attack against the Internet access provider PANIX.

  There have been a number of different solutions implemented to remedy this problem. Consult your vendor to get the appropriate patch.

- **Smurf** — The "smurf" attack uses forged ICMP echo request packets directed to IP broadcast addresses from remote locations to generate denial-of-service attacks. There are three parties in these attacks: the attacker, the intermediary, and the victim. The intermediary can be victimized by suffering the same types of problem that the "victim" does in these attacks.

The intermediary receives an ICMP echo request packet directed to the IP broadcast address of its network. If the intermediary does not filter ICMP traffic directed to IP broadcast addresses, many of the machines on the network will receive this ICMP echo request packet and send an ICMP echo reply packet back to the spoofed source address in the forged packet who is the attacker's intended victim. The result is that when all the machines at the intermediary's site respond to the ICMP echo requests, they send replies to the victim's machine. The victim is subjected to network congestion that could potentially make the network unusable.

Attackers have developed automated tools that enable them to send these attacks to multiple intermediaries at the same time, causing all of the intermediaries to direct their responses to the same victim. Attackers have also developed tools to look for network routers that do not filter broadcast traffic and networks where multiple hosts respond. These networks can the subsequently be used as intermediaries in attacks.

To prevent your site from being used as an intermediary in this attack, you must disable IP-directed broadcasts at your router — which will deny IP broadcast traffic onto your network from other networks — and configure your systems to prevent the machine from responding to ICMP packets sent to IP broadcast addresses.

In almost all cases, IP-directed broadcast functionality is not needed.

System Flooding

System flooding is the process of consuming a resource or resources on a system until it makes the system unable to do useful work. The resources consumed can be general resources, such as memory, storage, or computation or, more often, specific resources, such as buffers or queues, fill up. In many cases, system flooding will result in the system hanging or failing completely.

Mass-mailings

Mail flooding has become a very popular attack. Mail messages containing viruses can exploit powerful e-mail clients which provide powerful scripting languages and address books. These attacks generally forward infected mail messages to individuals from the address book. When the macro capability allows mail to be sent without user interaction, these attacks can overwhelm networks and mail servers.

Exploiting Vulnerabilities

Exploiting known vulnerabilities is the most common method of attack. Exploit tools are widely available and can be run without any knowledge of the vulnerability being exploited. These tools make it point-and-hack. There are basically two groups of tools: the tools which find systems with known vulnerabilities and those that attack the known vulnerability.

Scanners and Profilers

Scanners will look at many systems, making a preliminary evaluation of the software being run on them. They will usually sweep through address spaces looking for systems which are running services which may be able to be compromised. They are often able to determine the system hardware and what operating system is running, including the version of that operating system. They can determine what services are available on each system and what software is servicing those services. This information is often put into a database so when a new vulnerability is discovered in a specific version of software, all the systems which are running that software can be retrieved to create a list of systems which are likely to be able to be compromised. Some scanners can have the speed at which they scan a network adjusted to reduce the likelihood of detection.

Profilers take a more in-depth evaluation of a specific system to determine the type of hardware and software being used. They will attempt to identify the versions and patch levels so that a specific attack can be crafted. The processes of scanning and profiling are often combined.

Sniffers and Snoopers

A snooper is a program that watches data travel through the system looking for a particular type of information. The snooper may be attached to a network interface to watch all the network traffic or to a disk interface to watch all the data flowing to or from the disk. Snoopers can also be parasites, inserted inside a system, like the print spooler or login system, secretly gathering information.

To protect yourself from these types of attacks, you must monitor what is running on your system and the programs that are on your system, so you know if something is running that shouldn't be, or if programs have changed unexpectedly. You may also want to investigate an encrypted file system, that is, a system that stores all the files in an encrypted form. Encrypted networking can also be employed, so all the transmissions from your system are encrypted.

Generally, a system listens only to the network address which is for that system. However, a network sniffer put the network interface into promiscuous mode, so it will listen to all the packets. Then the sniffer decodes these packets.

Snort, created by Martin Roesch and included on the CD-ROM, is an open source network intrusion detection system capable of performing real-time traffic analysis and packet logging on IP networks. It can perform protocol analysis and content matching, and real-time alerting.

It utilizes a flexible rules language and a modular plug-in mechanism which allows it to be easily expanded.

Since Snort is freely available, it is quite popular with the hacker community for the very reasons it is popular with system administrators — it is easy to use and very powerful.

Security Tools

There are a large number of very useful security tools that test your system's configuration and permissions on critical files, as well as test for known security holes. These are excellent for identifying where your system has shortcomings and where to spend your resources to close these security holes. They are also invaluable tools to hackers. If you haven't run these programs or have neglected to repair a defect, a hacker can run these tools to determine how to compromise your system. Security tools should be kept on removable disk media, or on a disk that can be unmounted and powered off when not in use. You should not keep security auditing tools on the system; make the hacker bring his own tools.

More prudently, use all available security auditing tools to discover all security problems and fix them! Then continue to monitor and audit the security of your system.

Buffer Overflows

Buffer overflows are the result of faulty programs that do not adequately manage strings or buffers. Programmers tend not to test for overflows, since good data will not be a problem and the testing slows down the program.

A buffer overflow occurs when a program writes data beyond the bounds of allocated memory. This can occur when indexing beyond the end of an array, or indexing a pointer beyond allocated memory, or passing more data to a routine than it can handle. In each case, data is written in an unexpected location, causing unexpected results. Often the program will abort. However, there are cases where the overflow can cause data to be written to a memory mapped file, or cause security problems through stack-smashing attacks. Stack-smashing attacks target a specific programming fault: careless use of data buffers allocated on the program's run-time stack, namely, local variables and function arguments.

A creative attacker can take advantage of a buffer overflow vulnerability through stack-smashing and then run any arbitrary code. Common attackers exploit buffer overflows to get an interactive shell on the machine. In the most common attack, an intruder attempts to overflow the buffer of a remote daemon or service to inject his code into the program's address space and overwrite the return address of some function. When this function returns, it will jump into the intruder's code and perform the illicit code. The resultant shell will have the privileges of the program which was exploited.

File Permissions

A hacker can compromise a system by exploiting inadequately protected files. As we have seen, there are a great number of files that will open security problems if they are not properly secured. You should monitor the status of the file system with a tool that monitors file size, permissions, ownership, timestamps, and computes a strong checksum of the contents of the file. If you, the system manager, are not monitoring file permissions regularly, you will be susceptible to a permissions attack.

- **Directory** permissions protect all of the files and directories in the directory. Inadequate permissions on directories cause a trickle-down security problem, since the inadequate permissions grants access to the contents of the directory and any file or directory in the original directory can be modified. This allows a hacker to step down through all the contained directories within the directory tree and compromise any of the files within. This problem is greater when the weak permissions are closer to the root directory. Inappropriate permissions on the root directory, /, will allow access to the entire file system. How often do you check the permissions of the root file system?

- **Device files** control the access to the physical devices represented by these files. Insufficient permissions on these files can allow hackers to access the devices themselves. When these devices are modems, it gives the hacker the ability to use these devices to call out to other systems. Inadequate permissions on network interfaces enables hackers to sniff the network for valuable information. In the case of disk devices, this will grant access to all the files contained on the device. There are hacker tools that allow the hacker to traverse the file system on a disk by having access only to the device file that contains the file system. This tool does basically what the operating system does — it reads pointers and blocks of data from the disk and interprets the data it receives as directories and files. It also allows the hacker to change the permissions on any file on the disk to which he has write access to the device file. This can include other device files. If a hacker has access to the memory device, usually /dev/mem or /dev/kmem, he has access to everything that is in the system's memory: programs, data, and state information. Basically, this is the entire system. An open door like this will spell disaster.

Password Crackers

Passwords are most computer systems' primary method of authentication. You can gain access by identifying who you are, your login, and then by telling the computer a secret shared between only you and the computer: your password.

You are expected to keep your password secret by not telling anyone or by writing it down. The computer keeps the password secret by using strong encryption methods when storing the password.

Password Encryption History

Originally, UNIX password encryption was based on the M-209 rotor cipher that was used in World War II. However, by the late 1970s, computers had become fast enough for this algorithm to be executed very quickly, and this opened the door for password guessing.

In 1979, Robert Morris, Sr., and Ken Thompson wrote a paper, published in the *Communications of the ACM*, that described a new one-way function to encrypt UNIX passwords based on the National Bureau of Standards Data Encryption Standard (DES) algorithm. UNIX systems continue to use a variant of the DES algorithm today. The user's password is used as the DES key to encrypt a constant. The algorithm iterates 25 times the DES's internal 16 iterations for a total of 400 iterations, so the algorithm is slow enough to discourage guessing.

Since 1979, computers have continued to increase in speed at an accelerating rate. Today, single CPU systems are 150 times faster. This means that even a slow algorithm computes quickly. In addition, new implementations of the DES encryption algorithm have been developed that increase its speed. Where as the VAX® 11/780 could execute about 1.5 encryptions per second, today's multi-CPU systems have reported the ability to do millions of encryptions per second.

Many Possible Passwords

The input to the password encryption algorithm is the user's password. This is limited to the 7-bit ASCII character set, basically the printable characters that are available on a keyboard. There are 128 of these characters. The maximum length of the password is 8 characters, so there are over 72,000,000,000,000,000 possible passwords. Added to each password is a salt which is one of 4096 different values, which adds more complexity to the encryption algorithm. The password and salt are actually used as the key to the encryption algorithm. This key is used to encrypt the numeric value zero. The output from the algorithm is a 13-character string, the first 2 of which are the salt. The characters in this string are composed of characters from a 64-character set including the upper- and lower-case letters, the numerals, and the period, and the slash.

New password algorithms expand the number of possible passwords by allowing longer passwords. However, this is only helpful if the password selection uses the added features and longer passwords.

The encryption algorithm cannot be reverse-engineered, so passwords are actually guessed. This is an automated process of guessing the most likely passwords. This is successful because even though there are over 300 quadrillion possible passwords, users are rarely educated on the wise selection of passwords and select passwords from only a minuscule percentage of those possible passwords.

Password Cracking

The UNIX password encryption scheme is not actually broken cryptographically. Cracking is actually an automated process of guessing the most likely passwords. Usually a dictionary search is used with certain enhancements. These enhancements include the methods for improving passwords that have been promoted for years. Some of these are changing the letters S, O, and I for the numerals 5, 0 and 1. If the attack is against a machine in a specific industry, the attacker may utilize an industry-specific dictionary. A password cracker is a standard part of any hacker's toolkit.

Password Guessing

A password cracker will use all the information available about the user, trying the user's name, initials, account name, and any other personal information known. This information will be gathered from the GECOS field and from files in the user's home directory. This information will be processed through the permutations listed below.

A password cracker will try a dictionary search. The dictionary will be slanted based on the experiences of the hacker and the knowledge of the system being attacked. The dictionary will include common first names; characters, titles, and locations from works of fiction, television and film, cartoons, and computer games; sports terms; and terms based on the industry in which the computer is being used.

All of the above words will be permuted in the following manner:

- Varying of upper- and lower-case letters.
- Reversing the spelling.
- Substituting the numerals 0, 1, 2, and 5 for the letters o, i, z and s in the word.
- Appending a single digit to the word.
- Pairing two words and separating them with a special character.

Since passwords are the primary defense against outsiders, there have been numerous studies done on the subject. Studies show that between 25 and 30 percent of passwords will be cracked using this process.

Crack, one of the early password crackers, was developed by Alec Muffett and is still widely used. It institutes the variants described above to common words in the supplied dictionary. Crack takes as its input a series of password files and source dictionaries. It merges the dictionaries, turns the password files into a sorted list, and generates lists of possible passwords from the merged dictionary or from information gleaned about users from the password file. It is available on the included CD-ROM.

PART II

The Hacking Process

Today, hackers are much more skilled at attacking systems than in the past. Often they will have a plan and an objective. Sometimes a group of hackers will work together and attack a system with the precision of a military maneuver. First, they will do reconnaissance, gathering as much information as possible from a wide variety of sources about the organization they plan to attack. Then they will gain access to a system. From that point on, they will continue to gather privileges until they have total control of the system. During this process, they will monitor your activities as system manager, cover up any evidence that they were ever on your system and open back doors so they can return at any time. Once this beachhead is established, they will branch out to other systems. They will collect a number of systems to make tracing their activities as difficult as possible. Finally, they will make their way to their target system and achieve their goal of engaging in whatever malicious activities they have planned.

Understanding the hacking process is critical to the ability of information security professionals to prevent intrusions. Regardless of the intent of the hacker, there is a normal process that is performed to achieve their goals. The process by which information systems are attacked is very predictable. A typical attack pattern consists of gaining access to a user's account, gaining privileged access, covering his tracks, and using the victim's system as a stepping stone to expand his realm or to attack other sites.

Selecting the Target

Everyone is potentially the target of an attack. For the hacker, target selection is often the easiest part of the attack, while the victim may find it very difficult to determine why he was selected to be attacked. There are a number of common reasons why systems are attacked.

Who You Are

One of the key elements in being selected as a target is the visibility of the target. A very visible target will increase the status of the hack; it will increase the likelihood of publicity, which is what many of the attackers are after. Certain industries and businesses are more likely targets than others. Their level of visibility shines above the rest. It may be because of their dominance in the market, their position in the public eye, or their type of business.

What You Do

Attacks with personal motivation are most often selected because of what the organization does. It may be that the business or the industry in which the organization belongs is perceived as being involved in things of which the attacker does not approve. The perceived reputation is more important than the facts.

Sites which are expected to have good security are often targeted to illustrate the skill of the attacker. Companies which sell security products and services are prime targets as well as government and military sites.

Who Your Customers Are

An organization can become a target if its customers are targets. An organization who caters to a famous or highly-visible clientele will be of more interest to a hacker than another organization.

What You Know

An organization which has private information about its customers is a likely target. This private information can be as common as credit card information or as specific as personal itineraries. Credit card theft is one of the most common types of information theft. However, theft of more personal information — one's personal schedule or where one's children go to school — is much more alarming.

What You Have

If your site is selected as the ultimate target of the attack, it is because of something you have. It is something of value to the hacker. This could be monetary value, such as credit card numbers, electronic funds, or even the products you produce. All of these things can be turned into ready cash. It could also be that you have something the hacker wants to use. Sites with super-computers or other specialized computing equipment are targeted for this computing power which the hacker hopes to use.

Identifying the Systems to be Attacked

Systems are often attacked which are not the ultimate target of the attack. These stepping stone systems are selected because they will in some way assist the attacker in getting to his final target. It is rare that the target system is attacked directly or is the first system attacked. Most attacks use many stepping stones to get to their final destination.

Easy to Compromise

Overall, the most important criterion of why a system is attacked is its ability of it to be compromised. Attackers target systems for which they have the best ability to compromise and the least likelihood that they will be detected. Hacker tools can rapidly identify systems with known vulnerabilities and the tools which will successfully compromise them.

The further out-of-date a system is, the more likely it is to contain more vulnerabilities, but more importantly, this is an indication of the quality of administration the system is receiving. If a system is not updated, it is likely that there will be other administrative oversights in the configuration and management of the system.

Relationship to Target

Sites are often attacked because of the relationship between your company or systems and the hacker's target. The relationship may be based on network topology. The companies may use the same ISP, or have an extranet connection to support a business relationship. It could also be this business relationship which draws the attack. The hacker may want to disrupt the business process or strain the relationship between the businesses.

Other areas of commonality may be the reason for the attack. Companies may have outsourced part of their business to the same outsourcing company, especially computer operations. Companies who have common owners or members on the board may be targeted, as well as those who have common customer or suppliers, or are working as contractors on the same project.

Contain Valuable Information or Resources

Systems are attacked because the attacker believes that they contain resources or information which have value to him. Sometimes that which the hacker is after is obvious, such as credit card numbers or source code to yet unreleased software, while other times what the hacker wants is elusive to the victim. It is the hacker's perception of value which drives his actions. Therefore, every system needs to implement a level of security to deter hackers, and those systems which have unique or valuable resources or information need the level of security commensurate with the value of their contents.

Gathering Information

Gathering information is the most important part of hacking a system. Information is power. The more a hacker knows about a system, the more likely he will be able to achieve his goals and the less likely he is to be caught. Identification tools are used to locate and identify systems to be compromised. These tools will usually try to be relatively quiet in their activities so that they will not be noticed by intrusion detection software. Good reconnaissance reduces unsuccessful attempts.

Company Information

Many attackers will be targeting specific companies, but others will be looking only for systems which are easy to compromise. In either case, the attacker will want to know as much about the target as possible. Companies are targeted because of who they are, or what they do, or what they have, or with whom they associate.

Understanding a company's business will help the hacker with social engineering. It can help him locate systems with the information he is seeking. Knowing the company's organization improves his ability to find weaknesses to exploit.

Knowing the target company can determine the likelihood that the attack will be prosecuted and under which laws. Certain businesses and industries, such as government sites, have special protection.

System Information

Information about the specific system can be used to select specific targets that either are more likely to have what the attacker is looking for, or are more likely to be breached. The hacker will want to gather information about the target system — what kind of system it is, what software it is running, what it is used for. Determining who owns the machine, who uses the machine and who administers the machine can indicate the likelihood that it will contain the information the hacker is looking for. Information about the utilization of the machine and the quality of administration can indicate the ability to compromise the system without being detected.

Business Processes

Understanding the business process can highlight where valuable information is located and where there might be weak links in the process. It can also identify individuals who have access to valuable information. Knowing the business process can help identify the function of systems and what information they might contain based on the services that the systems support. Specific information about software services, such as version, can pinpoint what type of attacks can be successful.

Business Partners

Today, businesses are entering into partnerships more frequently and with more organizations than ever before. Often these partners are not well-known to the organization and their security policies even less known. Identifying business partners indicates possible alternate ways that an organization can be attacked. A partner's network may be more easily penetrated and lead to an easier access point.

User Information

The users of a system are often the weakest link in the security chain. They are given the ability to give access to the resources under their control to others, and the responsibility to select passwords which are many times the primary access controls.

The hackers want to learn about the users of a system in order to decide which accounts are safer to use. They are looking for accounts that have not been used in a long time or those that go for long periods of time without use. Accounts that are connected with a lot of idle time may be attractive.

Gaining Access

Access comes in a number of forms. It may be physical access, or access to the organization's network or computer systems, or it may be access to the information itself.

Corporate business has responded to the growth of the Internet by putting business sites on the Internet. These business systems must have open access so that customer can access them at any time from anywhere. They also have to be connected to internal systems for real-time pricing, inventory, and other functions. These sites are very attractive to hackers.

Network Access

Network access gives the attacker many more options in probing and attacking a system. Corporate networks are usually a guarded resource. Direct attacks on firewalls are usually noticed. However, network access can often be accomplished by less direct methods. Employees will often add modems to desktop systems so that they can get access to Internet sites which are not allowed through the firewall. These modems can be used to gain unsecured access from remote sites.

Companies which share building access with other companies may find that their physical security may be lax enough for hackers to gain access to the network. Utility closets are often shared among companies in the same building, granting access to almost anyone.

A hacker's system on the company's network becomes a peer in many network protocols and gives significantly better chance of successfully compromising systems.

Wireless networks also provide access to internal networks to those outside the physical security controls. Wireless networks have to be considered un-secure and require appropriate protection.

System Access

Computer systems, desktops, and servers are the most common targets in the information system. They are valuable resources in the information system. They are the repository of information and they give the attacker a foothold. Even when the computer is not the ultimate objective of the attack, it is usually necessary to compromise systems in order to gain that ultimate objective.

Access to Information

Information can be accessed from any source that has the information. This includes information systems, storage, communications, and people.

Acquiring Privileges

Privileges are required in order to utilize information system resources. All accounts, programs, and services have some privileges to perform their functions. Different elements will have different privileges, based on their requirements. The security model of least privileges says that only the minimum privileges necessary to perform a task should be given. Another tenet of security is isolation, so that the privileges given to one element cannot be used to compromise another. Both of these are difficult to implement, so often privileges can be acquired and utilized to leverage more privileges.

Information Access

Information is often the target of an attacker. Access to information enables the destruction of that information, the vandalism or other alteration of the information, or the theft of the information. He or she may want the information to use personally, or to otherwise profit from the possession of the information. Theft of information includes the theft of proprietary information, credit card information, personal information, and government secrets.

Resource Utilization

A system may be targeted for its resources. It can be because of the uniqueness of the resources, such as specialized hardware or access to unique peripherals, which the hacker wants to use, or it can be the abundance of resources which draws the hacker. A very fast computer system or a system with a very fast network is a tempting target. The hacker can use these resources for his own purposes and can go unnoticed if his consumption is relatively small compared to the total resources available to the system.

Avoiding Detection

Even though many hackers are looking for notoriety, they do not want to get caught. Their online life and notoriety are based on their online identity or handle. Most hackers do not want this to cross over into the physical world where they might be arrested. Many of the tools in the hacker's toolbox provide the hacker with some level of stealth. Some of these tools replace some system utilities with versions which do not report the presence of the hacker, his tools, or his activities. The goal of stealth tools is to keep the hacker from being discovered.

Realizing a Goal

It is likely that the goal of the attacker is to do more than just access information or utilize resources. Most hackers have a goal — there is a reason for their attacks. To achieve this goal, the hacker must compromise the system. Most of the time, hackers compromise systems by exploiting known vulnerabilities. These vulnerabilities can be software errors, improper configuration, or inadequate administration. Nearly all attack tools fall into this category.

Wealth

Computers have become a regular tool in the criminals' arsenal. Money flows through computers in the form of credit card numbers and electronic funds transfers, and enough personal information can be gathered about an individual to financially impersonate him or her — identity theft.

Notoriety

Notoriety is a key element in many types of attacks. Website vandalism, e-mail viruses, and denial-of-service attacks are staged only to get publicity. The publicity may be an attempt for personal fame or to draw attention to a cause.

Cause Harm

Some attacks are meant to cause harm to a business or individual. It may be financial harm such as theft of money or product or a denial-of-service attack which keeps the company from conducting business.

There have also been attacks against individuals. Computer networks have been used to harm people either directly by the one instituting the attack or through involving a third party.

## CHAPTER 5

Gathering Information

Information is your business and controlling access to it is what security is all about. Computer security is but one piece of information security. And it is complete information security that the company wants. Information must be protected in all its forms and everyone who has access to the information is responsible for its security. Everyone in the company must understand his or her role in information security — executives, managers, engineers, office workers, maintenance personnel — everyone. The employee's understanding of information handling procedures and security reporting procedures should be evaluated as part of an employee's performance review. It is the company's responsibility that each employee understand these things. There must be a continuing security awareness program aimed at all the employees of a company. A visible reporting process to record security incidents is required. Physical access procedures must be in place and followed. All the rules must apply to every rung on the corporate ladder — from the very top to the very lowest rung. Violations of security principles in order to make things easier for system managers or corporate executives just make it easier for hackers to hack at the highest level of the company.

The hacker gathers information to improve his chances of successfully attacking the system and achieving his goal. Hackers will use a wide variety of methods of gathering information and will be looking for information about the company, its employees, and the computer systems it uses. The computer systems will give up some information, and people will give up even more.

Public Sources

There is a wealth of information publicly available. Printed publications and websites often tout an organization's accomplishments and frequently provide extensive details. The entire community of industry analysts and corporate intelligence is built on gathering information which is publicly available. It is true in intelligence gathering that the sum of the parts is greater than the whole. Collecting and correlating information from many sources can build a more complete and detailed picture than any single source could provide. It is amazing how much information can be gathered, much of it without access or cost. People and systems are surprisingly willing to give away information.

Financial Reports

There are a number of public sources of financial reports about a company. There are public filings with the Security and Exchange Commission for publicly traded companies and the company itself will publish an annual report containing information about the company, its executives, its activities, and its partner relationships.

Public Websites

Websites often publish information without the level of involvement by corporate legal and public relations departments that printed material has. They will often report on new and exciting developments of the organization. They might highlight outstanding individuals or the types of systems which are used. Information is often published on websites without any review for sensitive content.

Domain Name Registration

The registration of domain names provides contact information for the owner, administrator, and financial contact for the domain. This contact information is often a specific individual, including e-mail and physical address. This may offer a strong foothold for social engineering or it may well indicate where the website is hosted and thereby indicate alternate methods of attack through other systems hosted at the same site.

Name Services

Name services publicly expose the hostname of internal systems, and broadcast the organization's internal structure, the size of its departments, the allocation of resources, and whether there is an expansion or contraction — all valuable information to competitors.

People

Technological solutions can address only technological problems. Everything else requires policies, procedures, practices, and education. People need to understand the importance of security in their day-to-day life and they need regular reminders through an awareness program.

People are social animals needing to communicate with others. They want to brag about their accomplishments and complain about their troubles, especially with those who are involved in similar pursuits, even if they are competitors.

All the computer security in the world will not help if the information that these measures are protecting is being gathered from people. People are generally more willing to share information than machines are.

Publishers

Individuals in the organization need to be kept aware of how the information that they make public may affect the organization. Today, the posting of resumes on the Internet has become common. These are full of useful information, not only about the individual, but also the systems he or she has been working with, the type of work being done, and more. Personal websites of employees boast of achievements and complain about the organization's shortcomings. All is valuable information to an attacker.

Eavesdropping

Hackers take every opportunity they can to look over the shoulder of someone who is entering "secret" information, whether it is a phone card number, an ATM PIN number, or a password for a computer system. Crowded areas are a prime location for these types of activities. All of us need education about the handling of information. You need to take the same care with company information as you would with personal information. You must be aware of your surroundings and pay attention to those around you.

There are also high-tech methods of eavesdropping. It has even been demonstrated that a laser can be bounced off a window and vibrations caused by the sounds inside the building can be collected and turned back into those sounds. The cost of high-tech surveillance has made it available only to the professional information gatherer. But as with all high-tech electronics, falling prices are making it more affordable for a wider audience. As in most other things, security is an economic issue. Security is the process of making it economically unfeasible to compromise the system or information.

Wireless networks are growing increasingly popular among companies, with uses that range from e-mail, instant messages and Internet access to file transfers and access to corporate servers and databases. But hackers have found that their errant signals often spill past office walls. They leak into adjacent businesses, ground floor lobbies of office towers, parking lots, even nearby streets.

Researchers told MSNBC.com that they had been able to "spy" on wireless systems used by such retailers as Wal-Mart and Home Depot. Best Buy followed suit by shutting down its wireless cash registers upon learning that it, too, had been monitored. [42]

---

[42]   Hornaday, Bill, "Team IDs possible hacker targets," *The Indianapolis Star*, 13 June 2002.

Socializing

It has long been said that it is easier to get information by buying someone a drink after work at the local pub than by trying to covertly gather it. Once befriended, people are very likely to talk about what is happening in their life, including office gossip. Why should a hacker steal information when all he has to do is ask for it? This technique requires the hacker to be a sociable person, which many computer hackers are not. However, this is the mainstay of the professional information-gathering industry.

Social Engineering

Social engineering is a confidence game; that is, gaining the confidence of the victim so he or she will give you the information you are requesting. Hackers can accomplish this through a number of methods. They will often start by calling the phone numbers around a modem number to find out what company owns the modem line. Once they identify the company, they will start to work on the employees.

A successful social engineer will use both intimidation and preying on people's natural desire to help people who ask for help. He will utilize new employees to get information from them and he will impersonate new employees to get information from help desks and other employees. He can befriend users who have privileges, or he can convince someone that he is a support person and he needs the information to debug a system problem.

Much social engineering will go unnoticed, since a hacker will ask one individual only a few specific questions and then move on. These attacks will be numerous inconsequential inquiries that add up to a great wealth of information.

> Unscrupulous account information brokers are obtaining custom-ers' account information from insured financial institutions through a practice known as pretext phone calling or social engineering. Brokers who engage in this practice call institutions and use sur-reptitious or fraudulent means to try to induce employees into pro-viding a customer's account information. For example, a broker may pose as a customer who has misplaced his or her account number, and may repeatedly call the institution until the broker finds an employee who is willing to divulge confidential account informa-tion. The broker may use information about the customer, such as the customer's social security number, that has been obtained from other sources, to convince the employee that the caller is legiti-mate. While there are no reliable estimates as to the extent of this practice, there is concern among the federal banking and law en-forcement agencies that it is becoming increasingly prevalent. [43]

[43]   "Pretext Phone Calling," *FDIC Special Alert*, 2 September 1998.

Trojan horses are a type of social engineering via software. Games that request passwords so that others cannot pretend to be you while playing the game will surprisingly often yield login passwords. Another common Trojan horse is the exciting new utility that does something very useful while giving your privileges to the hacker. These are just a few ways that a hacker can abuse the trust a user has put into him or his software.

Trusted Advisor

It is possible that a hacker will know more about the computer system than anyone else, including the system manager. If he is an employee, he has an advantage. He is already trusted, knows the people and the relationships, and can use his knowledge to build relationships with system managers, programmers, and other people who have privileges on the system by helping them with the problems they have with the system. In this manner he will become a trusted advisor, someone to whom these people turn when they need help. To facilitate this assistance, people will often allow him to access the system with their login, thereby giving him access to their privileges. Every employee should be aware of the importance of information security.

The lion's share of security incidents are caused by either current or former employees. This is why you must know the mood of your personnel. Most employee hackers are disgruntled employees who will cause trouble of some type; the computer is just a handy tool. Specific employees generally become disgruntled when there is stress in their life, either personal or business-related. However, if the company is going through change which has the employees concerned about layoffs or strikes, then you must be more alert to the possibility of in-house hacking.

You must impress upon your users the importance of not sharing logins and passwords. If a user needs special privileges, he should be given a special temporary login specific for the function that he is to do. This is required for accountability.

People need to understand the importance of security in their day-to-day life and they need regular reminders through an awareness program.

Going On Site

Local hackers will often take a field trip to their target's facility. They may appear in a tour of the facilities, or spend late hours going through refuse, or walk right in. Hackers have skirted physical security through a variety of guises. They have impersonated delivery people, telephone workmen, and office equipment repairmen: "I'll have to take this computer into the shop." A hacker news group has even given information on how to get a job as a janitor so the hacker can get uninterrupted, unsupervised access to an entire building.

Today the low price of "color technologies" — scanners, video capture and printers — has made it affordable for any hacker to produce very convincing company IDs. Quite often companies use PCs and software that are easily affordable to the public to create their official IDs. So, common identifiers may be too common. An ID on someone who acts as if he belongs is not enough to be certain that he does belong.

Every day there are people in your physical building who are not your employees. You often don't know who they are or if they should be there. Companies have planted people with competitors to gather information, as in this example:

Drive-by Sniffing

The growth of wireless technology, in both commercial and personal networks, has opened new avenues of attack. These are often installed without consideration of where the signals may be going. Hackers with a laptop computer and a wireless network interface can drive down the street and find unsecured wireless networks. They can use these networks to sniff data or to get unauthorized access. Many hackers are just looking for free Internet access, but if the wireless network is an internal network, your company could well be exposed.

> It has been a well documented fact that armed with a wireless-equipped laptop and antenna, hackers have no shortage of victims around London. But security firm I-sec recently demonstrated that using an empty Pringles tube as an antenna could boost the hacker's chance of picking up a wireless signal by as much as 15 per cent. Apparently the hollow tube shape combined with a tinfoil lining makes the empty crisps tin ideal for concentrating a signal.
>
> During a half-hour drive around the centre of London, almost 60 wireless networks were picked up. Around 40 of these had no security — a hacker would be able to use the company's bandwidth any way he liked, as well as browse the internal network. According to I-sec, the face of the Pringle man might not be the only household item in a hacker's arsenal. Objects from coffee tins to old satellite dishes have also been used to pick up wireless signals.[45]

Dumpster Diving

Dumpster diving is the term given to scrounging through the trash, since it often requires diving into a trash dumpster. A great wealth of information is thrown away by many organizations. This information can be in the form of computer printouts that may contain sensitive information; used carbon printer ribbons that can be unwound so all that was printed can be read; used media, that can still be read even if all the data were deleted or the disks reformatted; and computer manuals that not only contain information about the system but also quite often

[44]   Middleton, James, "Pringles: The Latest Hacker Tool," *vnunet.com*, 8 March 2002.

contain notes written in the margins by the users of these manuals. This information can be about the systems that are being used, proprietary or confidential information that was disposed of improperly, or even passwords written in the margins of user manuals.

This information is thrown away because people don't think of the consequences. Sometimes when a person quits or is transferred, all the material that was in his or her office is sent to the trash. In many cases, no one reviewed the material to see if it contained any confidential information.

You need to create an appropriate disposal policy. This policy should address all aspects of data disposal and should be part of a data handling policy. Data classification, access, storage, backup, and removal will also be included. It will define where data of specific classifications can be stored, and how this media, if it is removable media, disk, or tape, are to be labeled, handled, and disposed of. These procedures will vary, depending on the classification or sensitivity of the data. Information classification and handling procedures are important, regardless of the format of the information. They should apply uniformly, regardless of whether the information is on the computer, printed on paper, or on a marker board or drafting table. A marker board in an executive board room is no less susceptible to compromise than a piece of paper on a secretary's desk.

Snooping

Information exists in most offices in physical forms. This information is often left lying around on desks, or unlocked in file cabinets. Company *clean desk* policies exist to solve this problem, not to have clean desks. Whiteboards containing business plans and meeting notes are often left for the cleaning crew to erase. Company information decorates the walls of cubicles. In the open office environment, utilized by many companies, oral communications can be easily overheard. This includes telephone conversations.

Desktop Computers

With the greater distribution of information, physical security becomes even more important. When all the computers and information were in the data center, physical security was easy: It was localized. Now there is sensitive information on departmental servers and PCs on everyone's desktops and information is walking around inside laptop computers. So physical security and security control are much more complicated.

Computers must be secured from both access and theft. A survey reported that most of the laptop computers that were stolen in airports were not random thefts, but were stolen for the information they contained. Almost any security measure can be overcome if the hacker can get physical access to the computer system.

Computer Systems

Computer systems give out an amazing amount of unnecessary information about the services they provide and the versions of the software they are running. Systems which participate in cooperative networks are especially likely to release information. These systems which openly share resources have to supply a large amount of information to identify the resources being shared and the systems which use the resources.

System Information

Numerous commands freely announce information about themselves as well as about the system on which they are running. They often announce their revision and the versions of the operating system. This is very valuable information to the hacker. There is no reason that users' login names need to be public information. Making them public gives away half your system's primary protection — login and password security.

With many versions of UNIX systems and other emerging multi-tasking desktop operating systems, a skilled hacker will want to know what type of hardware and software are on the target system so he can design an attack plan and focus on those systems that he will most easily be able to conquer. The hacker-wanna-be, whose only skill in attacking a system is using tools written by someone else, will need to know what type of system his target is so he will know which tools to use.

Many programs on the system will give information to users who are not yet authenticated. Most login connections will announce the system's name and operating system revision unless configured not to.

User Information

A user's login name and password are items that the user is expected to keep confidential. In fact, it is these two pieces of information which are your primary defense against intruders.

A company has its own need to associate real people to user names on a system. However, there is no reason for this information to be available to anyone other than system administrators. Knowing a person's name, telephone number, title, and so on, gives a hacker a wealth of information that can be used for programmatic attacks, such as password guessing, or for social engineering. The more a social engineer knows about his victim, the more likely he is to successfully get his victim to believe his story and give him the information that he wants.

Application Information

Announcing what the system does helps the hacker locate the system that is most likely to have the information he is looking for. Even valid users should not need to know what system runs what application. The valid user should access the application from a menu structure that references only the application and not the system. This also gives the company the freedom to move an application from one machine to another or to use different machines in different departments for the same application without having to have different user instructions in different departments or having to notify all the users when a change occurs.

Over the Network

Even with these simple network connections, a hacker can use them to gather information and gain access to systems, even if all he has is a telnet connection. He may be able to make more than telnet connections to other systems. There are a number of network services that use simple character-based commands.

- **Banner scanning** is the process of sending connection requests to service ports on the system to evaluate the response for information about the type and version of the system and software.

- **Network profiling** is the process of identifying a system by how it responds to specifically formed TCP/IP packets. Since there are variations in the interpretation and implementation of the standards, there are differences in how systems respond. As a result, fine details exist in any particular implementation of a standard that may uniquely identify the vendor. By sending probes and looking at the results, hackers can determine which operating system is responding.

Security Experts

Hackers will read security advisories from the Computer Emergency Response Team and other security organizations. They will monitor security news groups and mailing lists. They will pore through security patches from vendors and read security books. Information is a double-edged sword: Any information about computer security can be used by hackers to their benefit. Many of the same tools used by system managers are also used by hackers.

However, security by obscurity does not work. It is shortsighted to think that hackers will not be able to discover flaws in your security just because you don't tell them. Hackers are much more creative about obtaining information and have the time to spend doing it, while system administrators are busy doing their jobs taking care of the system and its users. Security professionals' policy of keeping security issues to themselves tends to penalize the administrators of small systems and systems in small businesses who do not have access to these security professionals. These are the system managers who need security assistance most.

Mailing Lists

Security mailing lists and other broadcast forums are used to announce security vulnerabilities and solutions. These have been used as jumping-off points for creating attack tools and locating vulnerable systems. There is truly no need to disclose the vulnerability which has been discovered to the public. Only the process to eliminate the vulnerability is needed.

For security to improve, a move must be made from announcing vulnerabilities to a more efficient process of patching vulnerable systems to remove the security issues.

Customer Support

Support organizations exist to help users who are having trouble. These troubles can often be related to issues which are system vulnerabilities. Support personnel will often supply details of security issues in the support person's desire to solve problems beyond the normal scope of user issues. Hackers will contact support groups by impersonating a user and requesting help or information. This information may be used to develop exploit tools or to clarify how a vulnerability can be used to the hacker's advantage.

Self-help discussion groups have been frequented by hackers to identify vulnerable systems or to convince users with troubles that they can help if given more information or access. Users of these support group systems have been exploited by hackers.

Other Hackers

Hackers will spend a lot of time "surfing the boards": gathering information from hacker bulletin boards, looking for new tools to use to exploit a system, and absorbing "insider information" on the latest security bugs and patches. There are a large number of sites that have "hacker information," but they are not well-advertised. It will take the hacker some effort to find them, but when he does, he will find that hacker tools are available everywhere. In addition, many hackers informally associate and communicate findings, making it easier for "insiders" to learn from each other.

Computer security professionals need to learn the tricks and techniques used by the hacker. Hackers use information from security professionals to improve their craft; security professionals should learn from the exploits of hackers to improve security. Most companies would frown on security personnel interacting with hackers or surfing the hacker bulletin boards (BBSs). However, hackers have become public enough to gain some information without having to dive into the "forbidden" areas of the Net. There are regularly printed magazines like *2600*, a quarterly publication about hacking, as well as electronic journals like *Phrack*. There are even CD-ROM collections of software and information for hackers and, of course, there are news groups that specialize in the hacker culture. In France3, there is even a hacking academy.

Patrick W. Gregory was sentenced to 26 months in prison and $154,000 in restitution for telecommunications fraud and computer hacking.

Gregory was a member of two computer hacker organizations, "total-kaOs" and "globalHell." By using stolen unauthorized access devices, such as telephone numbers, PIN combinations and credit card numbers, Greg illegally accessed numerous teleconferences provided by such victims as AT&T, MCI, Sprint and others.

Gregory and other co-conspirators used the unauthorized access devices they stole to set up teleconferences so that they could communicate with each other and discuss matters relating to tele-communications theft and computer hacking. Gregory trafficked in authorized access devices by accessing illegal teleconferences using unauthorized PIN numbers he received from friends who be-longed to other online hacking organizations, and almost daily or-ganized hacking teleconferences lasting more than six hours.

He and his cohorts also trafficked in credit card information and computer password combinations that allowed them unauthorized access to multiple protected computer systems around the world, in which they would deface websites and intentionally crash sys-tems and delete data. [45]

---

[45]   "Major Investigations: Patrick Gregory, aka 'MostHateD'," *National Infrastructure Protection Center*.

## CHAPTER 6

Limiting Information Disclosure

There is no reason to give away information for free. This includes the system's name and its function and the company's name. Those who are authenticated to use the system know this information and those who are not don't need to know. Information may be the hacker's goal or it may be the means to the end. In any case, information is the hacker's most powerful tool. The hacker will want information on the kind of system, the applications that run on it, the users who use it, and the company that owns it. Every piece of information is just one more piece of the puzzle that must be solved for the hacker to achieve his goal.

Information systems can disclose a great deal of information if they are not appropriately administered. They are often built for maximum convenience and usability, not to prevent disclosing information without appropriate authentication. Disclosed information can be used to determine how to compromise the system. Databases of known vulnerabilities and software to exploit them are widely available and knowledge of the type of systems and the version of software can be used to attack the system.

Disclosure of information about users can aid in the process of password guessing or social engineering. Disclosed personal information can lead to personal security risks to the user and legal liability to the organization.

Public Information Sources

A certain amount of information is required for an organization to successfully participate on the Internet. This includes name services, which resolves names into physical addresses for public sites, enough information to successfully exchange e-mail and a web presence. These servers and services need to provide information without leaking unnecessary information which can be used to compromise the organization's information infrastructure.

Domain Name Service

Domain name service is a hierarchical organization of names used to identify systems on the Internet. Name services provide the correlation between a system's name and its address. Every system which requires public access from the Internet needs a unique name and address. However, systems which do not need to be accessed from users on the Internet do not need to have their addresses published to the public.

Split DNS is a method of dividing the name resolution between access from the internal network and those from an external network. In this manner, the external users see only those systems which are exposed to the Internet, while the internal users can resolve the names of all the intranet systems. Historically, this was accomplished by dividing public and private names by separating them onto different servers for inside and outside as mentioned in RFC 1918. Resolvers would receive different answers depending on whether they were on the inside or outside. BIND v9 implements another method (based on the IETF draft) to achieve the effect of local names that is more in tune with the concept of a single global DNS tree or at least the appearance of a single tree. Use of this approach is not required, and older techniques will continue to work.

Webservers

Webservers provide an organization with its presence on the Internet. They supply people with information about the company and facilitate e-business by providing shopping, ordering, and order tracking. The level of visibility of these servers have made them popular targets of hackers. Web servers often provide more information than what is needed. Enthusiastic web designers may publish unnecessary information, such as the type of systems and the tools used in the creation and support of the websites. Information placed on public websites should be limited to the business details needed for the site and should be evaluated before being made public.

Web development tools will often insert documentation into the code which they produce. These comments often identify the tool and the version of the software used to produce the web page. They may also include information about to whom the tool is registered, and the systems which were used to create the document. The output of these design tools should be examined to determine what information they are disclosing and this output should be stripped of all unnecessary information.

The web server software may also expose information about the vendor and version of software and hardware powering the website.

Announcements

Many of the services that are available on a system expose information about the system or the service. These announcements are rarely required by the protocol and do not require revealing the version of the software or the type or version of the operating system on which the service is running. These announcement banners can be removed or minimized to avoid releasing useful information.

Announcement banners have also been an issue with prosecution of hackers. Announcements which welcome you to a system can be perceived as granting permission to use the system. Today acceptable use warning banners are needed for legal defense.

Reconfiguring the Service

Many services are able to configure the information which is presented by the service. Some of these systems can be configured to not report this information or to report information supplied by the administrator. Any services which can be configured to disable its announcement banners should be so configured. Otherwise, it should be configured to expose the least amount of information possible.

- **telnet** provides terminal level access to a system. It requires user identification and authentication to grant access to the system. However, the default telnet banner reports operating system, hostname, operating system release, and version and the type of system hardware. One can override the default telnetd login banner.

  On Linux, the -h option is used to disable the host specific information in the banner.

  On HP-UX, the -b option will disable the information or you can supply a banner file to be displayed instead. For example, to use /etc/issue as the login banner, have inetd start telnetd with the following lines in /etc/inetd.conf. If *bannerfile* is not specified, telnetd does not print a login banner.

  ```
  telnet stream tcp nowait root /usr/lbin/telnetd telnetd -b /etc/issue
  ```

  The banner file can be used to present an acceptable use or warning banner.

- **FTP** provides file transfer capabilities to the system. It can be configured to require authentication or to grant anonymous access. The default banner reports the hostname and the version of the software. However, there are options which can be set in /etc/ftpd/ftpaccess which will suppress the banner output and the output of the *stat* command.

  On Linux, the entry is

  ```
  greeting terse
  ```

  On HP-UX, the needed entries are

  ```
  suppresshostname yes
  suppressversion yes
  ```

- **Sendmail** is the most common SMTP daemon provided with Linux and HP-UX systems. The default greeting message is configured to supply the system hostname, the version of sendmail, the patch level, and the current time. The information about the mail server is contained in the configuration file: `/etc/mail/sendmail.cf`. It can be removed by changing the following line in the configuration file from

```
SmtpGreetingMessage=$j Sendmail $v/$Z; $b
```

to

```
SmtpGreetingMessage=
```

Restricting the Scope of the Service

Restricting the scope of a service limits the locations which can access the service. This will limit the area where information can be disclosed. It also provides a level of security by limiting the locations from where an attack can be conducted.

TCP Wrapper

TCP Wrapper was developed by Wietse Venemand has been very popular among the UNIX community. It is a TCP/IP daemon wrapper package. A wrapper is used to give an existing program additional functionality without modifying that existing program. For example, if a higher level of security is desired for the FTP daemon, such as restricting access from a specific host, the wrapper program is put in its place and after access has been granted, the actual FTP server is started. The TCP Wrappers product suite provides an enhanced security mechanism for various services spawned by the Internet Services daemon, `inetd`. TCP wrapper, `tcpd`, package allows for the restricting of TCP services to specific interfaces or limiting requests to specific addresses. It does not require any modification to the existing network programs. It is a wrapper which is started from inetd and front-ends the actual service.

TCP Wrapper, tcpd, comes standard with Red Hat and FreeBSD. It is available on HP-UX 11i platform as a web upgrade.

TCP Wrappers uses `/etc/hosts.allow` and `/etc/hosts.deny` files as Access Control Lists (ACLs). These access control files are used to match the client and server entries with the request for a service. These files are based on pattern matching and consist of a set of access control rules for different services, which use tcpd.

Whenever a connection is established with inetd for a service, inetd runs the appropriate server program specified in `/etc/inetd.conf` and waits for other connections. TCP wrapper is installed by replacing the server which it is to protect in the configuration file with tcpd. Inetd then runs the wrapper program tcpd instead of running the server program directly. When inetd invokes tcpd for a service, it will read the `/etc/tcpd.conf` file and configure itself to effect its behavior for different features at run time.

Xinetd Security

Xinetd has the ability to limit the scope of the systems which will be allowed access to each service. The configuration file for each of the services has to be configured to select where the connections can be made. Connections can be limited to a specific interface. Client can be limited by IP address, either by inclusion or exclusion. Services can also be limited by time of day.

```
interface = 192.168.1.1
only_from = 192.168.1.0/24
no_access = 192.168.1.9
access_times = 09:00-16:30
```

inetd Security

The HP-UX inetd security feature is an addition to the internet daemon, `inetd`, and is a standard part of HP-UX. It provides controls similar to those available from `tcpd`, allowing selective access to services based on the address of the client. It uses the security file, `/usr/adm/inetd.sec`, to allow or deny access to services by host or network address. Each service can have a set of hostnames, network names, or address ranges which can be allowed or denied. The following line would allow logins the specified IP addresses and deny all others.

```
login        allow   10.3-5 192.34.56.5
```

Software Features

BIND, v8.1.2, included in HP-UX 11i, is much more configurable than previous releases. The new security features enable entirely new areas of configuration, `/etc/bind.conf`, with many options that previously applied to all zones which can now be used selectively. These mainly apply to such areas as access control lists and categorized logging.

BIND v8.1.2 protects all DNS client/server transactions with IP address-base ACLs. On a name server, ACLs control who can query the name server, initiate zone transfers from the name server, and request dynamic updates, as well as restrict the name servers to which queries can be sent. IP-address-based access control for queries, zone transfers, and updates may be specified on a zone-by-zone basis.

These access controls rely on the source IP address stated in IP packets to determine the identity of the transaction initiator. If no precautions are taken, IP address spoofing can subvert this control mechanism. This is one manifestation of the well-known security limitations of the existing Internet DNS version 8.1.2.

BIND v9 includes protocol enhancements necessary to securely query and update zones. The IETF is addressing the security limitations of the Internet DNS through the introduction of DNS security protocols, including DNSSec, TSIG, and TKEY. These protocols are implemented in BIND version 9. This version of BIND is a major rewrite of nearly all aspects of the underlying BIND architecture.

DNSSec is specified in the Proposed Standard RFC 2535. It provides data integrity and authentication to security-aware resolvers and applications using cryptographic digital signature. It prevents non-authorized access to DNS, and prevents name-to-address mapping tampering over the wire. These are the type of active network-level attacks to which DNS has been susceptible. DNSSec can also be used to safeguard DHCP dynamic updates. It restricts DHCP updates to those authorized to perform them. It guarantees the integrity of zone data, using digital signatures produced off-line by the owner of the data and stored in SIG Resource Records.

DNS Security Operational Considerations is covered by RFC2541, which covers the operational aspects for keys and signatures used in connection with the KEY and SIG DNS resource records.

- *TSIG,* Transaction SIGnature, can be used to cryptographically authenticate transactions. A key is shared by the resolvers and the name servers, and they use it to sign communications between them. Specifically, the integrity and origin of the data exchanged in a transaction are protected by HMAC-MD5, using a key shared by the servers involved. This key must be securely distributed to the participants by a manual configuration process.

- *TKEY* is a protocol which addresses the problem of distributing shared keys for TSIG by allowing participants in DNS transactions to establish shared secret material. Note that TSIG requires time synchronization between the name servers involved, and the name of the key (not just the key itself) must match on the servers. In addition, TSIG does not provide zone data integrity or secure binding of public keys.

Polling

There are a great number of information gathering services on UNIX systems that will supply information about the system and its users without requiring authentication. Many computer services are promiscuous when it comes to supplying information without authentication.

Disabling the Service

Disabling a service will keep it from disclosing information. It will also prevent the administrator from using the service to gather information. Each service should be evaluated as to its value to the administrator versus its value to a hacker. Any service which is selected to be disabled should be removed from the system to keep it from being re-enabled.

- **finger**, from BSD, has long been associated with hackers. The finger will list the user's login name, home directory, default shell, .plan and .project files; the information from the GECOS field in the password file; and the terminal's write status and idle time. You can gain information about a remote system by using the user@system syntax.

  Finger will also return information about users that are not currently logged on to the system.

  ```
  finger @target
  ```

  Generally the finger command is more valuable to hackers than it is to system administrators. You may want to consider removing it and the finger daemon, fingerd, from the system. While the finger command is more notorious than the rwho and rusers commands, they return very similar information.

- **rwho**, the remote who command, from BSD, reports who is logged onto all the systems that are running the remote who daemon rwhod. It displays the machine name, user name, to which line the user is connected, and the amount of idle time on that connection. It is accomplished through the utilization of the remote who daemons. These daemons communicate with every other machine that is running the daemon and exchange user information. This command will not work unless the remote who daemon is running on the machine where the command is executed.

- **rusers**, the remote users command from Sun, gives a list of users on every machine on the subnet. It does this by broadcasting a request to the remote users daemon, rusersd. This daemon is started by the internet daemon and can be limited by using the internet daemon security facilities.

- **SNMP**, Simple Network Management Protocol, supplies information to network management systems. The information needed by these management systems is also very valuable to hackers. The default read password on all systems is "public" and goes unchanged in most implementations. Some monitoring products expect that this will be the read password and provide no provision for altering it.

  Until the introduction of SNMP version 3, which has yet to gain widespread utilization, traffic between the monitoring and the monitored systems is transmitted as clear text.

Any remote monitoring should utilize a VPN technology to provide privacy for the management information.

Eavesdropping

Historically, listening to the network was not considered feasible because it required physical access to the network cable, the ability to tap the cable, and the ability to look through all of the packets on the network seeking the few packets that contained interesting information and reassembling them.

Today, however, with the wide use of twisted-pair networking and wireless networking, physical access constraints are all but eliminated and there are plenty of network protocol decoders that are widely available, either as a turnkey LAN analyzer system or in software. Most systems have some network monitoring tools to assist in troubleshooting network problems.

Network monitoring is the process of watching all the packets that cross the network. This can yield a wealth of information if you can filter the information you want. Passwords are passed across the network in plain text when logging on and when using FTP. Any data that is passed across the network can be captured, if you know where to look for them. Even something as simple as traffic analysis can give you information about the relationship between systems.

There are a variety of network monitors that are available. There are LAN analyzers that are specialized pieces of equipment that attach to the network and read packets and decode them. There is software for a variety of systems, including PCs, that will allow them to monitor all the network traffic.

The only way to protect information that travels over an unsecured network is encryption. Native encryption is available in the Internet Protocol, Version 6, (IPv6) and with IPSec in IPv4. It provides integrity and privacy for the data within the packet.

Physical Isolation

Physical isolation can significantly reduce the ability to eavesdrop. When networks are small and under the control of a single organization, physically isolating the networks between systems and their users from other networks can be accomplished. This is most often done when isolating networks with very high value information or isolating internal networks for the Internet. Physical isolation of networks requires discipline in granting users only the access which they need and not the access they want. A physically isolated network provides the greatest level of security.

Network Isolation

Separating physical networks reduces the possibility of eavesdropping. Complete physical isolation is not usually a viable option. Most networks need to be interconnected for basic communications needs, such as e-mail and Internet connectivity. So network isolation has to be implemented as controlled isolation. Network devices, such as firewalls and routers, can limit the scope of a service by blocking the service port from other networks.

- A **switch**, or switched hub, is a hub in a star network which isolates network traffic by maintaining a list of what addresses are on which segment and sending only the traffic which contains the target device to the segment. Most of these switches will revert to a hub, and send all traffic to each segment, if the list of addresses gets too large or the device gets conflicting address data.

- A **bridge** is a network device that is used to connect networks of different media types at a link level, such as coax and twisted-pair. These networks must be running the same protocol and be configured in the same address space.

  Some bridges filter the communication that passes across them by determining the machine's hardware addresses on the segments to which they connect and not transmitting packets for that machine to the other side of the bridge. This is called auto-segmentation. This isolates the network traffic and is generally used to improve network performance. It also adds to the security of the network by not broadcasting all the packets throughout the network. Some bridges also allow for programmatic filtering.

- A **router** is a network device that is used to connect networks of different protocol types at the network level. They can be of totally different topologies, such as Token Ring and Ethernet, and in totally different address spaces. A router uses software addresses, such as IP addresses, instead of machine addresses to forward the packets. It also isolates the network based on where the source and destination machines are located. Routers are also programmable with the ability to filter the packets and reject packets based on the information within the packets, the source IP and destination IP, source and destination port number, and the "direction" of the connection if it is a TCP/IP connection. Some routers also include encryption.

- A **firewall** is a method of isolating networks at the application level. It will authenticate all packets as they pass through the firewall. Application firewalls can do a great deal of authentication. A firewall can limit access by service, source, destination host, user, or any combination of these. A company can have many firewall machines, each servicing one or more applications. Firewalls may be set up within a company when organizations deem the information contained on their systems needs this level of protection.

Encryption

Encryption can be used to make the information presented unintelligible except to those who have the decryption key. Historically, the computational requirements limited the use of encryption. Today, cryptographic solutions are becoming commonplace.

A **virtual private network** (VPN) is a method of using encryption to create secure tunnels through an untrusted network (e.g., the Internet). A variety of VPN solutions exist; many are proprietary — requiring the same vendor's equipment or software on both ends of the secure tunnel — others are based on standards and are interoperable between different vendors' implementations.

A VPN can be implemented at any level of the network stack. Implementing encryption higher in the stack provides more selectivity in which traffic is encrypted, while implementing it lower in the stack provides less impact on applications and an increased level of security against traffic profiling.

- **Application layer** encryption can be used to protect the information used in the application providing that the client and server sides of the application can utilize the same encryption. Application level encryption is seen most often in e-mail applications. There are a number of differing and incompatible e-mail encryption systems.

  S/MIME, Secure Multipurpose Internet Mail Extension, is an example of application layer encryption. It is an encryption standard used to encrypt electronic mail and other types of messages on the Internet. It is an open standard developed by Rivest, Shamir, and Adleman.

- **Presentation layer** encryption is provided by the software which provides the look and feel for any of a number of applications. Remote display systems, such as X windows or the web protocol HTTP, are examples of presentation layer applications. Any encryption provided at this layer protects any application which uses this presentation service.

  S-HTTP is another protocol that provides security services across the Internet. It was designed to provide confidentiality, authentication, integrity, and non-reputability while supporting multiple key-management mechanisms and cryptographic algorithms via option negotiation between the parties involved in each transaction. S-HTTP is limited to the specific software that is implementing it, and encrypts each message individually.

- **Session layer** encryption creates a tunnel for each separate session. A single user may create multiple sessions between systems; generally each session of each program or service creates a separate tunnel. Wrapping or tunneling can be used to achieve a transport layer-like VPN with multiple applications sharing an encrypted tunnel.

  SSH, Secure Shell, provides support for secure remote login, secure file transfer, and secure TCP/IP and X11 forwardings. It can automatically encrypt, authenticate, and compress transmitted data.

- **Transport layer** encryption protects all the communication over a specific socket. This is the connection between two systems for a specific service. All requests for that service are encrypted at the transport layer.

  SSL, Secure Sockets Layer, is an encryption method developed by Netscape to provide security over the Internet. It supports several different encryption protocols, and provides client and server authentication. SSL operates at the transport layer, creates a secure encrypted channel of data, and thus can seamlessly encrypt data of many types.

- **Network** layer encryption protects all communication between two physical systems. All communication between the two systems is encrypted. It provides point-to-point encryption often used with a border gateway.

  IPSEC is an effort by the IETF to create cryptographically-secure peer-to-peer communications at the IP network level, and to provide authentication, integrity, access control, and confidentiality. An IPsec VPN generally consists of two communications channels between the endpoint hosts: a key-exchange channel over which authentication and encryption key information is passed (port 500), and one or more data channels over which private network traffic is carried. The format of the headers and packets used is described in a series of RFCs. The encapsulating security payload, ESP, is in RFC2406, and the authentication header, AH, is in RFC2402 and the ISAKMP key-exchange protocol is in RFC2408.

  A number of Linux implementations of IPSec are available. However, export restrictions on cryptography limit its distribution. The HP-UX implementation of IPSec is available as a no-charge add-on product.

- **Data Link** layer encryption provides encryption at the link level. Any communication of any protocol which travels over the link will be encrypted with the encryption at this level. Data link layer encryption is used to protect the information from security flaws in the transmission media, such are widespread broadcasts or media which are easy to eavesdrop.

Misinformation

Misinformation can be used to make the attacker waste time attempting attacks that will not work, since the type of systems and the version of the software reported are not an accurate representation of the actual system. Misinformation is often used as bait for intrusion detection systems. It is often easier to distinguish hacking activities from actual users when the former are attempting methods which are not appropriate for the type of system, than when the attackers are using appropriate services. Misinformation can also be used to draw attackers away from sensitive systems by making other systems more attractive. In any case, you should consult with your legal department before utilizing misinformation.

False Services

Services which can be configured to change the disclosed information can be configured to disclose false information. False services can be used to misrepresent the type of system or the software which it is running. They are also used to collect data on an attack by recording the attacker's activities against a service which is not being used by actual users.

Honey Pot

A honey pot is a system that has no valuable information, utilizes extensive logging, and is configured so that it is reasonably easy to compromise so that an attacker will be enticed to access this system which will notify the security administrator and track the attacker activities.

They are able to provide a great amount of detail about the attacks against the system. This can reveal insight into the tools and techniques used by hackers and can highlight when services start receiving new attacks.

Even though honey pots are very popular with the media, they are less popular with businesses. Honey pots require a significant investment in administration and monitoring. They provide information for intrusion detection, for which there are numerous other solutions, and evidence collection, which is a duty for law enforcement. System administrators are usually too busy to devote too much time to hacker research.

> While tracking hackers back to their bedrooms has largely been removed from the job description of security staff and cybernarks, there is at least one technique that aims to follow the movements of unwelcome visitors.
>
> A honey-pot is a server, or system designed to bait unweary hackers into what appears to be an "easy target". As the system is designed simply to attract would be hackers, any connection to the server triggers an alarm, and allows security experts to follow the intruder's movement through the site — looking for idiosyncrasies. On the one hand the intruder wastes valuable time breaking into what is essentially an empty safe, and on the other it allows security staff are able to use the information they gather to shore up their other charges.
>
> The honey-pot server approach forms part of a wider movement in cybercrime prevention by the name of Honeynet.[46]

---

[46]   Douglas, Jeanne-Vida, "Barbed Wire vs the Honey-pot: Methods of Tracing and Deterring Hackers," *ZDNet Australia* (www.zdnet.com.au), 26 October 2001.

## CHAPTER 7

Gaining Access

Gaining access is the most important step in an attack. The first contact is the most critical. It is at this point that the hacker has the most exposure, since it is at this point that he has the least information about the system. He doesn't yet know how well the system is managed, or if there are auditing or trip wires in place to warn the administrators of unauthorized access. He will try to quickly ascertain if the system is well managed or not, preferably before he has actually logged in to it or set off any alarms. This is when you need your best alarms.

If a hacker already has access to the machine, his battle is half won. This is the best time to halt the hacker, before he gets on your machine. Keeping a hacker off of your system is much easier than getting a hacker out of your system.

Outsiders

Your goal is to keep outside hackers out, but what exactly is "out"? You must decide what is in and what is out. This is accomplished by defining a security perimeter where information can flow and still be considered secure. The security perimeter is usually closely related to the scope of control of the security personnel. This definition must include computer hardware (computers, networks, terminals, printers, removable media), physical locations (buildings, wiring closets, cable runs), and software (what software can be used with what data). Things that will limit/define the security perimeter include things like removable media and public communication lines. When any of these perimeter limitations is reached, you have encountered a security perimeter.

It is at all these points of access to the security perimeter that perimeter defenses must be put into place. These defenses should keep information from going out unprotected and people and processes from coming in unless authenticated and authorized.

Even though attacks from outside an organization comprise a small percent of the successful attacks, it is these attacks that can be most devastating to a company. Outside attacks that go beyond simple exploratory probes usually have a very specific target. Even unsuccessful attacks can have devastating effects if the public relations are not handled well.

Network access should be limited by isolating networks through the use of bridges, routers, and firewalls. Firewalls should allow only limited secured services to pass through them. Filtered bridges and routers should be used to keep network traffic from traveling farther than necessary. It is not uncommon for a hacker to enter your facility, locate an unoccupied cubicle, and plug into an unused network jack to monitor your network traffic. With the correct level of filtering, this attack would yield no information. Without filtering, all the company's information will flow past so the hacker can take whatever he wants.

All systems should restrict access as much as possible. A system can limit access to services by host with the use of the security features of the internet daemon. This feature identifies from which hosts a service will accept connections. All network services that are started by the internet daemon can be protected in this manner. The internet configuration file lists these services that the daemon starts. You should use the internet daemon to start all network services.

You should remove the ability to reconfigure network devices in-band, that is, over the network. All administrative tasks on all devices, including computers, should require physical access to the device. Physical access is much easier to control than network access, and thereby easier to secure. Most UNIX systems have a secure terminal facility that allows you to limit access by the superuser to specific terminals, usually only the system console.

Insiders

Insiders are users who are authorized to have access to the system and perhaps the application and the data. Since the inside hacker is already on the system, you must monitor what he takes from the system. Data can be copied from the system by electronic means, such as copying a file to systems outside the company. This can be accomplished using FTP or e-mail. Connections that go outside the company should be logged by the firewall as to who made the connection, where the connection was made, and what quantity of data was transferred. This should include e-mail. An employee who e-mails a 500-megabyte message to a competitor might be considered suspicious. Data can also be copied from the system through physical means, on printouts, or removable media. Today gigabytes of data can fit into your pocket. This is why access to removable media and proper data handling procedures are so important.

Users should not be given free rein on a system; their access should be only through applications, where possible. User access should be restricted as much as possible. This can generally be done through the correct use of permissions. Employees must be taught to look at computers as tools just as they look at a telephone or typewriter. The company must make available the tools which its employees need to do their jobs. However, a company does not need to make services available to an employee that are not needed for his job. Restricting unnecessary services will limit the possible exposure that could come from the misuse of the service. Companies may have the right to monitor their employees. However, the company must maintain the correct level of monitoring. Job function, responsibilities, and years with the company all affect the level of monitoring that is appropriate.

To protect a system from someone who is a valid user on the system, you must set up an integrity check to validate the integrity of the system and the information on the system. You will also need to monitor activities to be sure there are no unauthorized processes running on the system.

The company needs to make the tools which the users need available to them so they will not go elsewhere to get them. Centralized servers with downloadable software can help maintain consistency among distributed systems, keeping all the software on the systems up to the same version. Using desktop machines that do not have removable media will limit your exposure to unauthorized software being brought onto your system and to having information removed from the system.

Back Doors

A back door is an unauthorized method of access. Once a hacker has access to a system, he will want to be able to continue to have access to that system even if he is discovered. To do this he will unlock a number of back doors. Back doors create an alternate method of gaining access if the primary access is cut off. The term back door is also used to indicate alternate methods of accessing data through back doors in application code.

Most back doors can be discovered if you do regular auditing of the integrity of the programs and configuration files on your system. A program that compares the current state of a file to a known good state of the file should detect any planted back doors. This program needs to validate the file's permissions, owner, group, size, and a digital signature using a strong cryptographic algorithm.

Anonymously

Anonymous access is any connection a service supplies without authenticating the identity of the user. A number of information system services allow anonymous access, usually limited to "safe" access. However, this "safe" access can often be used to gather information or can be exploited to gain more access than expected.

There is no accountability with anonymous access. Activities can be monitored. However, with no identification information about the person performing the action, there is no way to associate the activities with an individual. Sometimes there is information on the source of the anonymous connection, but it is often unreliable.

Active Sessions

An active session is a user's connection after he has authenticated his identity and has been granted privileges. If a hacker can access a session in this state, he can get access without the need for authentication. He can interact with the system as the user whose session it was.

Unattended Sessions

An unattended session occurs whenever a user leaves a session active when it is not being used. This allows anyone who has access to the terminal device access to that session. As far as the system is concerned, he or she is the person who left the session unattended. He or she has all the privileges of that user and will be able to perform any operation which that user could perform as that user. Unattended sessions generally occur when someone physically steps away from his or her terminal or PC without logging off or locking it. Setting automatic log-off or terminal locking features for idle sessions will help, but user awareness is critical to reducing this vulnerability.

Session Hijacking

Hijacking is the process of interrupting the communications between the server and the client systems so that the attacker is able to insert information into the session or completely take over the session. Hijacking is accomplished by being able to spoof the communication protocol. Some implementations of the TCP protocol use very predictable sequence numbers, which allows someone on the network to intercept and take over the session.

Researchers at the University of Maryland found that by using tools developed as part of the Open1x project, an open source implementation of the IEEE protocol, they could perform session hijacking and man-in-the-middle attacks on Wireless Lans. The wireless security standard brought in to replace the flawed Wireless Encryption Protocol (WEP)is just as defective.

Lars Davies, research fellow at the Centre for Commercial Law Studies, warned network managers to remain on guard where wireless was concerned. "If you use a wireless network, you are essentially open to the world."[47]

---

[47]   Allen, Paul and Millman, Rene, "Robust Wireless Standard is Flawed," *IT Week*, 22 February 2002.

Stolen Credentials

A user's credentials are the identifier used to distinguish the user and the information used to authenticate the identity. The first rule of computer security is: Do not share your password. However, stolen passwords continue to be a significant security issue.

Sniffing

Sniffing is the process of monitoring a communication media in an attempt to gather information. This process is used to find identification and authentication information. Password sniffing is effective because of the use of reusable passwords and the use of protocols which transmit user IDs and passwords across the communication media in clear text. This creates an environment where the process of stealing credentials is a trivial task.

Ikenna Iffih used his home computer to illegally gain access to a number of computers, including those controlled by NASA and an agency of the U.S. Department of Defense, where, among other things, he installed a "sniffer" program onto the system to intercept login names and passwords, and intentionally caused delays in communications.

He was charged with intentionally intercepting and endeavoring to intercept login names and passwords transmitted to and through a NASA computer.

Iffih was sentenced to 2 years of probation, the first 6 months of which must be served under home confinement. Additionally, the Court ordered him to pay $5,000 in restitution and to forfeit all computer equipment used to commit the crime. Lastly, Iffih is banned from using computers for any other purpose than work or school. [48]

Any password which is sent over a network in clear text has to be considered compromised. Even if the password is encrypted before transmission, password snooping can be used in conjunction with password guessing to extract a user ID and password pair. Numerous implementations have had weak encryption of passwords.

Snooping

Snooping is the process of observing a user's activity visually on his or her terminal device or with software. Trojan horses and parasites in the display software or input drivers have

---

[48]   "Boston Computer Hacker Sentenced for Illegal Access and Use of United States Government and Private Systems," *FBI Boston Field Office Press Release*.

been used to observe keyboard and mouse input in windows desktops, X windows displays and web browsers. The locally collected information can be stored or sent to the hacker. This type of attack is successful even with the use of encrypted communications, since the information is stolen before it is sent.

> Jesus Oquendo worked as a computer security specialist at Collegeboardwalk.com, which shared office space and a computer network with one of its investors, Five Partners Asset Management LLC, a venture capital company. Oquendo used this access to alter the start-up commands on the Five Partner's network to automatically collect passwords and e-mail them to himself.
>
> Using these passwords, Oquendo accessed Five Partners systems and the computer systems of RCS Computer Experience, where he deleted a database, costing RCS approximately $60,000 to repair. Finally, he left the victim a taunting message on their network: "Hello, I have just hacked into your system. Have a nice day." [49]

Social Engineering

Social engineering is the process of obtaining information through the use of a false pretense.

Asking an individual for his password may seem trivial to some experienced users, but there have been numerous reports of very simple techniques that have been successful. The request could come in the form of an e-mail message, a broadcast, or a telephone call.

> Intruders are using automated tools to post messages to trick unsuspecting users of Internet Relay Chat (IRC) and Instant Messaging (IM) services into downloading and executing malicious software. These messages typically offer the opportunity to download software of some value to the user, including improved music downloads, anti-virus protection, or pornography.
>
> This is purely a social engineering attack since the user's decision to download and run the software is the deciding factor in whether or not the attack is successful. Although this activity is not novel,

---

[49]   "New York City Computer Security Expert Convicted of Computer Hacking and Electronic Eavesdropping," *U.S. Department of Justice Press Release*, 7 March 2001.

> the technique is still effective, as evidenced by reports of tens of thousands of systems being compromised in this manner. [50]

The request may instruct the user to immediately change his password, usually due to testing or security issues. The user is further instructed to change the password to one that is specified in the message, or the user may be instructed to run a program, which will request the user to enter his user ID and password, which are then collected by the attacker. The message can appear to be from a site administrator or root. In reality, it may have been sent by an individual who is trying to gain access or additional privileges to the local machine via the user's account.

There should be a procedure to authenticate requests to change passwords or to run programs that request password information, so that the users are assured that these requests are legitimate. There should also be a well-defined process to report such attempts so that they can be tracked and the attacker captured.

Subverting Protocols

Computer protocols are well-documented to help with implementing them on differing platforms. These implementations are done by many people at many locations with differing skill levels. Some are implemented by students and others by hardware vendors. Some receive careful review while others have limited support. It is not surprising that the quality of implementations varies significantly.

Known Vulnerabilities

Most successful attacks utilize known vulnerabilities. New exploits are continuously being discovered. They are documented and shared in the hacker community. They are addressed and repaired, but the patches are often not implemented on systems, so they remain vulnerable after the problem should no longer be a problem.

> The National Infrastructure Protection Center released a summary of software vulnerabilities identified between December 12, 2000, and December 14, 2001. This 84-page report lists over 1200 exploits. Some of the exploits listed are not widely available on the Internet, but the potential vulnerability has been identified as a viable method of attack. [51]

---

[50] "Social Engineering Attacks via IRC and Instant Messaging," *CERT® Incident Note IN-2002-03*, 19 March 2002.

[51] "2001 Year End Summary," *National Infrastructure Protection Center CyberNotes*, Issue 2001-26, 31 December 2001.

Initially Unsecure

Many systems are shipped with security features turned off. This will often simplify the administration of the system and reduce the number of help desk calls. However, many administrators will be unaware that they need to do anything after the system is installed. The security implications are often not documented and the process of enabling the security features are not well-documented or easy to find.

> 3Com issued a security advisory stating that customers should immediately change the SNMP community string from the default to a proprietary and confidential identifier known only to authorized network management staff. This was due to the fact that the administrative password was available through a specific proprietary MIB variable when accessed through the read/write SNMP community string.
>
> The advisory was issued in response to the widespread distribution of special logins intended for service and recovery procedures issued only by 3Com's Customer Service Organization under conditions of extreme emergency, such as in the event of a customer's losing passwords. Due to this disclosure, some 3Com switching products were vulnerable to security breaches caused by unauthorized access via special logins.
>
> Customers were urged to log in to their switches and proceed to change the password via the appropriate password parameter to prevent unauthorized access to the accounts. [52]

Improperly Configured

Improper security configurations are responsible for a great number of system compromises. There are many reasons for improper configurations, including incorrect or incomplete documentation and under trained or nonexistent administration.

Even automated administration tools have been known to improperly or inadequately secure an environment.

Interactions between systems can lead to improper security configurations. Not all combinations or interactions are tested. Installing or configuring one system may alter the configuration file which is used by both systems.

---

[52]   "I-052: 3Com® CoreBuilder and SuperStack II LAN Vulnerabilities," *U.S. Department of Energy, Computer Incident Advisory Capabilities Advisory*, 20 May 1998.

Services Which Are No Longer Used

There are many protocols that are no longer in widespread use that are still installed on systems for compatibility. Many of these obsolete protocols predate any level of concerns of security. They may have been designed when direct connected or point-to-point dial-up access was the only available network. Many of these old protocols were migrated to LANs, but were not secured since they were rapidly replaced by newer protocols.

Many computer vendors started with proprietary operating systems. These systems expanded into networking before standards were available. DEC® created DECnet®, Apollo had Apollo Token Ring (ATR), HP had its network services (NS), and IBM® created a number of protocols. As each of these and other vendors moved into open systems, they had to implement the proprietary protocols on their open systems to allow connectivity. Many of these protocols are now obsolete but still exist in the versions of the UNIX systems from these vendors and are often installed and configured by default. Many of these proprietary protocols granted greater permissions with less authentication than current protocols.

Many of these protocols were proprietary and are not widely known. The programs which support the protocols are not part of the normal network start-up routines. An administrator will have seen the process running on all the machines of this type and not know what it does, only that it is always there. Even the vendor's help desk may not know.

In some cases, these protocols are enabled by default. Many of these early protocols have little or no security and may not be able to be adequately secured. Administrators may not know about them or what they are or what they do.

As a system manager, you must know what is installed and configured on your system. These programs may appear as unknown entries in the Internet configuration file or as daemons that are initiated during system start-up. These programs should be removed from the system if they are not being used. You must know what all the processes running on your system do, and why they are there.

## CHAPTER 8

Limiting Access

Halting the hacker before he gains access to your system requires a strong perimeter defense. At every spot where a hacker can gain access, you must put up defenses that require more than modest authentication. These spots should also have a fall-back detection scheme for all access and a notification scheme for those that are out of the ordinary.

A policy of least privileges should be enforced. No user needs more privileges than the privileges needed to do his job. A system need not provide services in excess of what are necessary for the proper function of that system. The key to managing this environment successfully is to keep abreast of what the users need to do their jobs and respond rapidly to supply these needs. This is a very difficult task given the rapidly changing environment in which most companies find themselves.

This is why most nongovernment organizations implement more relaxed policies.

Physical System Access

Physical security is fundamental to the security of an information system. Physical access to a system is the most compromising of any access issues. With physical access, one can physically damage the system, remove data storage devices, and, in most cases, gain access to the system's operations. Physical access needs to be limited to those who have a need to physically access the systems and it must produce a record of who had physical access and when.

Numerous sites have been plagued with stolen equipment and, in many cases, it has been memory modules, CPUs, and other internal components which have been stolen. This illustrates a need for locks on the computer cabinets as well as auditable locks on the rooms which house the computer systems. These locks must be able to identify the individual who entered and exited the room. This is usually accomplished with individually issued access cards. Integration of physical security into information security can simplify the management, monitoring, and correlation of security events.

This decentralization of systems means that more than just the computer operations staff must be made aware of physical security. The users must understand the importance of locking up their floppies and printouts and logging off or locking up their computers. A proprietary report requires the same security whether it is printed or on a diskette or in your computer.

Mobile computing users who use portable computers must be aware that the theft of their computer compromises all the information on that computer. Many corporate spies have found it easier to steal a portable computer than to break into a company's computer to get the desired information.

> An employee garnered a philanthropic reputation for treating his coworkers to pizza in the cafeteria on Friday afternoons. But while his colleagues munched on pepperoni, the employee's accomplice — the pizza man — stuffed his delivery bag with laptop computers and left the building without being challenged. [53]

Telecommuters, those employees who work from home, also add additional security issues, and they need the same level of security at home as they would have in the office.

Wireless communication adds a whole new area for hackers to exploit by eavesdropping without physical access. Cellular modems and wireless local area networks (LANs) have opened the doors to your data communication without a hacker having to physically attach to your network.

If your physical security procedures have not recently been reviewed, they should be. It is extremely important to review security procedures regularly to incorporate new equipment and technologies.

Network Equipment

The computer system extends beyond the physical box which contains it. The network to which it is connected also requires physical security for the network equipment and the junction points. Often network equipment is located in wiring closets which are shared with other functions, such as telephone equipment. The security of these areas are equally important to the security of the information system. Access to these closets are often given to repair personnel of other companies, such as telephone repairmen. This is why audited and monitored access is required. Unauthorized access to these areas enables a hacker to add unauthorized connections for eavesdropping or unauthorized access or to disable connections, causing disruptions in service.

---

[53]   Mello, Jr., John P., "Stop, Thief!," *CFO Magazine*, 1 October 1997.

Removable Media

Today, with tape backup technology allowing gigabytes of data to be stored on a tape that can fit into a shirt pocket, an entire data center's information can easily slip past normal physical security procedures. Much more attention than ever before must be paid to the sites that have removable media. With the decentralization of systems, removable media are everywhere.

Physical access precautions should be extended to anywhere there are removable media. Access to removable media devices allows a hacker to remove information from the system and the site without going through the network security which might otherwise detect it. Physical secure checkpoints are rarely adequate to detect the removal of information on removable media. The data density and physical size of tapes today make it easy to slip huge amounts of data past security checkpoints.

Once information is removed from the information system, the protection afforded by that information system, such as user authorizations and file permissions, does not apply. The information on removable media can be installed onto any system without regard to the security level or controls of that system.

Removable media are always a security issue. They create a porthole through which information can flow out of and into the system. Restricting the programs that can access these devices and the people who can run these programs will help limit this flow of information. Restricting the number of devices that have removable media and the number of people who have physical access to those devices will also help reduce the risk. Physical security will help limit this threat. So can appropriate labeling procedures.

It is wise to produce custom "company" labels that are specific to the classification of the data they will contain. When output devices are limited to a specific classification level, this can make for easy and rapid identification if the data are being handled correctly. In conjunction with a widespread employee security awareness program, this very simple concept can make a big difference in spotting inappropriate handling of information and having it reported.

System Backups

Backups can be both a blessing and a curse to the hacker as well as to the system manager. For a hacker, if gaining access to backups is easy, then accessing information from them may be easier than getting the same information from the system's disks. However, if the hacker's activity is logged and backed up, that may be just the evidence it takes to convict him. For you as a system manager, backups are your last safety net. You can never lose more data than that which has been created since your last good backup. When backups are stored off-site, you can recover from a physical disaster. However, if your backup and recovery policies are not sufficient, a hacker may be able to access your system's information from the backup or restore hacker code onto your system.

There is no bigger risk to your information systems than your system backups. Your entire system is on those tapes. If they are compromised, all the information contained on your system is compromised. Proper handling and storage of backups are critical to ensure the confidentiality and integrity of the information they contain. Nowhere are procedures more important than in the handling of removable media. Backups must be kept in a secure area. Anyone who has physical access to your backups can read them on another computer. If your backups are stored off-site, the transportation to and from the off-site storage must also be a secure process.

Procedures to request the mounting of backup media must be secure. This means a separate authentication of the requester. You need to understand the backup policy and procedures for your system, keeping in mind how they might be used by a hacker who plans to use your system to attack other systems or to plunder the information on your system.

Restricting Users

Reducing the number of user accounts on a system reduces the number of entry points into the system which can be exploited. Every authorized user must maintain the secrecy of his password and the administrator must provide a secure user environment and services. User accounts are often used by intruders as a place from which to work. Minimizing the capabilities of user accounts will minimize the intruder's ability to misuse the accounts.

Privileged Users

Privileged users are those accounts which are granted privileges above the minimum set of privileges for all accounts. These additional privileges give the user extra capabilities and are targets of hackers so that they can utilize these extra capabilities.

The root user, UID 0, on UNIX systems is an all-powerful user who does not have to obey the security restrictions which apply to all other users. For this reason, the root user's access should be limited to the system.

Securetty is a UNIX feature which defines secure terminals which the root user can use. A secure terminal is a configuration that limits the superuser's access to the system to a list of terminals that are considered secure. This limits only the login process. A user may still log in as a regular user and change to the superuser with the su command. Other access methods, such as X windows, do not adhere to the secure terminal settings.

It is advisable that root not be allowed to log in from any unsecured terminal. Only the system console, /dev/console, should be considered secure. Instead, require that users log in as themselves and switch user to root, thereby giving you a log of who is root. You can restrict root's access by using the secure terminal facility. This facility is implemented in a number of different ways, depending on the version of the UNIX operating system.

If the system is a System V derivative, such as Linux or HP-UX, it will have a file, /etc/securetty or /etc/default/login on Solaris, which will contain a list of the terminals that are considered secure. Only directly connected terminals whose connection does not leave the secured area should be included as a secure terminal. Often the console should be the only secure terminal.

If the implementation is a Berkeley Software Distribution (BSD) derivative, then you will need to add the secure parameter to the console line in the `/etc/ttys` or `/etc/ttytab` file. This line will look something like the following:

```
console "/etc/getty std.9600" vt100 on local secure
```

Time-based Access Control

With time-based access controls, the system administrator may specify times-of-day and days-of-week that are allowed for login for each user. When a user attempts to log in outside the allowed access time, the event is logged (if auditing is enabled for login failures and successes) and the login is terminated.

Most UNIX systems will implement time-based access controls through PAM features.

On HP-UX, enabling trusted systems enables this feature. A superuser can log in outside the allowed access time, but the event is logged. The permitted range of access times is stored in the protected password database for users and may be set with SAM. Users that are logged in when a range ends are not logged out.

Device-based Access Control

In the early days of interactive computing, the only connection to the computer was over serial lines. These serial lines allowed users to access the computer with terminals that were directly connected to the serial line or through a modem. Adding dialers to the modems allowed computers to dial out as well as receive incoming calls. Soon computers were calling other computers and serial networking was born.

Today most multiuser systems still use serial line access. The system console is almost always directly connected to the system by a serial line. If the system is a data entry system, it is likely that most of the users are using directly connected terminals. Also, many systems have modems attached to them. These are almost always attached via serial lines.

The `/etc/securetty` configuration file can be used to limit to specific terminals on which the root user can log in. The login program on Red Hat and Mandrake Linux also uses the `/etc/usrtty` configuration file to define from which terminals and from which remote systems each user can log in.

Dial-up Access

Trying to guess logins and passwords is the most dangerous and unproductive way for a hacker to access a system. This type of bell ringing, the repeated calling of a modem and attempting to login, will undoubtedly be noticed by any system manager. So unless the hacker has some insight into logins and passwords, it is unlikely that he will get anywhere. The attempts to log in will be logged, whether they are successful or not, by the accounting system.

Correctly configured, the system will hang up the modem after three failed login attempts and will also terminate a session that is disconnected.

For the login program to hang up the modem, the modem must be appropriately connected to the system, with a cable that supports full modem control, and attached to a port on the computer that also supports full modem control. The entry for the modem connection in /etc/gettydefs must also be correctly configured. The gettydefs entry must have a HUPCL (Hang-Up and Clear) entry in both sections of the entry as shown:

```
2400 # B2400 HUPCL IGNPAR ICRLN IXON OPOST ONLCR CS8
    CREAD ISIG ICANON ECHO ECHOK ISTRIP IXANY TAB3
    # B2400 HUPCL SANE CS8 ISTRIP IXANY TAB3
    # login:  #2400
```

Even with all these precautions, you must understand that phone lines are not secure: Some hackers are also able to hack the phone network, thereby being able to eavesdrop on communications, reroute calls, or steal a phone connection right out from under you, so the hacker is now connected to the session to which you were connected.

The ability to trace access through a dial-up line is now increased, since Caller ID® is available in most areas. This means it is no longer necessary to get a court order or file a harassing caller complaint to get the phone number of the calling individual.

Today Caller IDTM devices are available that will record the time and phone number of all the calls received. There are also Caller ID modems that present the computer with the phone number prior to connecting. These can be used to further authenticate users for a dial-back system, or to notify someone when there is an unauthorized access in progress.

One way to enhance the authentication is through dial-up security. This feature, which is implemented on some versions of UNIX systems, asks the user for two passwords. Even though this is referred to as dial-up security, it can be applied to any terminal or modem port on a port-by-port basis. The first password requested is the user's password; the second is a password based on the user's default shell. This requires the configuring of two files: /etc/dialups and /etc/d_passwd. The dialups file contains the list of ttys, terminal ports, on which the second password will be required.

```
/dev/tty0p0
/dev/tty0p1
```

The d_password file contains the default shell and the encrypted password for that shell. If a user's shell is not listed in this file, the dial-up password is not tested.

```
/bin/sh:dpscen80aKWa2:
/bin/ksh:dpJm/BwWmbsJg:
```

One of the difficulties with maintaining the d_passwd file is the process of encryption of the passwords. Here is a program that will encrypt a password given on the command line and write the encryption to standard out. This can be used to create the encrypted password in the d_passwd file.

```
main(argc,argv)
int argc;
char **argv;
{
  char *salt="dp"; /* use your favorite salt */
  printf ("%s",crypt(argv[1], salt);
}
```

Direct-connectTerminals

Compared to dial-up lines, direct-connect terminals have two disadvantages in keeping out a hacker. The first is a minor disadvantage — not having to redial after three failed login attempts. The second is a very real disadvantage — the ability of a hacker to get access to an unattended session when terminals are logged on and left alone. In a matter of seconds, a hacker can utilize an unattended session to gain access to a system or to gain privileges.

All inactive sessions should be logged off. This is generally more difficult than simply setting the shell time-out variable to a time-out value. This is because some programs' activity will not be measured and some applications will appear active to the shell even if there is no user interaction. In these cases, the terminal is allowed to lock while it is being used or to not lock when it is not being used. Some terminal locking software that has the ability to spawn a "screen saver" program may open back doors by using this feature if the spawned programs are not well-constructed.

On an HP-UX Trusted System, the system administrator can specify a list of users allowed for access each dedicated port on a MUX or DTC. When the list is null for a device, all users are allowed access. The device access information is stored in the device assignment database, /tcb/files/devassign, which contains an entry for each terminal device on the Trusted System. A field in the entry lists the users allowed on the device.

Over the Network

Attacking a system over the network gives the hacker a significant advantage over a serial line. On the serial line, the hacker has only the login program, and possibly UUCP, to attack. However, over the network, he has a plethora of programs offering services through different sockets on the network. Most of these services use simple text-based protocols that can be attacked, even if the hacker has only terminal access.

Dial-up access directly into a network is available only via a terminal server or a dial-up network server utilizing a serial line protocol, such as SLIP or PPP.

Terminal/Modem Servers

Network terminal or modem servers are devices that are directly attached to the network and allow for either direct-connected terminals or modems. The connection through these devices will generally give the user a prompt that allows him to connect to any device on the network. This connection will usually use either telnet or a proprietary protocol. In either case, the remote computer will see the user as a simple terminal connecting over the network. Many universities and businesses use terminal servers to consolidate the costs of modems and telephone lines into one location that can be utilized by everyone in the organization.

In many cases, a hacker will get a connection by simply connecting to the modem server. There may be no password required. He may then be able to connect to any computer that is on the same network or any system on which there is routing information. In either case, network terminal/modem servers are a very useful commodity to the hacker. Some of these network terminal servers will allow him to connect to the modem that is attached to the port and dial out using that modem. If that is the case, he has the ability to dial in and dial out, allowing him to put the long-distance call on your bill and to do connection laundering; that is, anyone who is tracing his activities to where he dialed out will come back to you, the owner of the terminal server, instead of directly to the hacker.

If you can require some level of authentication on your terminal server, do so. Giving free access to your network is asking for trouble. Restrict the systems to which the terminal server can connect. This will reduce your level of vulnerability. Utilize Caller ID on all modems. Institute callback security where possible. Where possible, do not allow dial-out from terminal servers.

Dial-up SLIP/PPP Servers

Today it is common to want to extend your network so you can facilitate users who work on the road or at home. This is usually done by having a dial-up SLIP or PPP server. This server gives TCP/IP connectivity to the system that dials into it.

This will allow the hacker to be a peer on the network. A hacker's system can utilize all the network tools at his disposal to probe systems. Gaining access over the network is much easier than over a terminal line. However, gaining access to a dial-up SLIP or PPP connection will generally be more difficult than a simple text connection. Text connections are often guarded by only a login ID and password. The dial-up SLIP will also require IP address information. Organizations should put stronger security on SLIP and PPP connections. These should include a hardware-based password system and some type of smart card, so access is not possible without physically having the smart card. This is termed two-factor authentication, because it is based on something you know, a password or PIN number, and something you have, a smart card or authentication token. It is also a very good idea to have Caller ID enabled on all dial-up connections.

Host-based Firewalls

A host-based firewall is a software product which evaluates each network packet that the system receives and determines if it should accept it, based on a variety of packet features including the source address and packet type. They have the ability to evaluate all types of packets, including UDP and ICMP.

When an IP packet is received, the software goes down a list of rules until it finds a rule matching the packet and then handles the packet in the manner that the rule specifies.

IPChain is a stateless firewall. This means the determination of accepting the packet is based solely on its source and destination addresses, port number, and protocol.

System administrators who already employ ipchain-based firewalls should begin to migrate their scripts to iptables before the release of 7.2. Red Hat 7.1 comes preinstalled with a 2.4.x kernel that has netfilter and iptables compiled in.

The following shell script configures ipchain to deny all access except SSH.

```
#!/bin/sh
PATH=/usr/sbin:/sbin:/bin:/usr/sbin
LOCAL_INTERFACE="192.168.1.1/32" # IP address
LOCAL_NETWORK="192.168.1.0/24"   # IP address/mask here
SSH_PERMITTED="192.168.1.2/32 192.168.2.3/32" # who allowed to ssh
# deny everything
ipchains -P input DENY
ipchains -P output DENY
ipchains -P forward DENY
ipchains -F
#permit ssh
for ipaddr in $SSH_PERMITTED;
do
ipchains -A input -p tcp -s $ipaddr -i $LOCAL_INTERFACE -j ACCEPT
done
# permit outgoing tcp
ipchains -A output -p tcp -i $LOCAL_INTERFACE -j ACCEPT
ipchains -A input -p tcp ! -y -i $LOCAL_INTERFACE -j ACCEPT
# all the other connection attempts
ipchains -A input -p tcp -i $LOCAL_INTERFACE -l -j DENY
ipchains -A input -p udp -i $LOCAL_INTERFACE -l -j DENY
ipchains -A input -p icmp -i $LOCAL_INTERFACE -l -j DENY
```

IPTables is part of the netfilter project and the replacement for ipchains in the Linux 2.4 kernel. Iptables has many more features than ipchains, including the ability to do stateful packet inspection, and a clean separation of packet filtering and network address translation.

```
#!/bin/sh
iptables -F
# permit outgoing connections
iptables -P OUTPUT ACCEPT
# deny inbound connections
iptables -P INPUT DROP
# allow packets on loopback interface
iptables -A INPUT lo -h ACCEPT
```

IPFilter is a stateful firewall package. It maintains session information so that it can associate each individual packet to the session to which it belongs. This allows for better selection of allowing or denying packets, since the additional information about the session is available. This session information can also be applied to sessionless connections, such as UDP and ICMP. IPFilter will associate these packets into a virtual session to which they belong and provide the additional security based on this session information.

IPFilter is was built on BSD based UNIX systems and is available on Solaris and Irix as well as HP-UX.

IPFilter/9000 (B9901AA) is a port to HP-UX of the popular BSD IPFilter program, which is a public-domain stateful inspection host-based firewall system. It provides for the filtering of selected IP traffic into or out of the system. The traffic can be selected by source address, destination address, protocol port number, packet features, or any combination of these. It is provided for use as a system firewall on hosts running HP-UX 11i.

A system firewall is a packet filtering mechanism that is built into the TCP/IP stack of a host and provides filtering functionality specifically configured for the protection of that particular host. This program uses a sophisticated stateful-inspection packet filtering technology to filter traffic that enters or exits an individual HP-UX host.

Multi-homed HP-UX systems can be configured to discard incoming packets that are received through one network interface but whose destination address is that of a different interface of the same host, as well as to block the sending of outgoing packets whose source address is not that of the interface through which they are being sent. This packet filtering feature characterizes the Strong End-System (ES) functionality described in RFC 1122 of the IETF.

It can also function as a limited application proxy, but it is not recommended or supported as a general-purpose application proxy.

Designed to be used as a firewall, it is quite capable of being used to protect a host from network attacks. By default, the product will allow all packets to pass both in and out. However, by adding the appropriate filters to /etc/opt/ipf/ipf.conf, all packets can be blocked.

It is supported on HP-UX 11, with appropriate patches, in both 32- and 64-bit mode. It is released as a no-charge software product on the application CD.

The following configuration file denies all except SSH:

```
# By default block all packets
block in all
block in proto tcp all flags s/sa
block in proto udp all
block in proto icmp all
# Allow packets on loopback interface
pass in quick on lo0 all
pass out quick on lo0 all
# Block all packets with IP options
block in log quick all with opt lsrr
block in log quick all with opt ssrr
block in log quick all with ipopts
# Block all packets with a length which is too short to be real
block in log quick proto tcp all with short
# pass secure shell
pass in on le0 proto tcp from 192.168.1.2/32 port = 22 keep state
# allow all outbound connections, initiated by me.
pass out quick proto tcp from any to any flags S keep state keep frags
pass out quick proto udp from any to any keep state
pass out quick proto icmp from any to any keep state
```

Packet Filtering

Packet filtering is a method of restricting network access based on the network service being requested and the hosts requesting the service. On specific machines, this is accomplished by disabling the service, using a wrapper program to deny access to the service, or using the internet daemon's security to limit the hosts that can use the service on systems that support it. Usually, you will want to do packet filtering on a network level instead of a host level. This can be accomplished with filtered bridges or routers. If your site isn't filtering certain TCP/IP packets, it may not be as secure as you think it is.

System managers, security managers, and network managers need to understand packet filtering issues. Due to the flaws in several TCP/IP services and chronic system administration problems, a site must be able to restrict external access to these services. It is recommended that the following services be filtered:

- **DNS zone transfers** can be used by hackers to request all the information contained in the Domain Name Services database. Permit access to this service only from known secondary domain name servers. This will prevent intruders from gaining additional knowledge about the systems connected to your local network.

- **TFTP** allows unauthenticated access to a system and lets the hacker put files on and get files from the system. A system with TFTP enabled can be used as a depot for the transfer of information or stolen information.

- **SunRPC** supports all the ONC®-based services.

- **NFS** (Network File System) has long been used by hackers to gain information and access to systems through inappropriate configuration and software problems.

- **rexec** is used to execute a program remotely. It always requires a password and leaves a minimal amount of log information. It is used by hackers who have initially compromised a system so they can regain access without leaving tracks.

- **rlogin** (the remote login service) uses Berkeley Trusted Hosts configuration and security.

- **rsh** remotely executes a program using trusted systems configuration and security.

  Both rlogin and rsh are used by hackers with the use of personal .rhosts files to create an intricate web of connections between systems and users on those systems. This can make it extremely difficult to track the hacker back to his origin through dozens of different machines, where he has utilized different user IDs on each one.

- **lpd** (remote printer daemon) allows unauthenticated access to the system's print spooler resources.

- **uucpd** allows UUCP to run over the network. Running this services opens all the UUCP security issues over the network.

- **X Windows** windowing system has been utilized to allow eavesdropping and capturing the keystrokes of the user on the system.

There are a variety of network analysis tools that will determine which sockets a system has active. These include SATAN and strobe.

If the site does not need to provide other services to external users, those other services should be filtered.

Restricting Services

Restricting the services that allow access to a system reduces the methods by which a system can be attacked. Exploiting vulnerabilities in services is the most common method for gaining access to a system, so if a system has fewer services, then there is less code to contain vulnerabilities.

Anonymous Access

Anonymous access is any access to the service without authenticating an identifier. Historically, there has been a number of anonymous services on UNIX machines. However, as the machines have become more reliable and the need for security has increased, these anonymous information services have dropped away. Today, there are few anonymous services.

Anonymous FTP is a configuration of FTP which allows someone who does not have an account on the machine to FTP files to and from the machine anonymously. This is done by entering either "anonymous" or "ftp" as the user name and anything as a password; by convention, this is the requester's e-mail address. Even though it is called anonymous and there is no user authentication, it is not always anonymous. There are a number of FTP daemons that log file transfer and the location from where the request was made. Some FTP daemons will validate that the given password is a valid user on the system that is making the request.

These transfers are restricted to the home directory tree of the user named "ftp." Anonymous FTP needs a partial file system configured in its home directory since it is a "chroot"ed process. This partial file system includes a password file. Some automated administration scripts, when creating the password file for anonymous FTP, will use the actual password file and set inappropriate permissions. Then a hacker can easily get the password file as follows:

```
ftp target
Connected to target.
220 target FTP server ready.
Name (target:hacker):  anonymous
331 Guest login ok, send ident as password.
Password: ******
230 Guest login ok, access restriction apply.
ftp>  get /etc/passwd
```

The messages from the FTP server can vary; however, the numeric values are standardized on all implementations.

Proper configuration of FTP is a must. Misconfigured anonymous FTP can open your system to both the theft and destruction of data. Anonymous FTP should be configured as follows:

The anonymous FTP account entry in the system's password file, /etc/passwd, should be similar to

```
ftp:DISABLED:500:500::/users/anon_ftp:/bin/false
```

The entry in the system's group file, /etc/group, and login group file, /etc/logingroup, should be similar to

```
ftp:DISABLED:500:
```

If the permissions of the FTP directory tree are not configured correctly, a hacker may be able to add an executable file to the bin directory or put a .rhosts file in the account's home directory and allow himself remote access via the Berkeley Trusted Hosts commands.

The anonymous FTP home directory and its subdirectories should have ownership and permissions as follows:

```
drwxr-x---  6  root  ftp  512 Jan 1 08:00 .
drwxr-x---  9  root  bin  512 Jan 1 08:00 ..
drwxr-x---  2  root  ftp  512 Jan 1 08:00 bin
drwxr-x---  2  root  ftp  512 Jan 1 08:00 etc
drwx-wx---  2  root  ftp  512 Jan 1 08:00 incoming
drwxr-x---  2  root  ftp  512 Jan 1 08:00 pub
```

If any of these directories is owned by ftp, then an intruder could compromise the system.

The optional incoming directory allows anonymous FTP users to store files on the system. Anonymous FTP is allowed write permission into the incoming directory. This directory has only write and execute permissions, allowing FTP to write into, but preventing FTP from listing, the contents of the directory. Having an incoming directory will allow an anonymous user to fill up your disk space.

FTP's password and group files should contain no information other than the lines for FTP, as in the following examples:

FTP's password file:

```
ftp:DISABLED:500:500:::
```

FTP's group file:

```
ftp:DISABLED:500:
```

Any commands in the bin directory should have the permissions --x--x--x so no one can interrogate the binary or replace it.

Trivial FTP, TFTP, is a file transfer program that requires no authentication. No user name or password is requested. This program will send and receive files to or from anyone who asks for them. The program is generally restricted to send only those files that are in the home directory tree of the user named "tftp." TFTP is generally used to boot up network devices such as network terminal servers, network-based printers, and X terminals.

If you do not require TFTP, disable or remove the TFTP daemon, tftpd.

If your system has network access, you should try to get the password file with tftp, because hackers will.

```
$      tftp
tftp> connect target.com
tftp> get /etc/passwd /tmp/target.passwd
```

Hackers may also be able to place a .rhosts file in the tftp home directory and then use trusted services to gain access to your system. Be sure the secure flag is set on the tftpd daemon in the internet configuration file, and there is a tftp user with a properly secured home directory.

This flag will limit TFTP access to the tftp user's home directory. The entry in the internet configuration file should be similar to this:

```
tftp dgram udp wait root /etc/tftpd tftpd -s /u/tftp
```

On some systems the secure flag may be "-r". Consult the manual page for TFTP. If your system does not have a secure flag, then try the above commands. If you can get your password file, so can a hacker. If this is the case, contact your vendor for a secure implementation of TFTP.

Since the tftpd daemon is started by inetd, you can use inetd.sec to restrict access to your TFTP services to specific machines.

Services Which Enable Trust

Trust is the situation where one system will trust the security of another system and relinquish control of security to that system. Usually trust is limited to user authentication, so that any user from a trusted system is considered to be trustworthy and no further authentication will take place. This is a user convenience giving users single-login, but it opens the door to hackers. Once one system is compromised, all the other systems in the chain of trust are directly vulnerable.

Berkeley Trusted Hosts is a subsystem that allows global authentication on a group of trusted hosts or equivalent systems. These systems are said to trust each other. Specifically, this means you can have access to all the trusted hosts without having to reenter your password. It also means that if a trusted system is compromised, then all the systems that trust the compromised system must be considered compromised.

Generally, all systems in a trusted host group are similarly managed, often by the same administrator. This is where the hacker is most likely to start to expand his realm. The /etc/hosts.equiv file will show him all the trusted hosts. The trusted hosts will generally all have the same user IDs. The .rhosts files will show him systems that users have added as trusted hosts; these are especially useful to the hacker; since they were added by users and not the system manager, the systems that are being trusted may not have the same level of security. The ".rhosts" files allow a user to define another user ID on another system to use the current system as the current user. Trusted systems are generally reciprocally trusted, so if a user has a .rhosts file on this system allowing access from another system, it is likely that the other system has a similar .rhosts file.

To find the home directories that have a .rhosts file use the following script:

```
cut -d: -f6 /etc/passwd | xargs -i ls -l {}/.rhosts 2>/dev/null
```

This command is the basis for any tool that needs to locate or process files in a user's home directory. The cut command reads the sixth field of the password file, which is the home directory entry, and then uses xargs to execute a command for each user's home directory.

Trusted telnet is a facility which allows telnet to utilize the Berkeley trusted hosts facilities, so one can log in to a trusted host without using a password. A typical configuration may consist of one or more secure front-end systems and a network of participating hosts. Users who have successfully logged onto the front-end system may telnet directly to any participating system without being prompted for another login. This option supports the TAC User ID (also known as the TAC Access Control System, or TACACS User ID), and uses the same files as rlogin to verify participating systems and authorized users, hosts.equiv, and .rhosts.

Enable the TAC User ID option. The system administrator can enable the TAC User ID option on servers designated as participating hosts by having inetd start telnetd with the -t option in `/etc/inetd.conf`:

```
telnet stream tcp nowait root /usr/lbin/telnetd telnetd -t
```

In order for the TAC User ID option to work as specified, the system administrator must assign to all authorized users of the option the same login name and unique user ID (UUID) on every participating system to which they are allowed TAC User ID access. These same UUIDs should not be assigned to non-authorized users.

Users cannot use the feature on systems where their local and remote UUIDs differ, but they can always use the normal telnet login sequence. Also, there may be a potential security breach where a user with one UUID may be able to gain entry to participating systems and accounts where that UUID is assigned to someone else, unless the above restrictions are followed.

Syslogd, the system logging daemon, can receive and store log information from other systems. There is no authentication required to send data to this service, so that any information sent to the syslog daemon will be written in the log files. On Linux systems, the remote logging feature has to be enabled. However, on HP-UX, it is enabled by default and has to be disabled with the "-N" option to disable this anonymous access.

File System Access

Remote file system access is a common service for networked computers. Many proprietary systems developed elaborate file-sharing protocols. Remote file sharing creates a significant security problem. Access and authorization must be uniformly enforced across a number of remote systems. This requires a consistent administration of systems and users. However, the use of these remote file system protocols does not require the enforcement of this level of homogenous administration. So there are many security issues with the use of remote file systems.

NFS

NFS streamlines file sharing between server and client systems by controlling access via the /etc/exports file. Entries in /etc/exports provide permission to mount a file system existing on the server onto any client machine or a specified list of machines. Once a file system is put into /etc/exports, the information is potentially available to anyone who can do an NFS mount. Thus, the NFS client user can access a server file system without having logged into the server system.

- **Server Vulnerability** — Server security is maintained by setting restrictive permissions on the file /etc/exports. Root privileges are not maintained across NFS. Thus, having root privileges on a client system does not provide you with special access to the server.

  The server performs the same permission checking remotely for the client as it does locally for its own users. The server side controls access to server files by the client by comparing the user ID and group ID of the client, which it receives via the network, with the user ID and group ID of the server file. Checking occurs within the kernel.

  A user with privileges on an NFS client can exploit that privilege to obtain unlimited access to an NFS server. Never export any file system to a node on which privilege is granted more leniently than from your own node's policy!

- **Client Vulnerability** — In earlier releases of NFS for workstations, the /dev inode had to reside on the client's disk. NFS now allows for the /dev inode containing the major and minor numbers of a client-mounted device to exist on the server side. This opens the possibility for someone to create a Trojan horse that overrides permissions set on the client's mounted device, by accessing the device via the file and inode number found on the server side.

  Although lacking permission to make a device file on the client side, a system violator wanting to sabotage the client can create an undermining device file, such as /dev/kmem, using root permissions on the server side. The new /dev file is created with the same major and minor number as that of the target device on the client side, but with the following permissions: crw-rw-rw-.

  The violator can then go to the client, log in as an ordinary user, and, using NFS, open up the newly created server-side device file and use it for devious means — to wipe out kernel memory on the server, read the contents of everyone's processes, or other mischief.

Common Internet File System

The Common Internet File System, CIFS, is the Windows specification for remote file access. CIFS had its beginnings in the networking protocols, sometimes called Server Message Block (SMB) protocols, that were developed in the late 1980s for PCs to share files over the then nascent Local Area Network technologies (e.g., Ethernet). SMB is the native file-sharing protocol in the Microsoft operating systems and the standard way that millions of PC users share files across corporate intranets.

CIFS is simply a renaming of SMB, and CIFS and SMB are, for all practical purposes, one and the same. (Microsoft now emphasizes the use of CIFS, although references to SMB still occur.) CIFS is also widely available on UNIX systems, VMS™, Macintosh, and other platforms.

Despite its name, CIFS is not actually a file system unto itself. More accurately, CIFS is a remote file access protocol; it provides access to files on remote systems. It sits on top of and works with the file systems of its host systems. CIFS defines both a server and a client: the CIFS client is used to access files on a CIFS server.

Samba, the Linux implementation of SMB, is supplied as part of the standard package on most Linux implementations and on HP-UX.

The HP-UX implementation of CIFS is CIFS/9000. It enables directories from HP-UX servers to be mounted onto Windows machines and vice versa. The HP CIFS/9000 server product consists of Samba source code which has been enhanced with ACL (Access Control List) mapping features. These mapping features allow you to change UNIX permission bits and ACLs from an NT client through the NT ACL graphical interface on NT clients.

SMB is a very noisy protocol. Servers announce their presence and identify their shared file systems to anyone who asks. This allows the "network neighborhood" functions to be "user friendly." Servers can be configured to not broadcast their existence, but anonymous access to share names is available to anyone who knows the server name.

UUCP

UNIX to UNIX Copy (UUCP) is a utility that is designed to facilitate transferring files, executing commands on remote systems, and sending mail over serial dial-up lines. There are two versions of UUCP: Version 2 that was written in 1977 at Bell Laboratories and is running on some older systems and the more common HoneyDanBer UUCP which was released in 1983 with UNIX System V Release 3. It is easy to tell which it is by looking in the UUCP directory, /usr/lib/uucp. If there is a file named Permissions, then it is HoneyDanBer; if there is a file named USERFILE, then it is Version 2.

The security of both versions of UUCP can be increased by creating different accounts with their own unique user names and passwords for each system that will be calling your system. Each account will have to have the same user ID as the uucp account. This gives you more accountability. You can tell when each system logs in and out and you can disable a specific machine by disabling the account.

There are a number of configuration files that identify with which other computers to communicate and what permissions those computers have on your system. These files must contain appropriate configuration information and be properly protected.

The Systems file (L.sys in Version 2) contains the system name, phone number, uucp login name, and password for systems that the system calls. Even if the permissions are set correctly on this file, a hacker can get into this file by using the uuname command to get a list of systems that are called by this system, and using the debug option of cu or uucico to determine the phone numbers and uucp logins and passwords.

The Systems file should be owned by the account "uucp" and be readable only by uucp. The debug options for cu and uucico should be disabled if possible; otherwise, the command uucp should be executable only by the account "uucp," and cu removed from the system, unless needed.

In Version 2, the L.cmds file contains a list of commands that can be executed by the specified remote system. All unnecessary commands should be removed.

The USERFILE is used to set local access permissions. It identifies for each system what directories that system has access to. It also will indicate if dial-back is to be utilized for the system.

The directories that can be accessed should be restricted. You should not allow access to any user's home directory or any directory that contains configuration information. Altering this information could compromise your system.

The HoneyDanBer system combines the functionality of these two files into one file, the Permissions file. The Permissions file is made up of a number of name/value pairs. Each line will define the accessible directories and available commands for a MACHINE that your system calls or a LOGNAME for a system that calls your system.

A hacker may try UUCP access to the system. If your system supports anonymous UUCP, this will let him browse. You should try the following hacker trick to make sure your system is secure:

```
uucp target!/etc/passwd /tmp/target.passwd
```

If the target system has not limited the scope of the file system access, this will get the password file. A machine that is not properly configured may allow a hacker to update the system's configurations.

Today, most sites have replaced their use of UUCP for point-to-point access with SLIP or PPP, a point-to-point networking protocol. However, most systems still have the UUCP software loaded.

If you have UUCP on your system, whether you use it or not and whether you have modems or not, you must validate that the Permissions file is configured appropriately. An inappropriately configured UUCP can be used to gain privileges on the local system. If you are not using UUCP, remove it from your system.

## CHAPTER 9

Getting Credentials

Identity information is the piece of information which is used to uniquely identify an entity anywhere within the enterprise. An identifier is what a user, which wants to utilize resources, uses to differentiate itself from all other entities. Without identification, there is no basis for granting authorizations or maintaining accountability. An identifier must uniquely represent only a single individual, so that any of the activities performed by the identity are the responsibility of the individual. In most computer systems, this is the user's login name.

Most organizations are primarily concerned with the identification of individuals. However, people are only one type of user. In today's networked client/server environment systems, software, hardware, and networks also need positive identification to assure information security.

- **Unique** — Identifiers must be unique so that the user can be positively identified. Identifiers should be global, that is, an identifier should belong to one user throughout the enterprise. Any specific user should have only one identifier, even if the user performs multiple roles in the organization. This simplifies the association of individual identity for both the user and for the information system. It simplifies management and issuance of identifiers and reduces confusion in tracking the user and controlling which resources he or she uses. This allows for individual accountability and ensures that the individual is the person represented by the identifier. Identifiers must not be shared; otherwise it is not possible to promote personal accountability. This is especially important for effectively controlling access to information with high integrity or confidentiality requirements.

- **Universal** — The same type of identifier should be available from all users — individuals, systems, or programs — anything that requires access to the information. One identifier should be ample to identify one user anywhere for any reason. Identifiers must not be context-dependent, meaning the use of one identifier in one circumstance and another identifier in a different circumstance. (This does not mean that there will not be different methods to verify the identifier based on the specific situation.) This simplifies the process of validating the identifier. It also simplifies electronic storage and allows all users to be controlled in the same manner by having identifiers that are all of the same type and format.

• **Verifiable** — There should be an easy and standardized process to validate the identifier so that simple standard interfaces can be constructed. The verification process should be highly available, since without verification no privileges can be granted. There should be multiple verification methods that can be used at different times to give different levels of identity assurance or in case a specific method of verification is suspected of being compromised.

Stealing a user's identity requires acquiring both the identifier and the authenticator. The protection of this information is critical. In most cases, a hacker's first access to a system will be through a user account with limited privileges. Generally he will gain the identity of another account by getting the login name and password for that account by coercing the trusted computer system to gain access to the account or by taking advantage of a vulnerability in the software or hardware.

Identity Management

It has become common practice that user identifiers are public information. However, there is no reason to expose this information. Since, in most cases, the identifier is half of what is needed to gain access to a system, it too should not be public information. The association of identity and user is important only to the administrators of the system. It is needed to assign responsibility and billing of consumed resources. Otherwise, the actual identity of the user is not necessary to be made public.

Users' identifiers are made public in a number of ways. They are used in reports generated by the systems and are used for identification on printouts.

E-mail

A user's e-mail address should not be the user's identifier. The e-mail system's mail transfer agent should associate a simple human name to the user's identifier and make only this name externally available. This can be the individual's actual name, for example:

```
John_Doe@BigCompany.com
```

This makes the e-mail address simpler to remember and protects half of the information needed to authenticate to the system, providing better system security.

Sendmail provides for relating these external identities to actual user identifiers through the use of aliases and the generics table. The alias file maps inbound mail addresses to actual accounts and the generics table remaps addresses on outbound mail to reflect the external identifier. Uncommenting the following entries in the sendmail.cf file will enable the ability to map both inbound and outbound addresses.

```
O AliasFile=/etc/mail/aliases
Kgenerics dbm -o /etc/mail/genericstable
```

Account Management

Account management is a very large part of a system manager's job. It includes the assigning of accounts for new users, retiring accounts when the user is no longer authorized, and disabling accounts when the account is temporarily not going to be used. Unfortunately, account management is often considered administrative drudgery — day-to-day work to be delegated.

Good account management can go a long way toward keeping a hacker from making your system his home. Appropriately retiring an account and disabling an account when the user will not be using it for a period of time, for example, during his vacation, and monitoring an account while it is not being used will often catch hackers who are using these accounts.

UNIX accounts are defined in the password file /etc/passwd and are the base element of accounting; that is, all processes are owned by an account and all of the resources that are consumed on a system are assigned to an account. Each account has a login name, an optional password, a numeric user ID and numeric group ID, a home directory, and a start-up shell. It is the numeric IDs that are used by the system; the character login name and group name are there for human convenience.

User Accounts

Accounts exist for all users of the system, as well as entities that are not users, per se. All accounts can own system resources. This ownership gives the account special privileges with the resources. There may be accounts that exist for subsystems, such as databases or networking services. These accounts generally do not have the ability to log in; that is, they have no valid password. However, they still have all the rest of the attributes of the account.

Every account should be for one specific function or user. Sharing an account creates group accountability and defeats the ability to assign resources and accountability to a specific individual. Most systems will have a one-user, one-login policy so all the resources can be traced to a specific individual.

Guest Accounts

A guest account is an account that has either no password or a well-known password. Generally these are set up so a "guest" can have limited access to a system. Guest accounts are created for someone who will be accessing the system for a short time. This way, the system manager does not have to create a new user, only to remove this new user a short time later. Some systems come with guest accounts built-in. The two most common are guest and demo.

Guest accounts provide anonymous access and no accountability. The perceived trouble to add and remove a user who will be on the system only a short time is much less than locating and correcting problems that can be created by an anonymous guest user. Guest accounts are extremely useful to hackers to get a foot in the door of the system and look around. Generally the guest accounts have very limited capabilities. However, even with limited capabilities there are numerous ways the hacker can use them to get more privileges.

Default Accounts

A default account is an account that is created by the hardware or software vendor by default. These accounts may be required for particular software to operate, or they may be for the convenience of support personnel, or they may be included because they have always been there. Many of these accounts have either no password or they have default passwords that have become well-known. This is a quick and common attack of a system, often used by hackers to judge the quality of administration of a system. Here is a list of some of the well-known default accounts.

- **root** is the default name for the superuser's account.
- **daemon** is the account that owns all the UNIX background processes.
- **bin** and **sysbin** are accounts that own the executable files on the system.
- **adm** and **sysadmin** are accounts for administrative activities. They generally own the system logs and accounting information.
- **rje** is the account for all IBM mainframe networking products.
- **guest** and **demo** are accounts that by default have no password and exist to allow anyone to access the system through a guest account or run the demonstration programs with the login demo.
- **lp** is the account for the print spooler.
- **uucp**, **nuucp**, and **uufield** are accounts for the UUCP serial networking protocol. The account names uucp and nuucp have both been used for anonymous accesses via UUCP. The uufield account is an account used by the hardware vendor for field support, so field support engineers can access customer systems and get and update files.

All default accounts, except for root, should be removed or disabled. To disable an account, you can change the encrypted password field in the password file to LOCKED. If you are using shadowed passwords, this will have to be done in the shadow password file. Most system management tools have the ability to lock an account and automatically manage both the password file and the shadow password file.

If your hardware or software vendor says that a default account is required, find out its purpose. Does it have to be on the system only when there are support people accessing it? Can the name be changed? Minimally, change the password!

Captive Accounts

A captive account is an account that is created to offer information to someone without logging on. It directly executes a noninteractive command or program. These accounts generally have no password to make them more usable. Some historic captive accounts are date, which shows the system's current time and date; who, which shows who is currently on the system; and backup, which performs a system backup. A system administrator may have created a captive account for simple processes or to restrict a user. Quite often if a user performs only one function on a system, it makes sense to restrict him to running only that one program. However, if that program is not well-designed, the user may be able to escape from the program and have access to the system in a more direct manner.

Captive accounts are dangerous because they allow anonymous access, even if it is limited. They also have a home environment that can be exploited with trusted systems. Remove all captive accounts.

Dormant Accounts

A dormant account is an account that has been created and either has never been used or has not been used for an extended period of time. This may be because the person has changed job responsibilities or is no longer employed, or the account may have been made for a project manager or sponsor who really did not need access to the computer. In any case, these are valuable accounts for hackers: Since no one is using them, no one may notice his misuse of them, since most computer misuse is noticed by regular users and not the system managers. Dormant accounts should be retired.

This points out the importance of having and enforcing a computer access authorization policy. This policy will require proper authorization for adding a new user and require that the security manager be notified on the termination of any computer-authorized users.

This also is a reason for a comprehensive computer security training for all computer-authorized personnel. They need to know how to tell if there is something suspicious going on with their account and they need to know whom to notify if they are concerned.

Disabled Accounts

A disabled account is a account that does not have a valid password. Accounts may be disabled because a user is on leave, or it may be disabled until the account and the associated files are removed. Generally system managers will disable an account by putting an asterisk, or the word "DISABLED" or "LOCKED" in the password field. Any entry in the password field that is not 13 characters long will effectively disable the login. If you are using shadow passwords, the system administration tools should allow you to disable accounts.

Disabled accounts are still valid accounts. They can still own files, and run processes. They can have access via the Berkeley Trusted Host mechanism.

Some systems have the ability to automatically disable an account if the account has a given number of successive failed login attempts. This is an attempt to thwart password guessing at the login prompt.

This is a useful tool to the hacker because he can easily lock users, and sometimes the system manager, out of the system by entering bad passwords at the login prompt. With a complete list of user names, he could deny service to all users on the system.

Any automated response system must be carefully thought out to see if it can be used by a hacker to attack a system, yours or another. In this case, automatically disabling accounts can rapidly be turned into a denial-of-service attack.

Retired Accounts

User IDs should never be reused. They are assigned to a specific user and are contained on backups and logs even after that user is no longer allowed on the system. When an account is not going to be used again, it should be retired and disabled, and files owned by the account reassigned. Retired accounts should not own anything.

Repositories

The identity and authentication information is usually stored together in an authentication data repository. This repository can be as simple an in a password file on each individual system, or it can be implemented as a service to enable enterprise administration.

Files

On UNIX systems, the default storage location for passwords is the /etc/passwd file. This file is required to be world readable so that there is universal access to user and group IDs. This file contains seven fields separated by colons. The fields are user name, encrypted password, numeric user ID, numeric group ID, GECOS, home directory, and start-up program.

- The user name is eight characters or less; the initial character must be a lower-case letter and cannot contain the characters # or @. These two special characters are used as the delete character and delete the entire line characters. This is the only editing that is allowed at the standard UNIX login prompt.

- The encrypted password is not actually an encryption of the password; it is the encryption of the value 0 using the password and the salt as the key. The field is 13 characters; the first 2 characters are the "salt," composed of 2 characters, which is appended to the password to make the key. This adds an additional 4096 possible encryptions for the same password. The salt adds a little spice to the algorithm. This field may be suffixed by a comma and two characters which are the password aging element. The first character denotes the maximum number of weeks for which a password is valid. The second character indicates the minimum number of weeks before the password can be changed. The character set used in the encrypted password field is composed of 64 characters representing the values from 0 to 63. In order, the characters are the period, the slash, 0 through 9, the upper-case letters, and the lower-case letters.

No account should be allowed without passwords. A user without a password is easy to spot since the password field in the password file will be blank. This script will print out all the accounts without passwords.

```
awk -F: 'length($2)<1 {print $1}' < /etc/passwd
```

- The third field is the user ID (UID) field. It is a 16-bit integer. It is this value, not the user's name, that is used to identify ownership and grant access to resources. A UID of 0 indicates superuser privileges. The UIDs of -1 and -2 are used by NFS®. The UID of -1 is for an unauthenticated user and is referred to as nobody; the UID of -2 is used for the root user of another system who is accessing a file system for which he does not have root access.

- The fourth field is the group ID (GID) field; it is a 16-bit integer. Groups are used to group users together so they can share files among the individuals in the group without allowing everyone access.

- The fifth field is the GECOS field. This is a comment field that, by convention, contains a comma separated list of user's "real-life" name, location, office phone number, and home phone number. This field is used by the finger command, as well as a number of other commands that display a user's real name.

  GECOS information should never be included. Not having this information may be an inconvenience. You will have to manually convert a user's login name to his real name. However, the GECOS information is some of the most valuable information your system has to aid a hacker in password cracking. It gives the hacker more information about users that can lead to insight into guessing passwords. Some of the system management tools will request the user's name, telephone number, and organization information and fill in the GECOS field.

- The sixth field is the user's home directory, generally limited to no more that 64 characters.

- The seventh field is the user's start-up program. It is generally limited to 44 characters.

NIS

Network Information Service (NIS®) was developed by Sun Microsystems® to provide a centralized repository for common system configuration files. These configuration files generally include the password file, group file, and many others. Since many of these contain sensitive information, access is limited to those clients that know the NIS domain name.

Security for NIS is based on only a single password: the NIS domain name. Any system with the NIS domain name can read any of the information in the NIS database since there is almost no authentication between clients and servers. The NIS domain name is generally easy to guess by using the same techniques as those used in guessing passwords. You must select a domain name that is difficult to guess. This is your only protection on all your NIS databases. Selecting a good password is not enough when the systems will tell you the password when it is requested.

If the system is running the NFS diskless boot daemon, a simple program can be written to access the boot server and receive the NIS domain name in the response; it can then be used to compromise the NIS system. The Remote Procedure Call (RPC) that requests the resources is illustrated below.

```
callrpc(server, BOOTPARAMPROG, BOOTPARAMVERS, BOOTPARAMPROC_WHOAMI,
        xdr_bp_whoami_arg, &arg, xdr_bp_whoami_res, &res);
printf("%s has NIS Domain name:  %s\n", server, res.domain.name);
```

Once a hacker knows your NIS domain name, he can access any of the information in the server's NIS maps by utilizing a simple RPC query, even when he is outside the subnet served by that server. The program ypx which has been posted on Usenet News does just that. It will transfer any NIS map from any host that is running the ypserv daemon.

NIS also requires that each file on each client computer have a special entry that tells the system to access the server for the information for that file. This entry starts with a plus sign. For example, a password file may look like the following:

```
+::0:0:::
```

In this case, all passwords are pulled from the NIS server. However, if this system does not bind to a NIS server because it cannot talk to the server, a hacker will be able to log in as "+" and have root privileges. A system may be unable to reach a server for any of a number of reasons, including a server failure, a network failure, or routing error.

It is imperative that the NIS client files be configured correctly. The above example should be:

```
+:LOCKED:88:88:::
```

Then if the system could not bind to its server, you would be unable to log in to the system as "+". Even if the password field is omitted, you would not be able to get superuser access. Because of the long-standing security problem with NIS, some vendors have implemented special rules pertaining to the NIS configuration. Check your vendor's documentation for specifics.

If a hacker can gain access to the yp master files by mounting the ypmaster directory or compromising the NIS master system, he can control all the systems that are in the NIS domain. Any changes to the NIS master will propagate to all the clients. The ypmaster directory is usually `/var/yp` or `/usr/etc/yp`. The subdirectory that contains the data is the same name as the domain name.

One feature on HP-UX specific to NIS security is the `/var/yp/secureservers` file. This file can be used by NIS clients to specify a list of valid IP addresses (i.e., NIS servers) for which the client can bind. This file helps to eliminate the threat of a client binding to unauthorized, rogue NIS servers.

NIS+

NIS+ manages the same information about usernames, passwords, groupnames, and hostnames, but does so with greater emphasis on security. The enhancement to security include greater control of access to data and both client and server authentication. NIS+ uses a combination of public and secret key cryptography to authenticate clients and servers. However, the key exchange implementation limits the effectiveness of the security implementation. All nodes within the domain must be running NIS+ (not NIS) or all security enhancements are disabled. It is also more complex to administer and this is where many security issues arise.

LDAP

LDAP (Lightweight Directory Access Protocol) is a proposed open standard for accessing global or local directory services over a network and/or the Internet. A directory, in this sense, is simply a data repository which associates an attribute to an identifier. Requests for an identifier return the attribute. It is typically used to associate names with phone numbers, e-mail addresses, and user credentials. LDAP directories are designed to support a high volume of queries, but the data stored in the directory do not change very often.

LDAP can be used as an authentication service via the pam_ldap module. LDAP is commonly used as a central authentication server so that users have a unified login that covers console logins, POP servers, IMAP servers, machines connected to the network using Samba, and even Windows NT/2000 machines. Using LDAP, all of these login situations can rely on the same user ID and password combination, greatly simplifying administration.

OpenLDAP is present in Red Hat 6 and newer releases and supports LDAP as an authentication method. HP-UX introduced LDAP as an authentication method at release 11 and provides Netscape LDAP server for intranet uses.

Monitoring the Network

There are numerous ways you can monitor the traffic on a network. There are specific instruments that analyze the traffic on a LAN, as well as software that allows your computer to see all the packets on the network. This listening to all the packets on a network is often referred to as having your system in "promiscuous" mode. Many systems come with a network-logging tool for diagnostics that can work for this purpose.

Just watching all the packets on a network will not yield much useful information. A hacker must be able to filter out the packets that he doesn't want and capture and reconstruct the communication he is looking for. What he is looking for are telnet, rlogin and ftp packets that will contain the user name and associated password. These are passed across the network in clear text.

Network monitoring software has become widespread and available for all types of computers. Many vendors will include a network sniffer as part of the diagnostic software that comes with the system. Many of these programs are not built with security in mind; they are created to collect information to solve a particular problem. However, it is often the same information that a hacker is looking for.

Controlling network monitoring is a very difficult task. Anyone who has access to your network can monitor the packets on the network. Any of the data in the packets can be captured. The only defense to this is to encrypt the data that are traveling over the network. However, in a standard UNIX environment, user data can be encrypted, but the login names and passwords which are part of the control environment cannot. There are a number of packages available to increase the security of the login process.

On Linux systems, the promiscuous mode can be enabled or disabled with the ifconfig command. The output from the netstat -i command will display the status of the interface as illustrated below.

```
netstat -i
eth1  Link encap:Ethernet  HWaddr 00:90:27:3A:E3:67
      inet addr:10.0.0.3  Bcast:10.0.0.255  Mask:255.255.255.0
      UP BROADCAST RUNNING PROMISC  MTU:1500  Metric:1
      RX packets:50361 errors:0 dropped:0 overruns:0 frame:0
      TX packets:16 errors:0 dropped:0 overruns:0 carrier:0
      collisions:0 txqueuelen:100
      Interrupt:17 Base address:0xfcc0
```

ARPA Services

The ARPA services of telnet and FTP are two of the oldest protocols still in use today. They date back to the very beginning of computer networks. The entire session is transmitted in clear text. There is no encryption utilized, even for the login password. This makes these protocols hazardous to use today with the availability of network sniffers. Security-enhanced versions or secure replacements for these protocols should be used to get remote system access and to transfer files.

Kerberos is an authentication service for authenticating users or services across an open network. It authenticates entities without sending plain text passwords over the network. The Kerberos protocol uses strong cryptography (DES) so that a client can prove its identity to a server (and vice versa) across an insecure network connection, and assure privacy and data integrity in the communications. It works by assigning a unique shared secret key and issues a token called a ticket to each client that logs on to the network. The ticket is then embedded in messages to identify the sender of the message.

Under Kerberos, a client (generally either a user or a service) sends a request for a ticket to the Key Distribution Center (KDC). The KDC creates a ticket-granting ticket (TGT) for the client, encrypts it using the KDC key, and sends the encrypted TGT back to the client. The client uses the TGT to obtain further service tickets, which provide the proof of the client's identity.

PAM Kerberos, PAM-KRB5, is supported on the HP-UX 11i system. It is based on Kerberos Authentication System V5, developed by Massachusetts Institute of Technology (MIT). The PAM Kerberos module is compliant with IETF RFC 1510 and Open Group RFC 86. HP-UX PAM Kerberos is implemented under the PAM (Pluggable Authentication Module) framework. PAM Kerberos works with Microsoft Windows 2000 and MIT Kerberos V5 KDC. However, it is not intended to work with the HP-UX DCE KDC.

To support single sign-on between HP-UX and Microsoft Windows 2000 or other UNIX systems running MIT Kerberos, HP-UX provides PAM Kerberos that integrates HP-UX login with any Kerberos 5 Server, such as Microsoft Windows 2000 Key Distribution Center (KDC) and MIT KDC.

Secure Shell

Secure shell provides terminal access (ssh) and file transfer (sftp) in a secure manner. If SSH is used for remote shell logins and file copying, these security threats can be greatly diminished. A server's digital signature provides verification for its identity. The entire communication between client and server systems cannot be used if intercepted, because each of the packets is encrypted. Attempts to spoof the identity of either side of a communication will not work, since each packet is encrypted using a key known only by the local and remote systems.

Since servers can be configured to allow different types of authentication, this method gives each side the optimal amount of control. The server can decide which encryption methods it will support based on its security model, and the client can choose the order of authentication methods to attempt from among the available options. Thanks to the secure nature of the SSH transport layer, even seemingly insecure authentication methods, such as a host-based authentication, are safe to use.

For SSH to be truly effective in protecting your network connections, you must stop using all insecure connection protocols, such as telnet and rsh. Otherwise, a user's password may be protected using ssh on one day only to be captured when it logs in the next day using telnet.

POP and IMAP

Post Office Protocol (POP) and Internet Message Access Protocol (IMAP) are two protocols which are used to access e-mail which has been stored on a server.

These protocols both suffer from transmitting unencrypted passwords and data over the network. The common solution to this problem is to wrap the protocol in an encryption protocol, such as SSL or SSH.

Linux systems can enable SSL-wrapped IMAP and POP3 by using the sslproxy program supplied by openssl. The services would need to be added to /etc/services, and the program invoked from inetd. To do this, add the following lines to /etc/services:

```
imaps 993/tcp
pop3s 995/tcp
```

and these lines to /etc/inetd.conf

```
imaps stream tcp nowait root /usr/sbin/tcpd sslproxy -t 3600 -p imap
pop3s stream tcp nowait root /usr/sbin/tcpd sslproxy -t 3600 -p pop-3
```

FTP Sessions

FTP, File Transfer Protocol, allows you to transfer files between computers. In general, the user must have an account with a valid user name and password on both machines. The FTP protocol passes the user name and password over the network in clear text, so that any network sniffer can see this information. Disable or remove the FTP daemon ftpd if FTP services are not needed.

Users can be restricted from using FTP by entering their user names into the file /etc/ftpusers. The superuser account, all accounts with extra privileges, such as database administrators, all default accounts, and captive accounts should be listed in the /etc/ftpusers file. Since the FTP user's file is an exclusion file, each time a user is added that does not need FTP access, it must be added to this file.

Although most systems can log these attempts if logging is turned on, most sites do not log bad passwords that are entered via FTP, so hackers see this as safer place to do password guessing than at the login prompt.

SMTP

A hacker can use the Simple Mail Transfer Protocol (SMTP) command `vrfy` to verify if a user login name exists on a system. This command will also give him the person's real name from the GECOS field of the password file, and the address to which the mail is forwarded, if the mail is forwarded. The following entries in the sendmail.cf file can eliminate a great deal of SMTP-based snooping:

```
novrfy
noexpn
goaway
```

A user who has his mail forwarded to another system may be a limited user of the system. This may indicate a good user ID to exploit. Checking common user IDs, such as root or postmaster, may indicate who administers the system and where his home system is.

A company should discourage the use of e-mail addresses that address specific users on specific machines. Instead, the company should set up one e-mail gateway that has an e-mail address for all of the employees. This gateway would then relay the inbound e-mail to the appropriate machine and user. This would hide the specifics of a machine name and user login ID. It would also have the benefit of giving a uniform appearance to all the company's e-mail.

Social Engineering

Social Engineering is the process of getting someone to divulge information through the process of using a false pretense. Most social engineering is done by people who will use a variety of tactics to get the target to divulge information. Some of these tactics include playing on the victim's sympathies, using intimidation, expressing that it is an urgent situation, and using the 5-til-5 syndrome, which is contacting the victim just before it is time to go home in hopes that he will hurry through with the request, skipping security checks, etc., so that he can get it done and get home soon.

There are also programs which use social engineering tactics to get information or to gain privileges.

Spoofs

A spoof is a program that impersonates another program in order to gather information. A spoof is generally used to gain information by fooling a user or another computer into volunteering information. A spoof that simulates the login sequence can be planted by logging onto a terminal and running the program with the `exec` command. It will then appear to be a login session. After the victim enters his user ID and password, the program will tell him that the login is incorrect and will exit leaving the real login to reprompt. A careful eye will notice that most login spoofs do not prompt three times for login and password before the banner is reissued.

To limit this type of spoof, users should get in the habit of hitting the break key before logging on. Simple spoofs will not reissue a login after a break is sent. It may also be advisable to hit the return key a few times before logging on to be sure that the login process is acting properly.

There have been numerous login spoofs written and published in hacker publications. They vary from simple shell scripts to very involved programs that utilize the original source code.

Trojan Horse

A Trojan horse is a program that appears to be a useful program, and often is, but it actually has an alternate purpose. It works by getting someone to run the program unknowingly.

> Recent Trojan horses are arriving at your computer as e-mail allegedly from someone you know offering you an interesting attachment. However, the attachment is actually malicious code. The effects of the malicious file are activated only when the file in question is executed. These attacks have used "VBS/OnTheFly" malicious code — a VBScript program that spreads via email.
>
> The most famous of these is probably the "Anna Kournikova" Trojan. It purports to contain naked pictures. When the malicious code executes, it attempts to send copies of itself, using Microsoft Outlook, to all entries in each of the address books. So far these Trojans have only caused congestion on networks and e-mail servers.[54]

Some Trojan horses get victims to run them by having the same name as a known program or being advertised as a program that would be difficult to live without. Trojan horses are often touted to be useful utilities or games.

Monitoring User Input

Eavesdropping on users, either looking over their shoulder or by electronic means, is a proven method of gathering information. It is easy for an individual to be alert, when entering private information, to the people around them who might be trying to see what is being entered. However, awareness of electronic eavesdropping is more difficult.

---

[54]   "VBS/OnTheFly (Anna Kournikova) Malicious Code," *FedCIRC Advisory FA-2001-03*, 12 February 2001.

Keystroke Monitoring

Keystroke monitoring is the process of electronically looking over someone's shoulder and watching what they are entering on the keyboard. It is accomplished by having a program monitor the terminal port that the terminal is attached to. Keystroke monitoring has become popular with businesses. It can be used to monitor the work habits of employees. It can also be used by hackers to watch what a user types into the computer, including login IDs and passwords.

Keystroke monitoring is often implemented by system owners to monitor the activities of their employees. A compromised monitoring system can be utilized by a hacker to gather invaluable information.

Covert software for keyboard and mouse monitoring has been found which invades web browsers. Once infected, the value of any encryption is lost since the data are intercepted before they are encrypted for transmission.

Remote Display Systems

A system that is running a remote display system is vulnerable to attack if the protocol to transmit the remote display is vulnerable or if the remote system is vulnerable. Remote display servers, such as the X windows system, offer service through a well-known port. Monitoring this port can enable a third party to capture or watch windows, user keystrokes, and more.

Remote display systems need to be able to adequately protect the communications and strongly authenticate the client host and user. Preferably, the system would limit the access based on both the user and the location from which the user has attached. Even with adequate user authentication, all the information passes over the network and generally remote display systems do not encrypt their communications.

## CHAPTER 10

Controlling Authentication

Authentication is the process of validating the identity of the entity in question. Usually we think of authenticating users, but systems, programs, data, etc., also have a need for authentication.

Authentication information is that piece of information which can be used to verify the accuracy of the identity. This information which is used to authenticate the user's identity must be protected so that it cannot be used to forge an identity. The factors that can be used to authenticate the identity of an entity are those factors that are unique to that specific entity. The factors must be known or derivable to both the entity being authenticated and the process authenticating the entity. The following are three basic factors that are used in authentication. These basic factors are available to all types of entities.

- **Something you know** — a shared secret, a password, something both the user and the authenticator know. Password authentication is relatively inexpensive and easy to implement, which is why almost all systems that perform authentication use passwords. The most common password problem is a weak password — if users can select them, they are generally not long enough, not random enough, or not changed often enough, to keep them secure. In addition, many systems do not store passwords in a secure location or with strong enough protections to prevent common password attacks.

- **Something you have** — a physical ID (e.g., an identification card). Using a physical item increases the likelihood that its loss or theft will be noticed and reported.

- **Something you are** — a measurable feature (e.g., fingerprint, facial characteristics, voiceprint). The measuring of a physical characteristic is called biometrics. If the entity that is being authenticated is a program or a system, the measurement can be a cryptographic checksum.

Authentication Management

Authentication management is a combination of user education and appropriate use of technology. Users have to understand the importance of protecting their identifier and password and how to select good passwords. Technological solutions need to be implemented to help the user select good passwords and to be able to apply the appropriate level of security to the resources as needed.

Password Selection

The selection of passwords is still paramount to system security. A good password is a password that is not cracked by a password cracking method and is easy to remember.

Password management is primarily a user issue. Education of users is paramount in the maintenance of password security. This education should include how to set passwords, how to select good passwords, and the importance of passwords. Users must understand that poor passwords jeopardize their work, as well as the work of everyone else who uses the system.

System managers should be vigilant about passwords. Password cracking is the most effective method of gaining privileges in a system. You can run password crackers against your system, but this takes a lot of computing resources and requires that there be a copy of the cracking software and a customized dictionary on the system that could fall into the wrong hands. It has been suggested that these dictionaries can be preencrypted and stored on tape, so you do not have to run the password cracking software. You only have to match the encrypted passwords to encrypted words from the tape. This would utilize less processing time but require more time for the tape processing.

It may be better to take the proactive choice of installing a package that evaluates the quality of a password when the password is entered. This does not require the computational resources, because the password is captured as plain text and can be rapidly evaluated. There are a number of tools to choose from including Password+ and npasswd. The tool you select should be flexible enough to allow you to customize your environment with the inclusion of special dictionaries that have words and phrases specific to your industry, or to your company, or to your employees.

Password cracking, the difficulty users have in selecting good passwords, and the widespread proliferation of network snooping that will compromise even good passwords, have made reusable passwords of limited value locally and a major security issue over an untrusted network. That is why reusable passwords are falling into disfavor and so much effort is being put into onetime passwords.

A study done in 1989 by Dan Klein at Carnegie-Mellon University used these methods to attempt to crack a list of 13,797 actual passwords from a variety of sources. The total dictionary utilized was comprised of 62,727 words. This process guessed 3,340 passwords.

Table 10-1 Sources of Passwords[55]

Source of Password	Search Size	Number of Matches	Percent of Total
User/account names	130	368	2.70%
Character sequences	866	22	0.20%
Numbers	427	9	0.10%
Chinese	392	56	0.40%
Place names	628	82	0.60%
Common names	2239	548	4.00%
Female names	4280	161	1.20%
Male names	2866	140	1.00%
Uncommon names	4955	130	0.90%
Myths and legends	1246	66	0.50%
Shakespearean	473	11	0.10%
Sports terms	238	32	0.20%
Science fiction	691	59	0.40%
Movies and actors	99	12	0.10%
Cartoons	92	9	0.10%
Famous people	290	55	0.40%
Phrases and patterns	933	253	1.80%
Surnames	33	9	0.10%
Biology	58	1	0.00%
Unix dictionary	19683	1027	7.40%
Machine names	9018	132	1.00%
Mnemonics	14	2	0.00%
King James Bible	7525	83	0.60%
Miscellaneous words	3212	54	0.40%
Yiddish words	56	0	0.00%
Asteroids	2407	19	0.10%
TOTAL	62851	3340	24.30%

Table 10-1 contains the information revealed by the study about the source of passwords selected by users.

[55] Klein, Dan, "Foiling the Cracker: A Survey of, and Improvements to, Password Security," 1989.

Cracking Passwords

One of the most common ways to get privileges is to crack the password file. Password cracking is the process of determining the authentication information from using the cipher that is used to verify the password to guess or crack the password. On UNIX systems, passwords are not actually cracked; the passwords are guessed. Standard UNIX passwords are up to eight characters long. Many systems require a minimum of six characters and the inclusion of a numeral or special character. However, the superuser can override these minimums. Often when accounts are created, the superuser will create them with a simple password or no password at all.

No account should be allowed without passwords. As a system manager, you should set the user's initial password, using a good password as an example to the users. You should not e-mail the new password to the user. Many hackers scan mail looking for keywords like password or secret.

Generally, getting access to passwords is very simple for the hacker. The password file is readable to all users, so the hacker can easily copy it to his system to crack. The only way to secure the password file is to use shadow passwords.

Changing the Algorithm

Password cracking requires knowing both the cryptographic algorithm and the resultant cypher in order to be able to compare the result of using a guessed password to the actual cypher. Changing the algorithm can diminish the ability of the hacker to crack the password.

Altering the crypt library routine on UNIX systems will change how the password is calculated. This will give you a password file that is nonstandard, causing password guessing to fail. This, of course, requires that you have the source code to your operating system. The simplest change is to alter the number of times which the cryptographic routine is run against the cipher. Altering the cyrpt routine will not only make password cracking ineffective on other machines, it will also make the password field of no use to other machines which do not have the same alterations. So, to support an enterprise-wide identification environment, all the systems must be identically modified. If you plan to use NIS to share passwords, you will have to do the same modification on all the systems that are involved. The cracking routines can still be run on a system which has been modified to crack the passwords, since the cracking tool will call the modified crypt function.

Red Hat Linux allows the use of the MD5 algorithm to encrypt passwords. This algorithm allows a long password to be used (up to 256 characters), instead of the standard eight letters or less and is much more difficult to crack.

Slackware Linux systems are easy to enable MD5 by editing the /etc/login.defs file so that MD5_CRYPT_ENAB line says yes instead of no.

Shadow Passwords

Shadow passwords remove the encrypted password field from the public password file and put it into a file that is accessible only to root. The location of the secure password file will vary depending on implementation. This deters cracking methods, because the encrypted password is not available to ordinary users. Some implementations will allow access to the encrypted password via the getpwent or the getspwent subroutine. You need to validate that this program will return only encrypted passwords if it is run by the superuser. If either of these subroutines will return the encrypted password to nonsuperusers, then your shadow password system is not offering you the protection it should and you need to petition your vendor to fix this security problem.

HP-UX implements shadowed passwords as part of its trusted system base. The /etc/lbin/tsconvert command is used to convert the HP-UX system to a trusted system. The shadow passwords are stored in user directories within the /tcb/files/auth directory structure by username. Trusted HP-UX does not support NIS, but it will support NIS+ with some limited functionality.

Shadow passwords are available in HP-UX 11.22 without requiring trusted systems. The 11.22 HP-UX release of Shadow Passwords is based on the *defacto* standard provided in Sun Solaris, Linux, and other UNIX flavors. The pwconv command can be run to move encrypted passwords from the publicly readable /etc/passwd file to /etc/shadow, and replace the password fields in /etc/passwd with 'x'. Afterwards, pwunconv can be run to convert back to a standard system. In 11.22 shadow passwords are not supported with NIS, NIS+ nor LDAP.

Current versions of the standard PAM for Linux supports shadow passwords without modification. Early versions require selecting a specific PAM module for shadow support, generally unix+shadow.

Finding Passwords in Clear Text

There are a number of places on a system where a hacker is likely to find passwords unencrypted, thereby not needing to utilize intense password cracking. There are also a number of ways that he can electronically look over a user's shoulder as the user types in his password. A hacker may also use social engineering to convince a user to give him his password.

FTP Configuration File

There are configuration files for FTP that are often overlooked or misconfigured. The .netrc file in each user's home directory is used by FTP to allow a user to connect to another machine without entering the user name and password for that machine. It accomplishes this by keeping a copy of the user name and password in this file.

The .netrc file in each user's home directory is the first place a hacker will look for unencrypted passwords. This file contains system names, user names, and passwords of other systems in clear text. It is a convenience file which allows users to FTP to other systems and not enter their login or password. This information is gotten directly from the file.

The following command will list the contents of all the .netrc files in the user's home directories:

```
cut -d: -f6 /etc/passwd | xargs -i cat {}/.netrc 2>/dev/null
```

Since the .netrc file is a convenience file and a major security risk, not directly for your system but for other systems, it should not be allowed. If you must allow it, it must be read-only only for its owner and no permissions for anyone else.

Disable or remove the FTP daemon if FTP services are not needed.

UUCP Configuration File

The systems file for UUCP, either Systems or L.sys, contains the name of remote systems, their UUCP login name and password, and their phone number. This is enough to enable an attack against these systems.

Permissions on the UUCP systems file should be read-only for its owner, which should be the account "uucp," and there should be no permissions for anyone else.

If the debug option is available on the cu or the uucico command, it can be used to retrieve the information that is contained in these files, even if the permissions are correct.

The debug option should not be allowed on these commands except for the superuser. UUCP should be removed from the system if not required.

Bad Login Attempts

A hacker will check the /etc/btmp file for passwords that users have inadvertently entered instead of their login name. It is not that uncommon for users to type in their password instead of their login name. This is usually because that they are not paying attention and are out of sync with the login program. The hacker can find out whose password it is by looking at the times of other bad login attempts and good login attempts from the same terminal. The user will generally get logged in once he sees what he did.

The /etc/btmp file should be owned by root and should have read and write permissions for root only. This file should be monitored for those who are trying to guess passwords and reset on a regular basis.

Game Passwords

There are a number of very common multiplayer games on UNIX systems that will let you suspend your session and return to it at a later time. These games will ask for a password so you can be authenticated upon your return. Many people will use their login password as the password for the game because it's easy to remember. Many of these games store these passwords as clear text.

You must be aware of all the programs utilized on your system. There may be more than just games that want a password, such as databases, for example. These passwords must be encrypted. UNIX systems have the password encryption function, crypt, available. Users should be reminded that they should not use their login password for any other password. It would be best if these programs checked to make sure that the password that was entered was not the login password. This can be accomplished on some systems by using the getpwent function.

The Future of Passwords

There are only three things that can be used for authentication: something you know, something you have, or something you are. Combining two or more of these things yields a stronger authentication. Passwords are something you know. Keys are something you have. An access card that requires a PIN number combines both something you have and something you know. Reliable and accurate systems to identify something you are, such as fingerprint or hand-print scanners, voice identification equipment, or retina scanners, are very expensive and have yet to prove themselves.

The two major security risks to passwords today are password guessing and password snooping. These two risks have made the current UNIX password system suspect, and it is apparent that it will soon be ineffective. The following password methodologies address one or both of these issues.

Computer-generated Passwords

Since the main problem with passwords is that users choose ones that are easy to guess, one approach to improving password security is to use passwords that are created by the computer. Computer-generated passwords render password guessing useless, since the passwords selected by the computer are not found in any dictionary. But that also means that the passwords are difficult for users to remember. So users will usually write down their passwords, opening a door to other types of snooping.

Writing down a password in a "time management system" or in your "pocket computer" may not be much of a security risk, since you will know if your time management system or your pocket computer is lost or stolen and can notify the system managers to change your passwords. However, most users will write down their password on a piece of paper and keep it close at hand near their terminal (in their desk drawer, under the keyboard, stuck to the edge of the terminal monitor), thereby leading to the general consensus that writing down your password is a bad idea.

Pass Phrases

Since the number of possible passwords grows exponentially with the length of the password, some sites have replaced the standard UNIX password system with a system that uses pass phrases. A pass phrase system allows the user to type in a long password where every character must match to be granted access. This allows the user to use a phrase that can be remembered and reduces the success of password guessing.

Challenge-response Systems

Some sites have addressed the issue by having the user answer a series of questions. Then when the user logs in, one of the questions is presented to the user and he must give the matching response to gain access. In this case, if a password is compromised, it opens only a smaller window of vulnerability, since the hacker may receive a challenge that is not the one to which he has the correct response. Generally, these systems will continue to give the same challenge until a correct response is supplied, keeping a hacker from retrying until the challenge he has the response for is presented.

Onetime Passwords

Onetime passwords eliminate the security issues of snooping and password cracking by not using a password more than once. So getting someone's password does not help a hacker get access to the system.

Today, onetime passwords are implemented either with a book of precomputed passwords that the user carries with him, and the system prompts the user for a specific entry from the book, or through the use of smart cards that compute the next password in the smart card. Outfitting thousands of users with smart cards may be cost-prohibitive.

Implementing Strong Authentication

There have been many solutions and implementations for providing strong authentication. Some of these solutions replace daemons and are for specific systems, while others do not address all methods of access to a system, and others require that the user's terminal be a PC. These restrictions and limited functionality have prevented them from becoming the next-generation authentication scheme.

A good authentication scheme has to be ubiquitous so it can be used everywhere. It has to be universal so that all access methods to a system are supported. It has to be flexible enough to support the specific needs of any system.

Modern implementations of UNIX systems are shipped with a unified authentication scheme called PAM.

PAM

The Pluggable Authentication Module (PAM) [OSF RFC 86] is an industry standard authentication framework. PAM gives system administrators the flexibility of choosing any authentication service available on the system to perform authentication. The PAM framework also allows new authentication service modules to be plugged in and made available without modifying the applications. Programs requiring user authentication pass their requests to PAM, which determines the correct verification method and returns the appropriate response. The programs do not need to know what authentication method is being used. Login authentication, account checking, and password modification use the PAM interface.

PAM defines four authentication module types: User Authentication (auth) which verifies the identity of a user and sets the user-specific credentials, Account Management (account) which retrieves the user's expiration information and verifies that the user's account and password have not expired, Session Management (session) which provides functions to initiate and terminate sessions, and Password Management (password) which provides a function to change passwords.

Control is available on both a system-wide service and an individual user basis. In the newest version of PAM, the system-wide configuration files are in the /etc/pam.d directory in files named for each service. Earlier versions use /etc/pam.conf to define system-wide and service-specific authentication methods. The /etc/pam_user.conf file is used to specify individual user methods.

The **system-wide configuration** file, /etc/pam.conf, defines the security mechanisms that are used to authenticate users. Its default values provide the customary operation of the system.

There is an entry in the file for each area of authentication for each service.

The entries in /etc/pam.conf have the following form:

```
service-name module-type control module-path options
login     auth  required  /usr/lib/security/libpam_unix.1
```

The **peruser configuration** file, /etc/pam_user.conf, allows individual users to be assigned different options. /etc/pam_user.conf is optional. It is needed only if PAM applications need to behave differently for various users. This can be used to isolate the administrative user accounts. For each login-name listed, the options listed replace any options specified for the module-type/module-path in /etc/pam.conf.

The entries in /etc/pam_user.conf have the following form:

```
login-name module-type module-path options
```

Multiple-authentication methods can be utilized simultaneously. The methods will be tried in the order in which they are listed. All "required" methods have to be successfully passed for the user to be authenticated. An authentication which successfully passes a method which is defined to be "sufficient" is considered authenticated at that point.

In combination, they can be used to allow for local users and global users. This would generally be used to have local administrative accounts and global user accounts. It is best to have no overlap between user identities between the password file and the LDAP. However, when there is an overlap, the first listed has priority.

This example indicates that the UNIX password file will have priority. Thereby, if a root user is added to the LDAP, that user will not have access to the system because there is a local root user.

```
login auth sufficient /usr/lib/security/libpam_unix.1
login auth required  /usr/lib/security/libpam_ldap.1 use_first_pass
```

The "use_first_pass" option uses the password entered for pam_unix for pam_ldap as well. Without this option, the user would be re-prompted if the pam_unix was unsuccessful.

In a more complex environment where multiple PAMs are utilized, there are specific ordering issues.

PAM modules can do more than just define new authentication methods. They can be used to restrict or enhance the other PAM authentication methods. Required modules can be added which limit access to the system based on resource quotas, or time of day, or any definable restriction. PAM modules can be added to password management to test the quality of the password selected. Stacking these modules can create any number of useful user controls.

- **HP-UX** supports PAM starting with HP-UX release 10.20 for authenticating CDE components and at 10.30 PAM was extended to provide authentication for system commands on standard HP-UX, Trusted Systems, and the Distributed Computing Environment (DCE) and to allow third-party modules. With Release 11i, PAM processing was extended. It now supports telnet, login, remsh, ftp, rexec, rlogin, dtlogin, and rcp.

  Table 10-2 lists the available HP-supplied PAM modules for 11i, which reside in `/usr/lib/security`.

Table 10-2 HP-supplied PAM Modules

libpam_unix	Standard HP-UX authentication
libpam_dce	DCE authentication
libpam_ntl	NT LanManager authentication
libpam_ldap	LDAP authentication
libpam_krb5	Kerberos V5 authentication, i.e., MIT Kerberos and Windows 2000
libpam_updbe	Enable user specific PAM configurations

In the System Administration Manager (SAM), you can use the Authenticated Commands subarea of Auditing and Security to manage the PAM configuration file, `/etc/pam.conf`. For each type of PAM authentication — User Authentication (auth), Account Management (account), Session Management (session), and Password Management (password) — you can add, modify, or remove service names from the PAM configuration file.

SAM is not able to manage the peruser file, `/etc/pam_user.conf`, or the DCE interface; you must modify these by hand.

- **Linux** support for PAM is gaining rapid acceptance and support for most current Linux releases. The open source community has produced a number of PAM modules to incorporate additional authentication methods which are available in most Linux distributions. Table 10-3 shows common PAM modules found on most Linux systems.

Table 10-3 Linux-supported PAM Modules

pam_cracklib	This module performs strength-checking for new passwords by stacking it before other password modules. It requires the cracklib library, libcrack, to compile.
pam_ftp	This module checks to see if the user is "ftp" or "anonymous." On finding this to be the case, it prompts for an e-mail address for a password, and proceeds to set the PAM_RUSER item with this value.
pam_group	This module extends the /etc/group concept by granting group privileges based on who the user is and when or from where he is requesting a service, as well as, what he is trying to do.
pam_limits	This module sets the resource limits for a service.
pam_listfile	This module authenticates users based on the contents of a specified file.
pam_nologin	This module always lets root in; it lets other users in only if the file /etc/nologin doesn't exist. In any case, if /etc/nologin exists, its contents are displayed to the user.
pam_passwd+	This module performs password strength-checking.
pam_pwdb	This module is a plug-in replacement for pam_unix_* that uses the Password Database library.
pam_radius	This module performs RADIUS authentication, using the Password Database library.
pam_rootok	This module authenticates the user if his real UID is root (intended for use with the sufficient control flag).
pam_securetty	This module implements /etc/securretty access controls.

Table 10-3 Linux-supported PAM Modules (cont.)

pam_shells	This module requires that the user's shell be listed in the /etc/shells file.
pam_tally	This module keeps track of the number of times an attempt is made to login.
pam_time	This module authorizes users based on when the from where they log in.
pam_unix_*	This module implements standard UNIX authentication.
pam_wheel	This module enforces the wheel group privileges.

These include some widely used authentication schemes, such as NDS, SecureID, Radius, IMAP, TACACS, S/KEY and SQL databases.

The following excerpts from the Red Hat Linux documentation illustrate and explain a default PAM configuration file:

```
#%PAM-1.0
auth       required /lib/security/pam_securetty.so
auth       required /lib/security/pam_pwdb.so shadow nullok
auth       required /lib/security/pam_nologin.so
account  required /lib/security/pam_pwdb.so
password required /lib/security/pam_cracklib.so
password required /lib/security/pam_pwdb.so shadow nullok use_authtok
session  required /lib/security/pam_pwdb.so
```

The first line is a comment. (Any line that starts with a # character is a comment.) Lines two through four stack up three modules to use for login authorization. Line two makes sure that if the user is trying to log in as root, the tty on which he or she is logging in is listed in the /etc/securetty file if that file exists. Line three causes the user to be asked for a password and the password to be checked. Line four checks to see if the file /etc/nologin exists, and if it does, displays the contents of the file, and if the user is not root, does not let him or her login.

Note that all three modules are checked, even if the first module fails. This is a security decision — it is designed to prevent the user from knowing why his or her authentication was disallowed, because knowing why it was disallowed might allow him or her to break the authentication more easily. You can change this behavior by changing required to requisite; if any requisite module returns failure, PAM fails immediately without calling any other modules.

The fifth line causes any necessary accounting to be done. For example, if shadow passwords have been enabled, the pam_pwdb.so module will check to see if the account has expired, or if the user has not changed his or her password and the grace period for changing the password has expired.

The sixth line subjects a newly changed password to a series of tests to ensure that it cannot, for example, be easily determined by a dictionary-based password cracking program.

The seventh line (which may be wrapped) specifies that if the login program changes the user's password, it should use the pam_pwdb.so module to do so. (It will do so only if an auth module has determined that the password needs to be changed, for example, if a shadow password has expired.)

The eighth and final line specifies that the pam_pwdb.so module should be used to manage the session. Currently, that module doesn't do anything; it could be replaced (or supplemented by stacking) by any necessary module.

Note that the order of the lines in the file matters especially when "sufficient" and "requisite" modules are used.

## CHAPTER 11

Gaining Privileges

Once a hacker has access to your system, keeping him from gaining more privileges is the hardest thing for a security administrator. Determining if the person using an account is the authorized user or not is a difficult task, especially if you have no reason to suspect a user. If the hacker is an official user, the task becomes even more difficult. His legitimate physical access and relationship with other users and system managers can all be exploited to his benefit.

An experienced hacker who can gain access and privileges on your system will be difficult to detect without diligent efforts. If he has gotten this far, you can be sure that his skills and knowledge will be a match for yours. He will probably know the software on your system well, but you will have better knowledge of the behavior of your system.

Building user profiles can help you identify hackers. These profiles are a database of normal work habits showing how and when each user uses the system. Automated collection of information from accounting, auditing, and logs can be analyzed to create statistical norms and notify security when there is significant deviation. Expert systems are becoming available in the marketplace to help in this endeavor.

The variety of methods and plethora of software on the system make plugging all the holes a continuous, impossible task. The hacker's ego is usually his downfall. Most hackers want to be recognized for their brilliance in outsmarting the system with their hacking exploits. They will feel compelled to tell people about their exploits, so they can be held in awe.

Awareness is the best defense for keeping hackers from gaining more privileges. It is not only important for the system administrator, but for ordinary users as well. Educating your users about security issues will create many allies to assist you in your endeavor.

The hacker will want to gain more privileges so he will have access to more of the system's resources. Privileges are allocated by account, so to gain more privileges he will either gain the identity of another user, whose account has more privileges, or get a user who has more privileges to run programs on his behalf.

Having Another User Run a Program

A hacker is always looking for someone else to do his work for him and to take the blame. When the hacker can accomplish this, he can utilize the other person's privileges. The main way a hacker will get another user to run a program for him is through the use of a Trojan horse or by inserting the program into the user's start-up scripts. However, there are a wide variety of ways for a hacker to get other users to run programs on his behalf.

Compromised Software

There are a number of ways to compromise software so that it behaves differently from how it was designed to behave. Virus software infects the host code so that when the host code is executed, the virus is also executed. Virus software can be sophisticated code which inserts itself into binary executables or simple macro command files which are attached to data files. Once executed, the virus code has the privileges of the user who unknowingly executed it.

Trojan Horse

A Trojan horse is a useful or apparently useful program containing hidden code that, when invoked, performs some unwanted function. Trojan horses can be used to accomplish functions indirectly that an unauthorized user could not accomplish directly. When the Trojan horse is executed by the unsuspecting user, it inherits all the privileges that the user who executed it has. It will then use these privileges to perform functions which were unavailable to the hacker. This is why Trojan horses are often impersonating system utilities or other functions which privileged users are likely to run.

Trojan horses have also been introduced in the packaging of software itself. Software can be packaged in a "shar" format, which is un-"shar"ed by sending the package as input to the shell. Commands can be inserted into a shar file that will be executed when the package is un-"shar"ed.

Recently, the World Wide Web has been targeted by hackers who have created web pages that appear harmless, yet deliver more than expected by utilizing undocumented features in the browsers and exploiting Java applets.

You can reduce the risk of Trojan horses by creating a quarantine system. This is a system that is not connected to your network and exists only to unload and test software that is from an untrusted source. This will catch the Trojan horses that are in the packaging and will give you a chance to examine the code and test the software in a safe environment.

Spoof

A spoof is a particular type of Trojan horse; it duplicates the action of an existing command and it is run unknowingly by the user.

Spoofs are generally invoked because of an inappropriate PATH variable. The PATH variable should never contain a "." or a blank field "::". These both indicate current directory.

The PATH list should be ordered from most secure to least secure. This will prevent system commands, like ls, from being executed from a public directory instead of a system directory. This is very hard to police, since users can change their PATHs and many now build their PATHs with scripts that are dependent on terminal type, character-mode terminal, or X terminal. The minimum you can do is validate the PATH variable in all users' start-up scripts and the PATH in system start-up scripts. All scripts should be checked. Another danger is the listing of a directory that does not exist in the PATH. This could allow for the creation of that directory and the inclusion of numerous spoof programs. All shell scripts should set their own path in the script.

Spoofs also require that the spoofing program have the same name as an existing program, so you may want to search for files that have the same name as common utilities. However, this effort may outweigh its usefulness.

Software Start-up / Shutdown

When software is started, it can read an initialization file that can affect the behavior of the software. There are also a large number of programs that support macros. These macros are generally initialized when the program starts and often have access to all the information to which the user has access. These macros can be disastrous to an unsuspecting victim. They are often written within the context of what they are intended to do and are not evaluated for security risks. In many cases, they have access to command interpreters which have complete access to the system. The values in this initialization file may compromise the security of the user who is running the software or it may cause unexpected results.

For example, there are configuration files for the X windows system that can include values that will allow anyone to access the X terminal. There are also a large number of word processors that support macros. These macros can be disastrous to an unsuspecting victim. For example, the vi editor has a start-up script, .exrc. This file is processed as input commands to the vi program, so you can use the shell escape to insert shell commands that will be executed when the user runs vi.

```
!chmod 666 /etc/passwd
```

You can keep the vi editor from running the .exrc file by setting the EXINIT environment variable. If this variable is set, it will be executed instead of the .exrc file.

All start-up files should have read-only permission for the owner, who should be the owner of the home directory that they are in.

User's Login / Logout

Every time a user logs in to the system, there are a series of start-up commands that are executed. Some of these commands are executed for every user, while others are specific for specific users. These scripts are generally used to personalize the user's environment and notify users of any critical communications.

A user's login and logout scripts are a fruitful area for hackers. These scripts are often written by the user and have permissions that are lax, or call programs without the use of fully qualified path names, making them vulnerable to Trojan horse attacks.

There are many access methods available to access a system, so there are many login files which have to be modified to support peruser features. Table 11-1 lists the files associated with each shell.

Table 11-1 Shell Start-up Script Files

Shell Name	Global Login Script	User-specific Login Script	Shell Invocation Script	Logout Script
BASH (bash)	/etc/profile	~/.bash_profile	~/.bashrc	
Bourne (sh)	/etc/profile	~/.profile		
C Shell (csh)	/etc/csh.login	~/.login	~/.cshrc	~/.logout
Korn Shell (ksh)	/etc/profile	~/.profile	~/.kshrc	

All these files must have proper permissions. Those in the user's home directory, which are often created or modified by the user, are especially susceptible to permission errors. If there are script files for shells other than the user's default shell, they too must be checked, because the default shell can be changed with the change shell, chsh, command. Some versions of UNIX systems may limit valid login shells to those listed in the file /etc/shells. Limit the shells to only those you utilize.

System Start-up

Each time a system is booted up, it executes a specific set of start-up procedures with superuser privileges. Initially, the operating system is loaded into memory from the file system. The system generally has a default operating system file or kernel, but any properly configured file can be used. Then the initialization process, init, is started.

The initialization program executes the programs and scripts as directed by its configuration file. Any programs or scripts that are run during this start-up procedure are an area that can be exploited because they generally run as the superuser.

If the permissions are such that any of these programs can be replaced, a hacker has the ability to alter the system in any fashion. This is a place where a Trojan horse can be used if the program search path is not set correctly or properly secured.

You need to fully understand this process, as well as all the programs that are executed during a system start-up. First of all, if the boot file is replaced or removed, the system will either not boot up or will boot up differently from its intended method. All the programs that are started from the initialization program and all the subsequent programs must have their permissions checked. All programs and scripts executed during system start-up should be owned by root and be readable only by root. All programs that are executed from these scripts should either use fully qualified path names or the path variable should be set in the script. All of these scripts and the programs that they execute should be periodically checked to validate they have not been tampered with.

System Shutdown

Each time a system is shut down, it goes through a specific set of shutdown routines. These routines, either a series of scripts or a directory containing a number of scripts, are automatically executed at system shutdown. These scripts normally execute with root privileges. This allows for the orderly shutdown of software subsystems before the system's shutdown.

Quite often these scripts are not closely monitored for security. Just like the start-up scripts, subverting any of these scripts, or any of the scripts or programs they call, will allow a hacker to subvert the entire system the next time that the system is shut down.

These scripts are as important as system start-up scripts and are vulnerable to the same type of attack. Unfortunately, they are often overlooked by the automated security checkers. Any script that is executed during system shutdown should be readable only by root. All programs that are executed from these scripts should either use fully qualified path names or the path variable should be set in the script. All these scripts, and the programs that they execute, should be periodically checked to validate that they have not been tampered with.

Exploiting Permission Vulnerabilities

File permissions are a common security problem on most systems. File permissions, even though a simple concept, are often misunderstood. The security of a file is based on both its permissions and the permissions of its parent directory. There are also variations in the implementation of special permission bits and in the implementation of access control lists.

- **Discretionary access controls**, DAC, are those access controls by which the information owner has control over who gets access to the files he owns. DACs are usually implemented with permission bits which define the levels of access or an access control list, ACL, which specifically details what users have which permissions. The owner of a file is usually the person who creates the file. However, ownership may be assigned to an information curator and not the creator.

- **Mandatory access controls**, MAC, are those access controls that are controlled by the system. They are either built into or configured into the system. Mandatory access control is a method by which the system administrator defines a series of access rules that must be met to allow access to the file. These controls are usually in addition to discretionary access control. Traditionally, mandatory access controls are not seen outside the military and government. However, today many businesses are looking at these controls, especially as businesses venture into the area of highly interconnected networks, such as the Internet.

Here are some common permission problems that cause security issues.

Default Permissions

The built-in shell command umask is used to set file creation permissions. When a file is created, each bit in the file mode creation mask that is set causes the corresponding permission bit in the file mode to be cleared. Each invocation of a shell will have an independent "umask" that can be set by the user.

Generally, there is a system "umask" that is set in one of the start-up scripts. This mask is the default unless a user either has invoked the command directly or has it in his personal start-up script. It is advisable to set the global umask value to as strict a value as possible. A value of 037 will allow the owner to read and write the file while the group will have read permissions and all others will have no permissions. The actual value you set should be dependent on your data security policy.

Directories

Inappropriate permissions on directories will not only compromise the information in that directory, but also all the information in all the subdirectories below this directory. Once a hacker has access to a directory he can subvert any subdirectory by creating a new subdirectory and copying all of the old directory into the new directory, replacing the files he wants, then removing the old directory and replacing it with the new directory.

Directory permissions are very important since one mistake can compromise dozens or even hundreds of files. The higher in the directory tree, the more compounded the problem. When additional physical disk drives are added to a system, they are mounted on a directory. This directory is referred to as a mount point. Special attention should be paid to these directories; these are often under-secured. Also check the root directory; if it is compromised, the whole system is at risk.

When the sticky bit is set on a directory, it prevents any regular user from deleting any file in the directory which he or she does not own even if the permissions of the directory would allow it. This feature can add an additional level of security to public directories, such as /tmp.

Home Directories

Your home directory is the directory you are assigned when you log in. This directory has your personal start-up files and configuration files for the programs you run. It is also the location that is generally used for any work in process. Users' home directories are some of the most important directories and need to be properly secured.

Any user's home directory that has permissions that will allow a hacker to write into it will allow him to alter the user's start-up files. With this capability, he can alter program start-up scripts and configuration files that will allow him to masquerade as that user or gain that user's privileges.

It is very important to monitor the permissions of both the users' home directories and the configuration files in those home directories. Users' home directories should be owned by the user and should not be writable by anyone else. The configuration files in the home directory should not be writable or readable by anyone other than their owner. The only exception to this is when the account is a restricted account, which means that the user is not allowed to change his environment. Generally, these are user accounts that are defined to have a very limited scope of abilities, such as "ftp" and "tftp" accounts.

Device Files

Any device file that is insufficiently protected will allow a hacker to gain access to the information on that device. If it is a terminal, he can monitor keystrokes or plant a spoof. If it is a backup device, he may be able to read and rewrite backup tapes and may well be able to modify the information on the backup. If he can read the disk device, any file on that disk can be read. With write access to the memory device file, the hacker can change anything that is in the system's memory, including his own privileges.

Device file permissions are the most important of all file permissions, since access to one device file gives you access to all the information on that device and possibly control of the entire system.

Device files should be limited to the /dev directory. The following command will find device files which are not in the /dev directory.

```
find / -type b -o -type c -print | grep -v ^/dev/ 2>/dev/null
```

Symbolic and Hard Links

Links are a method of giving the same file more than one name that can be in different directories. Hard links are created by having multiple directory entries that point at the same file and thus the permissions and the ownership are reflected the same in each entry. However, a symbolic link is just a file that points to another file by name. There is no other association between these files, so a file and a symbolic link may have different owners and permissions. Symbolic links can also be used to point to directories.

Links are not inherently a problem; however, since a symbolic link can point to a directory, a misplaced chmod -R (due to its recursive nature) can change the permissions on the files in the subdirectories pointed to by that symbolic link which can be anywhere in the file system. The following command will find all symbolic links on a system:

```
find / -type l -print 2>/dev/null
```

Exploiting Hardware Vulnerabilities

Hardware vulnerabilities are generally caused by the exploitation of features that have been put into the hardware to differentiate it from the competition or to aid in the support and maintenance of the hardware. Some features that have been exploited include terminals with memory that can be reread by the computer, and downloadable configuration and password protection of all types of devices, including printers. It is the hacker's creative misuse of these features that can turn a feature into a vulnerability.

Smart Terminals

A smart terminal is a terminal that has some local processing capability that is generally used to off-load the processing from the host system.

Some terminals have memory and the ability to access that memory via escape sequences. A hacker may be able to send an escape sequence to the terminal that will make the terminal send him the information that is in the terminal's memory. It may also be possible to send a command string to the terminal and force the terminal to send it to the program that is running on the terminal. The program will not have the ability to tell that the command was not typed at the terminal. This can be extremely valuable to a hacker if root leaves a session unattended. If the hacker is desperate, he might try to do these "screen gymnastics" right in front of the root user while he is logged on. This feature can also be used to send letter bombs. A hacker can send e-mail that has the escape sequences for the terminal; then, when the letter is read, the "commands" are run on the terminal. He may be able to reconfigure the terminal and possibly password protect the terminal's configuration.

First, you must educate the users on the importance of never leaving a terminal session unattended. A hacker can gain your privileges by accessing your unattended terminal, either physically or from the computer. Secondly, whenever anyone logs on, he or she should set messages off. Each user's start-up script should include the command

```
mesg n # Turn off messages
```

This command will keep other users from sending data to your terminal.

The log-off process should clear all of the terminal's memory, not just the visible screen memory, so that this type of program will not get any useful information.

Graphics Display Systems

An X terminal is a graphics terminal that runs the X protocol. Originally, all the X programs ran on another computer system; now many of the standard X clients are available to run on the X terminal itself. As X terminals continue to become more powerful, with X clients running locally and with attached peripherals, they become a more inviting target of subversion.

Many of the X terminals that allow local clients will allow you to execute the clients via a remote shell or other protocol and route the output to any X terminal. So a hacker can run terminal software on another person's X terminal. He may also be able to get remote access to the peripherals that are attached to another X terminal. These may include floppies, CD-ROMs, or scanners. If the remote access is not properly restricted, this will open a security issue.

System Start-up

Every time a computer system is started, whether it is a server system or a workstation, the boot ROM has to search for a device from which to boot the system. This boot ROM is also programmed so that a system manager or support engineer can interrupt the standard boot sequence and alter the boot path. This may be required due to hardware failure or a change in configuration. This may be as simple as inserting a support disk or tape so the system will boot from it or there may be a user interactive implementation of the boot ROM so that the system support personnel can enter the information directly into the boot ROM. In either case, if physical access to a system is permitted, the standard boot process can be interrupted with an alternate boot.

Any system can be compromised if physical access is allowed. Even those vendors who advertise a secure boot process must have a way to override this in the case that the secure option is set and there is no useful boot device available. Physical security is a must.

Hackers may be able to override the boot process by introducing a removable disk or tape into the system and rebooting the system. Most boot ROMs have the ability to disable booting from removable media. This feature should be enabled. Boot ROM passwords should be set to prevent the systems boot parameters from being changed. Boot ROM passwords require strong passwords, since there are password cracking tools for boot ROM passwords.

On PA-RISC systems, the ability to interrupt the boot ROM can be disabled by setting security on at the ISL prompt of the boot ROM. The following ISL command disables the ability to interrupt the boot process:

```
Secure ON
```

Even with these precautions, a system can be compromised if physical access is allowed. Disconnecting all drives from the system will make it fail the boot process and return it to the ISL prompt.

The Linux Loader (LILO) is the primary mechanism for booting Linux. This loader can be password protected by editing /etc/lilo.conf and adding the following lines after the "prompt" line:

```
password = lilo-password
restricted
```

where *lilo-password* is the password in clear text. Since the password is in clear text in this file, the permissions should be 600 for this file. To make this change take effect, execute the command:

```
/sbin/lilo
```

Red Hat 7.2 has introduced a new boot loader, GNU GRUB, GRand Unified Bootloader. It requests a password during install. The GRUB configuration information is located in /boot/grub/grub.conf.

Exploiting Software Vulnerabilities

This area has the most successful attacks on systems. Almost daily there are reports of new bugs, or variations of old bugs, in system software. Patches for repair are released as soon as the bug is discovered. However, many system managers do not keep current on operating system releases and applying patches, especially security patches.

Because this is changing on a daily basis, it is not possible to give timely information pertaining to software vulnerabilities in a book. By the time the book is printed and distributed, the problems discussed will have been repaired and an entire new crop of problems will exist. However, we will take a look at some "classic" software vulnerabilities and software attacks that are not based on bugs.

PATH Variable Attacks

PATH variable attacks are based on the fact that many programs are dependent on your path variable to locate subprocesses that are required for the program. This allows the program to be independent of the path name of the directory where it and its child processes reside. This includes both programs and scripts.

If a hacker can read your scripts or has read permission to your binaries so he can use the strings command on them, he will be able to locate programs that are executed with either a relative path or no path, thereby depending on the path variable. Shell scripts and programs should execute programs using a fully qualified path name only. Short of this, they should set the PATH variable themselves, eliminating the dependency on an appropriately configured user environment. Removing the read permissions from binaries and scripts will make it more difficult for the hacker to utilize this method of attack. Some implementations require that read permissions be allowed to execute a shell script.

File Name Attacks

File name attacks are instigated by creating a file whose name will be interpreted by the system as something else by embedding command delimiters into the file name. Since UNIX systems have no restrictions on what characters can be used in a file name, you can insert terminators and spaces into a file name. For example, a file could be called

```
core;rm -r /*
```

Even if this file is discovered, just getting rid of it could be perilous. If this file is processed by any command that uses the shell to expand the file name, the semicolon will be interpreted as a shell delimiter and the part of the file name that follows the semicolon will be interpreted as a command. In the previous example, the command after the semicolon is the command to delete all the files on the computer. It would be devastating if this command were run by the superuser.

File attacks are especially effective for systems that are fairly well managed. These systems that have a good system manager, who may not be a great security manager, will have automated many of the repetitive tasks, such as deleting core files, consolidating log information, and so on. Most of these activities will have been automated using cron, so they are done on a regular basis. And some of these jobs will be run as the superuser.

cron

Cron allows for time-based scheduling of jobs. Many of these scheduled processes will run with superuser privileges or with other special privileges. In System III-based systems, all cron processes are run by root and are stored in the file /usr/lib/crontab. In SystemV-based systems, each user can have his or her own cron processes; these are stored in files with the name of the user in the directory /usr/spool/cron/crontabs.

This is a prime location for hackers to gain more privileges and to check to see if automated system monitoring exists. Jobs set up in cron to monitor logs and gather other information are a prime signal that the system is being monitored. A hacker can use permission problems with the cron jobs directory or with any of the processes started from cron to substitute his own process and gain the privileges of that job.

One of the major advantages that a system manager has over an outside hacker is the knowledge of his system. It is important to know what your system's cron jobs are and what they do. You should periodically check the permissions on both the crontab files and the programs they execute.

There are also two permissions files used by the cron system. The first permission file is /usr/lib/cron/cron.allow. If this file exists, then all the login names listed in the file are allowed to use the cron system. If this file does not exist, then the second permissions file, /usr/lib/cron/crontab.allow, is used. If this file exists, then all users except those listed in the file are allowed to use the cron system. If neither file exists, then only the superuser can use the cron system.

at

The at command is similar to the cron system; it allows you to schedule a job at a specific time in the future. The System III Version runs an associated program, atrun, that is shipped with the setUID bit set. In this case, the system can be subverted using the at command. The System V Version also has two permissions files: at.allow and at.deny. They operate in the same manner as the cron permission files.

## CHAPTER 12

Controlling Authorizations

Authorizations are the privileges given to users and programs which allow them special rights. These rights limit how resources are utilized and help ensure appropriate use. Authorizations can be used either to restrict access or to grant selective access. Controlling authorization is the primary method of managing the resources which are available to users. The finer the granularity of the authorizations, the more control in assigning the right privileges for the right job. The following are some basic principles in building authorization models which support the kind of security model you have.

- **That which is not specifically denied is allowed**. This open environment model requires prior knowledge of everything that is to be denied so that it can be specifically denied. This creates an environment which is very difficult to adequately secure. This model is often the result of the evolution of an environment without security implementing some basic security measures. Most security signature scanning technologies, such as virus scanners, work within this model. They cannot stop an attack until they know what the attack looks like. Anything is allowed until it is determined to be dangerous.

- **That which is not specifically allowed is denied**. This is a closed model. Some would call it paranoid. However, it prevents unknown attacks. It also prevents users from doing anything which has not been defined as acceptable. This may slow the implementation of new systems and aggravate users. Businesses can use this model to control the consumption of resources — requiring a business justification before allowing a behavior. Most security professionals agree that this model is required to build an environment where malicious attacks are a threat.

- **Provide the minimum privileges required.** This strategy of giving the minimum privileges necessary to perform the task for the minimum amount of time that they are needed is called least privileges. This minimizes the chances of misusing privileges.

User Authorizations

Users should be given only the authorizations needed to perform the tasks that they must perform for their duties. Minimizing the users' authorization minimizes the damage, accidental or malicious, that they can cause.

Carefully design the user and group relationships on your system to allow for the most restrictive permissions possible. There should be no access allowed except at the user and group levels. Users can be allowed to have access to multiple groups through supplemental groups that are configured in /etc/logingroup. You want to restrict your system as much as possible but still allow the system to operate correctly. Generally speaking, the read and write permissions should be removed from all executable programs. However, some implementations require read permissions on shell scripts.

Identity-based Authorizations

Most authorizations are based on individual identity. Individual identities will be given specific privileges. It provides the greatest level of flexibility: Every user can be given unique authorizations based on his or her specific needs. It also requires the greatest amount of administration.

Group-based Authorizations

Users are often put into groups and authorizations are applied to these groups to simplify the administration of authorizations.

The newgrp command allows a user to change his group association if he is allowed to by the /etc/group file. The group file is composed of four colon-separated fields. The first is the group name, followed by the group ID, followed by an encrypted password field, followed by a comma-delimited list of login names that can change their group affiliations to this group.

The following example illustrates a group called "admin" with the group ID of 100. The users root, nathaniel, and jocelyn have the ability to change their group affiliation to this group with the newgrp command with the correct password.

```
admin:100:dpBIMfa.UshYc:root,nathaniel,jocelyn
```

This file must be readable by all users, but it should be writable only by root. If you are not using the new group feature, you should not have any users in the group file. Some automated administrative tools will add these users automatically. In any case, you should disable the newgrp command by setting the password field to LOCKED.

Some UNIX implementations support supplemental groups with the use of the file /etc/logingroups. This feature allows a user to be associated with more than one group at a time. Properly administered, it eliminates the need for the newgrp command. Each of the user's login groups is used to evaluate whether the user has access to a resource. This file has the same format as the system group file. Some documentation suggests linking these two files.

Role-based Authorizations

A user may perform many roles in an information system. A user's needs are based on the role that she is performing at that time. The role may be based on the relationship to the file or process (e.g., owner).

Controlled by Rules

Rules can be used to add greater granularity and flexibility to the levels of authorizations. The rules can incorporate additional information and relationships. They can add restrictions based on dynamic information, such as the time of day or the phase of the moon. Rules generally are represented by a list of relationships which all have to be met for the privilege to be granted.

Program Authorizations

Some programs need to have permissions regardless of the permissions that the user running the program may have. Setting authorizations on programs gives those authorizations to the program. Program authorizations can also be used to isolate a system from other systems and minimize the requirements on user privileges.

Set-User-ID and Set-Group-ID

Set-User-ID, SetUID, is a permission that a program can have which sets the effective user ID to a specific user, instead of the actual user who is running the program. This is often used to grant privileges to a program so that anyone can run the program and it can still have the necessary permissions and ownership rights to perform its function. The Set-Group-ID, SetGID, is very similar to SetUID except it sets the effective group id.

The set-user-on-exec, setUID, and the set-group-on-exec, setGID, permissions on a program file allow a user to get the privileges of the specified user or group for the execution of that program. This allows a user to get access to resources only under the control of the specific program. This is referred to as an effective user ID and effective group ID.

You will want to inventory all of the setUID and setGID files on your system. This process should be run regularly and any changes to the list should be investigated. You can inventory the setUID and setGID file with the following commands:

```
find / -perm +4000 -print
find / -perm +2000 -print
```

If the system will allow a user to change the group or ownership of a file, a hacker may be able to set the file as a setUID or setGID file and then change the group or owner of the file. These commands may not reset the SUID or SGID permission bit. This would leave you with a SUID or SGID program. To test this you should create the following file called uid_test.c:

```
main()
{
  return(system("/bin/sh"));
}
```

Compile the program with the command

```
cc uid_test.c -o uid_test
```

Now that you have an executable file uid_test, you can change the setUID and setGID bits and ownership and the group. If any of the ls -l commands shows that the program is either setUID or setGID, then this is a security issue.

```
chmod 2111 uid_file
chgrp root uid_file
ls -l uid_file
chmod 2111 uid_file
ls -l uid_file
chmod 4111 uid_file
chown root uid_file
ls -l uid_file
```

If the problem exists on your system, contact your vendor. You may want to limit the access to the change owner, chown, and change group, chgrp, commands. The change owner command can also be used to give the ownership of a file to another so that your accounting and bill-back system will charge that other person for the space consumed by the file.

On many systems, the UUCP command, uudecode, will create files with setUID or setGID permissions. This command, in conjunction with uuencode, is used to convert binary files to ASCII text files and back so that they can be transmitted over the UUCP network. The following code illustrates the UUCP header which contains permission information:

```
begin 4777 filename
```

A hacker may also be able to introduce setUID and setGID programs if he has mount capabilities by having the system mount a file system that contains a setUID or setGID file. On some systems, users are granted mount capabilities because they need to mount floppies or CD-ROMs. These capabilities can be granted through specific commands that mount the floppy or ROM. Investigate this because, if these are not standard commands, they may have flaws.

Mounting file systems should be done only by system managers. All file systems should be mounted with the no setUID flag set, so that any setUID or setGID file on that file system will be disabled.

If a hacker is able to have files restored onto the system, he may be able to have them restored into different directories or with different permissions than they were stored with. He may also be able to have files restored from a tape that was created on another system. This method will allow him to introduce any programs with any permissions and ownerships which he desires.

Your data handling policy must address the issues of authentication and permissions for the backup and restoration of data, especially with tapes that are removed off-site or brought on-site.

Compartmentalization

Program isolation is one method of controlling program authorizations by limiting the scope of access. It is an important step in keeping programs secure.

UNIX Protected Subsystem

The UNIX protected subsystem is a process of isolating a software system through the utilization of group permissions. A protected subsystem is a group of programs which provide a particular service or group of related services that require more authorization for access to data files and devices than those of the users who need the service. For example, the mail and printing systems on most UNIX systems are implemented as protected subsystems.

Each protected subsystem has its own user ID and group ID used only by its programs and files. The protected files and devices allow no access except through the group permissions bits and the programs all run with their effective group ID set to the subsystem group ID. No users are allowed access to the group used by a protected subsystem.

The following steps will create a protected subsystem.

1. Create a user ID and a group ID for the protected subsystem.

2. Change the ownership and group for each file that is to be protected to the user "bin" and the group ID which was created.

```
chown bin:protected protected_file
chown protect:protected protected_program
```

3. Set the permission bits on the files in the protected subsystem so that they are accessible only from the protected group.

```
chmod 060 protected_file
```

4. Set the set-group-on-exec bit on the programs in the protected subsystem.

```
chmod 2001 protected_program
```

All parts of the protected subsystem need to be in directories with sufficient protection so that the files which are part of the protected subsystems cannot be altered or their permissions altered.

chroot Environment

The chroot environment is a method of isolating a software system by creating a separate directory tree for each system to reside. The chroot forces the process to view the sub-tree as the root file system. Software which runs in a chrooted environment has no access to the system outside the chroot directory tree.

The following steps produce a chroot environment.

1. Create directory for chroot environment.

```
mkdir /chroot/ProgramDir
chmod ugo-rw /chroot/ProgramDir
```

2. Load the software into the chroot environment.

3. Create necessary directories within the chroot environment.

```
mkdir /chroot/ProgramDir/{etc bin tmp opt}
```

4. Set appropriate permissions on the directories.

```
chmod 666 /chroot/ProgramDir/tmp
chmod +t /chroot/ProgramDir/tmp
```

5. Create needed system files within the chroot environment.

```
echo "chrootid:*:2000:2000:Chroot User:/home/chrootid:/bin/false" \
>/chroot/ProgramDir/etc/passwd
```

6. Set appropriate permissions on the files.

```
chmod 444 /chroot/ProgramDir/etc/passwd
```

7. Create special files needed within the chroot environment.

Protecting Files

Information itself will often have associated authorization definitions that indicate which users are allowed which access rights.

All access to files in UNIX systems is controlled by the permissions of that file, and everything in UNIX systems is a file. There are a variety of types of files, including a regular file, which contains either text or binary data or programs; a directory, which contains information about the location of a file; a device file, which may be either a block or character device and represents a logical or physical device; a named pipe, which is used for inter-process communication; and a symbolic link, which is a file that points to another file. Some implementations may expand this list of file types to include sockets, mounted directories, or others.

Discretionary Access Controls

Discretionary access controls are those access controls that are controlled by the information owner.

Discretionary access control is a method by which a user has control over the access of the files which he owns. Standard UNIX file system permissions are discretionary access controls.

With standard UNIX file system permissions, every file has a list of three permissions for each of three groups of users plus three miscellaneous modes. Each of these three groups of users can have a differing set of these permissions to this file. They are user (the owner of the file), group (the users in the group to which the file belongs), and world (all other users).

The owner of a file is usually the person who creates the file. However, on some systems you can change the ownership of a file with the chown command. This is disallowed on some systems because it would allow you to hide your disk utilization by giving large files to someone else while retaining access rights and the ability to remove the file.

The chown command allows the owner of the file to give the file to another user by changing the owner of the file. This can also be used to give a file, and its associated costs, to another user. The owner of a file can change the file's group association by using the chgrp command.

The group is the people whose group ID in the password file matches the group ID of the file. A user can temporarily change his group affiliation with the newgrp command if he is listed in the /etc/group file or belongs to a number of groups with the use of the /etc/logingroup file.

The world permission bits apply to all users who are neither the file owner nor are in the group with which the file is associated.

UNIX file permission bits define the access rights of read, write, and execute to the file's owner, group, and everyone else. These coarse grain access rights are the fundamental access rights on UNIX systems.

There are three permissions: read, write, and execute. For a regular file, these permissions are fairly obvious. They allow the user to read the file, write to the file, and to execute the file.

If the file is a directory, the meaning is a little more involved. Read permission means that you can access the information about the files in the directory, write permission means that you can change the information about the file, including renaming or deleting the file, and execute permission means that you can access and search the directory. Only the owner of a file (and the superuser) can change its permissions.

The permissions are generally represented by a string of nine characters, three characters for the permissions for each of the three groups of users. The characters are "r" for read, "w" for write, and "x" for execute.

For example the string "rwxr-x---" means that the owner of the file has read, write, and execute permissions, while the people which belong to the same group as the file have read and execute permissions, and everyone else has no permissions. This is very straightforward for files.

The three miscellaneous modes are set-user-ID on execute, set-group-ID on execute, and sticky bit. Originally these three modes were pertinent only to program files, that is, files that are either binary executables or shell scripts. The set-user-ID and group-ID modes change the effective user or group-ID of the program that is executing so it appears to the program that it was executed by that user or group.

The sticky bit tells the program scheduler to keep the program in virtual memory because it is likely that the program will be executed again soon and it will not have to be reloaded from disk, possibly across the network, if it is still there.

Some vendors have disabled the set-user-ID and set-group-ID modes for shell scripts because of the related security problems.

Some vendors have extended these modes to represent other behaviors when applied to other files. One common extension is that if the sticky bit is set on a directory, then only the owner of files in that directory can delete them.

The built-in shell command umask is used to set the shell's default file creation permission mask. When a file is created, each bit in the file mode creation mask that is set causes the corresponding permission bit in the file mode to be cleared. This means that any file created will have the permissions bits set that are not set in the umask mask. This mask can be set by the user and it remains active until the user changes it or the user's session is over. Each invocation of a shell will have an independent mask that can be reset by the user.

Generally there is a system mask that is set in one of the start-up scripts. This mask is the default unless a user either has invoked the command directly or has it in his personal start-up script. It is advisable to set the global mask value to as strict a value as possible. A value of 037 will allow the owner to read and write the file while the group will have read permissions and all world will have no permissions. The actual value you set should be dependent on your data security policy.

The chmod command allows the owner of a file to set the file's permissions, which can be done with either a symbolic or numeric syntax.

- **Setting Permissions with Symbolic Modes**

  When you are using the symbolic mode to set permissions, you are always adding to or removing from existing permissions. The symbols used for the symbolic mode are "r" for read, "w" for write, "x" for execute/access, "s" for set-id-on-exec, and "t" for the sticky bit. The user who owns the file is indicated by the character "u," the group to which the file belongs by the character "g," and the world, all others, by the character "o." These symbols are connected by using either the plus sign "+" to add the permission or the minus "-" to remove the permission. So if you want to remove the write access from the users in the group that owns a file, the command would be

  ```
  chmod g-w filename
  ```

  Both users and permissions can be combined so you can grant one or more permissions to one or more users in one command. For example, if you want to grant read access to both the users in the file's group and all other users, the command would be

  ```
  chmod go+r filename
  ```

- **Setting Permissions with Numeric Modes**

  This method always sets the absolute permissions of a file. With numeric modes, the permissions are converted into octal numbers, with read set to 4, write set to 2, and execute/access set to 1. The permissions are combined by adding their values. It then uses three digits to represent the users — the first digit for the owner, the second for the group, and the last for the world. Table 12-1 shows the values for these permissions.

Table 12-1 UNIX Permissions in Symbolic and Numeric Modes

Owner			Group			World		
r	w	x	r	w	x	r	w	x
4	2	1	4	2	1	4	2	1

In addition to the permission bits, there is an optional leading digit which is used to represent the set-userID bit (4), the set-groupID bit (2), and the sticky bit (1).

To set read, write, and execute permissions for the owner, read-only for the group, and no permissions for world users the command would be:

```
chmod 740 filename
```

Exploiting Permission Vulnerabilities

File permissions are the primary security problem on most systems. File permissions, even though a simple concept, are often misunderstood. The security of a file is based on both its permissions and the permissions of its parent directory. There are also variations in the implementation of special permission bits and in the implementation of access control lists.

Here are some common permission problems that cause security issues.

Some Interesting Examples

In the following examples the columns in the listing are permissions, user, group, size, time, and file name. The two-line listing indicates the permissions of the directory, indicated by "." and a file in that directory, named file*n*. This listings could be made by using the command

```
ls -ld . file?
```

These examples illustrate the interaction between the permissions on a directory and the files it contains.

- **Example 1**

  Bob thinks he is allowing the users in his group to read his file, but not allowing them to modify it in any manner.

  ```
  drwxrwxr-x 2 bob software 512 .
  -rw-r----- 1 bob software 200 file1
  ```

  The group permissions on the file allow all the users in the "software" group to read the files but not write to them. However, the permissions on the directory will allow anyone in the software group to rename or delete the file. The world permissions on the directory allow anyone to list the names of the files in the directory, but without access rights to the file.

  Bob did the right thing on the file permissions. It is the directory permissions that are too lax. To allow anyone to list the files, and to allow only Bob to change the files in his directory, the directory permissions should look like this:

  ```
  drwxr-xr-x 2 bob software 512 .
  ```

- **Example 2**

  Barb thinks that she has allowed the users in the "admin" group to list the files in her directory and has restricted them from access to her files by removing the write permission to the directory.

  ```
  drwxr-x--- 2 barb admin 512 .
  -rw-rw---- 1 barb admin 128 file2
  ```

  The users in the "admin" group cannot rename or delete the file. However, since the file is writable by the "admin" group, anyone in the "admin" group can modify the file, including deleting all the information out of the file, leaving an empty file.

  In this case, Barb set the permissions on the directory correctly. However, the file permissions are too lax. The permissions that she should use are

  ```
  -rw-r----- 1 barb admin 128 file2
  ```

- **Example 3**

  Bill thinks that he has protected his files by removing the read and write permissions from the directory.

  ```
  drwx--x--x 2 bill dbase  512 .
  -rw-rw-r-- 1 bill dbase 1024 file3
  ```

  All the users in the world have access, "x," permission to the directory, but they cannot list the contents of the directory. However, if they know the name of the file, anyone can read it and the users in the "dbase" group can modify the file.

  The removal of the read and write permissions from the directory has made it so that no one other than Bill can list the files in his directory or add, delete, or rename any of his files. The directory permissions should not include access permissions unless you want to grant that right. The directory permissions should be

  ```
  drwx------ 2 bill dbase  512 .
  ```

Access Control Lists

Access control lists, ACLs, are lists that indicate which users have what access rights to the information. ACLs were developed to meet the requirement where many selective users and groups need different types of access to files. ACLs provide a mechanism by which file access privileges can be defined for selected users and groups.

ACLs are an extension to the UNIX mode bits, required for "B3" security rating, allowing for more granularity of access control by allowing specific permissions to be applied to specified users. ACLs are defined as triples with the first element being a user identifier, the second, a group, and the third, permissions. ACLs are available on some UNIX systems. However, currently there are no standards on how ACLs are implemented.

Many implementations regard them as an addition to the mode bits so that if a user does not get access with the UNIX permission bits, the ACLs are checked to see if the user can be granted permission. Some implementations may test the ACLs before the UNIX mode bits. The ACLs may grant permissions on the basis of the first ACL that the user matches, therefore making them order-dependent, or they may define a "best match" for the user and grant those permissions. Some implementations add the ACLs as an additional lock so that you must successfully pass both the UNIX mode bits and the ACLs.

Posix ACLs

Posix ACLs were defined in the IEEE 1003.1 POSIX standards for discretionary access controls. ACLs did not gain broad acceptance with UNIX vendors. However, recently more systems are becoming available with ACLs, many of which do not comply with this standard. There are a number of projects in the Linux arena which are involved with implementing ACLs for a Linux file system.

The VERITAS File System™ (VxFS©), which is also known as the Journaled File System, or JFS, implements POSIX ACLs. HP JFS 3.3 is included with HP-UX 11i.

ACLs are supported as a superset of the UNIX operating system discretionary access control (DAC) mechanism for files, but not for other objects such as inter-process communication (IPC) objects. ACLs allow the file owner or superuser to permit or deny access to a list of users and groups other than the file owner and owning group, which is available through permission bits. An access control list (ACL) consists of a set of one-line entries associated with a file that specifies permissions. Each entry specifies for one user-ID or group-ID a set of access permissions, including read, write, and execute/search.

- **ACL Notation** — The user and group ID fields, uid and gid, can contain either numeric user or group IDs, or their corresponding character representations. The perm field indicates access permission either in symbolic form, as a combination of r, w, x, and -, or in numeric form, as an octal value of 0 through 7 representing the sum of 4 for read permission, 2 for write permission, and 1 for execute permission.

Supported commands that manage JFS ACLs recognize the following symbolic representation:

[d[efault]:]u[ser]: [uid]:perm

[d[efault]:]g[roup]: [gid]:perm

[d[efault]:]c[lass]:perm

[d[efault]:]o[ther]:perm

An ACL entry prefixed with d: or default: can occur only in a directory's ACL, and it indicates that the remainder of the entry is not to be used in determining the access rights to the directory, but is instead to be applied to any files or subdirectories created in the directory.

- **Base ACL Entries** — When a file is created, four base access control list entries are mapped from the file's access permission bits to match a file's owner and group and its traditional permission bits.

  u::perm   Base ACL entry for the file's owner

  g::perm   Base ACL entry for the file's group

  c::perm   Base ACL entry for the file's group class

  o::perm   Base ACL entry for others

- **Optional ACL Entries** — Optional access control list entries contain additional access control information, which the user can set to further allow or deny file access. Up to thirteen optional ACL entries can be specified. For example, the following optional access control list entries can be associated with our file:

  u:mary:rwx   Grant read, write, and execute access to user "mary".

  user:george:---   Deny any access to user "george".

  g:writers:rw-   Grant read and write access to members of group writers.

- **Class Entries** — In an ACL that contains more than one user entry and/or more than one group entry, the class entry specifies the maximum permissions that can be granted by any of the additional user and group entries. If a particular permission is not granted in the class entry, then it cannot be granted by any ACL entries, except for the owner entry. Any permission can be denied to a particular user or group. The class entry acts as an upper bound for file permissions.

- **ACL Uniqueness** — Entries are unique in each ACL. There can be only one of each type of base entry, and one entry for any given user or group ID. Likewise, there can be only one of each type of default base entry, and one default entry for any given user or group ID.

- **ACL Inheritance** — When a directory's ACL contains default entries, those entries are not used in determining access to the directory itself. Instead, every time a file is created in the directory, the directory's default ACL entries are added as nondefault ACL entries to the new file.

HP-UX HFS ACLs

ACLs were first implemented on HP-UX on the HFS file system. These ACLs are not Posix-compliant. However, they offer the same basic capabilities to limit access to files by specific users and groups. With HSFACLs, an additional 13 sets of file access permissions can be defined above the standard three sets of permissions (owner, group, world) that are provided with standard UNIX operating systems.

The notation used with ACLs to define file access is: (user.group, permissions) where the following symbols can be used in the **user.group** fields:

%   Any user or any group

@   The current file owner or current file group

*   Used for ACL pattern matching, includes % and @

Some standard UNIX commands have additional parameters, such as the "-acl" option to the find command, or new commands which perform the same function on files with ACLs have been created, such as the lsacl command which performs a ls displaying ACLs. Not using the appropriate command or command option may lead to the accidental deletion of the ACLs.

Changing the ACLs on a file is done with the chacl command. The chacl command allows file permissions to be granted or restricted to specific users or groups. The following example shows two ACLs being added for myfile:

```
chacl "(%.bio,r--)" myfile
chacl "(alex.%,r--)" myfile
```

The chacl command can also be used to *delete* an existing ACL:

```
chacl -d "(%.bio,r--)" myfile
```

Use the following syntax to replace all existing ACLs on a file with a new set of ACLs:

```
chacl -r "(%.users,r-x)" myfile
```

It is also possible to copy ACLs from one file to another:

```
chacl -f myfile myfile2
```

Finally, if a file's ACLs are no longer needed, they may be *zapped* with the following:

```
chacl -z myfile
```

Mandatory Access Controls

Mandatory access controls, MAC, are a layer of security on top of discretionary access controls. Mandatory access controls cannot be changed by the users; the system enforces MAC consistently. Each access control method must grant access before access is given. If any of the methods denies access, then access is denied.

Even though most UNIX vendors have a secure UNIX operating system that has mandatory access control for government accounts, few bring these security features into their business UNIX offerings for commercial accounts.

Hewlett-Packard offers a couple of operating system options which provide MAC controls.

- Virtual Vault is a commercialized version of its military grade HP-UX operating system. This operating system, VVOS, offers a number of added security features designed to provide extra security for the e-business environment. VVOS uses a modified Bell-LaPadula model where every file and process contain a tag, which is composed of a compartment and a classification. A process can write to a file only when the process's tag is equal to the tag of the file. However, the process can read the file if the process's tag dominates the file's tag.

- Secure Linux is a compartmentalized version of Red Hat Linux. In general, this means that every process on the system is assigned a compartment label and can access only other processes with the same label.

Secure Linux implements mandatory access controls through the use of compartments. It disallows any access from outside the compartment without special permission, and uses a file control table to identify the type of authorizations (read, write, append) that a process which is within the compartment has with respect to the file.

Read-only File Systems

Making an entire file system read-only can be very beneficial to a system. It can reduce the need for the management of individual files which are on the read-only file system. On UNIX systems, files which can be read-only are usually grouped into directories which can be put on read-only file systems.

Read-only Media

Many types of storage media can be physically configured to be read-only with jumpers on hard drives, or write-protect tabs on tapes, or WORMs and CD-R. These read-only media can be very useful, since they provide an extra layer of security for static files, such as executables. Read-only media makes it impossible to alter these static images.

Read-only Mount

Mounting a file system as a read-only file system prevents writing to the files in the file system. However, this protection method can be circumvented if there is access to the device file which contains the file system, or a privileged user can unmount and remount the file system without the read-only option.

## CHAPTER 13

Avoiding Detection

Alittle paranoia is a good thing for both the hacker and the system manager. The hacker is committing a crime, so he should be aware that there may be people observing what he is doing. Whenever he is on a system, he must be very aware of what is happening on that system. He should be aware of who is on it and what they are doing, and if the system is running any new background tasks. Those tasks could be monitoring the system if the system manager thinks someone is using it. A good system manager cannot assume that his system is safe, or that there is nothing on it that anyone would want to steal. He must realize that computer hacking and electronic espionage are not just in fiction — both happen regularly. The system manager must always be on the lookout for hackers.

When a hacker is on a system, one objective is to make as few tracks as possible. The next step is to erase as many of those tracks as he can. Finally, he needs to make the tracks that have to be left behind as confusing as possible. The hacker does not want to be caught, so the longer it takes for a system manager to follow those tracks to his discovery, the longer he has to accomplish his goal.

The amount of effort required to cover his tracks is going to depend on the level of monitoring the system receives from its administrators. If the system is receiving minimal monitoring, it may be sufficient for the hacker merely to be logged in and running processes when no one else is on the system. If the system is heavily monitored, he will have to walk softly and use all the tools at his disposal.

Monitoring Connections

There are many commands that can be used to monitor user connections. Generally, the commands used by a hacker to watch what is happening on a system are the same commands that a system manager uses to see the activity of a system. These commands report who is connected, how long they have been connected, and from where they are connected. They can also show what programs the users are running.

Connections can be monitored at many levels. At the lower levels, information about which interface, what port, or on what phone line the connection was made can be captured. At the higher levels, you can determine the user ID and the resources being used.

For most hackers, it is almost reflexive to check to see who is on the system as soon as they log in to determine if there is anyone on the system who might notice their presence. The system manager should also get into this habit, to see if there is anyone there who should not be on the system. Knowing what activities are appropriate on a system is the systems manager's greatest advantage.

Active Connections

Active connections are reported from the information in the log /etc/utmp. This file contains information about the current users on the system. All the programs that list the users currently logged in utilize this file. The login programs are responsible for logging this information into this log. There are some services which have options which do not report the connections and thus provide an easy method of connecting stealthfully. Hackers will replace system programs with Trojan horse programs which do not log their connections, and there are a variety of hacker programs that modify utmp. A system manager cannot trust the commands which report active connections to be reliable, especially if the system is suspected of being compromised.

Auditing provides an additional method of logging connections. The system manager should audit the connections to the system, which will indicate who logged on and from where, and this record can be compared to the utmp log to find the discrepancies.

Completed Connections

System logs record the activities of users and processes on a system after they have completed. The /etc/wtmp log contains connection information for completed connections. However, connection information can also be logged into the standard syslog facility, which can write logs to remote servers where they are less likely to be altered.

Dial-up Lines

Today, with the widespread availability of Caller ID, dial-up access can log not only the time and the user ID being used to gain access, but also the phone number from which the connection was made. You can use a printing Caller ID device which prints the time and telephone number or there are modems available that support Caller ID. These modems can be used with a modified login program to log the calling phone number into the standard logging environment.

This is a great help when it comes to tracking down the hacker. However, it does not eliminate false leads from connection laundering or from hackers who are able to hack the telephone system.

Network Connections

A socket is a connection between two systems over a specific port. Socket connections allow for program-to-program communication over the network. Sockets are the basis for all network-based processes. The network statistics command, `netstat`, with appropriate options, will show which sockets have active connections and to what systems the connections are made.

Monitoring Processes

Processes are started by either "forking" them, that is, creating a new process that is a child process of the process that forked it, or by "execing" them, which replaces the first process with the second process and in so doing destroys the first process. In both cases, the new process inherits a number of characteristics from the parent process. Some of these characteristics are the owner of the process, including privileges, priority, and the user's environment.

Process monitoring comes in two varieties: first, monitoring processes while they are running, and second, monitoring processes after they have completed. The first is generally done with the processes status command, `ps`, the second with process logging.

Running Processes

To be able to monitor what is currently running on a system, you must be able to look into the system and examine the system's tables. These tables include the process table, which is a list of the processes in the system.

In order to look into the system, you must have appropriate privileges to examine the system's memory where these tables are stored. These privileges are either granted by setting the permissions on the memory device file, `/dev/mem`, or by having the information-gathering program run with enough privileges to access the system memory.

There is a long list of programs that can be used to gather information about the system's current status. These are generally classified as performance tools. The simplest way to see what is running on the system is to use the process status, `ps`, command.

The options for the `ps` command vary based on whether the system is a BSD or SYSV derivative. In either case, this command can report all the processes currently running in the system. It can display the owner of the process, the amount of CPU time consumed, the associated terminal, if any, its parent process, the name, and all the parameters to the process.

Completed Processes

To be able to gather historic information about what has been running on a system, the system has to record and store this information. There are a number of levels within the system where this reporting occurs and for a number of reasons.

The most common is system logging. Historically, however, system logging has been the most proprietary area of a UNIX system. Each vendor implemented its own low-level logging for each hardware platform and interface.

Today, most systems utilize the system logging facility syslog. The syslog facility creates a single logging environment that is system-independent. It allows messages to be sorted by their source and importance, and the messages can be routed to a variety of destinations.

Session accounting is a UNIX utility that records resource utilization by user for billing purposes. It measures user connect time, CPU usage, printer usage, and disk usage. The commands used by BSD and SYS-III derivatives differ significantly even though they report the same basic information.

Auditing, a relatively new feature for most UNIX implementations, is a method of monitoring specific activities as they relate to specific system calls or specific users. Auditing is a requirement for a C2 security grade operating system as defined by the U.S. Department of Defense's Orange Book.

Auditing allows you to monitor user access to objects. Specifically what is auditable will vary between implementations, but it will include system calls, administrative commands, and network connections. The audit will report which user invoked the call and whether the call was successful or not.

These audit logs can be used to identify security breaks and attempted security breaks. These are well-known to hackers and are often targeted to remove evidence of the hacker's activities.

Security logs, that is, information that is logged specifically to report on the security health of a system, are currently found as a collection of specific tools that address specific security issues or third-party products. There are a number of products that do security logging, but there is no standard set of integrated tools that is widely utilized throughout the industry. Many of the tools are written with the ability to utilize the system logging facility, syslog. If the syslog system has been secured, it is a good method to control and manage the security log messages. These messages must be regularly reviewed.

Command Histories

The shell history is a file that contains a command stack of all the commands entered by the user. It is generally configured to a specific size so that it holds a finite number of commands; after that point, they fall off the stack. Depending on the size and activity, the history file may be more or less than the last session. The hacker uses the history file to monitor a user's activities while he is not online.

Shell histories can also be used by system administrators to see what a hacker has been doing on the system. Once you have determined that a specific account is being used by a hacker, reviewing that account's shell history file may reveal what the hacker has been doing.

All this information may be of limited value if you do not know what each user should be doing on the system. That is why user profiles are so important to security.

Monitoring Information

Once a hacker has gained access to your system, he will want to know if you are aware of his presence. He will focus his interest on any information that indicates that the system is suspected of being compromised. He will be as interested in the activities of the system administrators as they will be in him.

Administrator's Mailbox

A hacker, with appropriate permissions, will read root's e-mail. This will allow him to keep current with what the system administrator knows. Most of the time, the system administrator does not discover a hacker's presence by himself; usually a regular user notices that his response time is slower, or a loss of available disk space, or someone using his login. Communications from users, possibly through e-mail, may be the first indication to the system administrator that there is a problem. The appropriate procedures to report suspected security incidents should be defined in the security policy and should be well understood by all computer users.

System Console

The system console is where it all happens. Most of the systems log errors to the system console, so this is where you see problems and alerts. Anyone who logs on to the system console is probably a system administrator since he or she has physical access to the system. A skilled hacker will always keep an eye on the system console in order to see log messages and what the system administrators are doing.

There are a number of ways to monitor the system console. One such way is to access the console via a program that attaches itself to the data stream that is going to and from the console device. One such program is xconsole. This program is an X windows program that will create a window on an X windows display that will contain all the input and output that comes to and from the system console. This program is used by many system administrators so they can monitor the system console without having to be in the computer room.

All the convenient programs you have to monitor the system can also be used by hackers to monitor the system as well. You must keep this in mind when you install system management tools. They may have more value to a hacker than they do to you.

Another method of monitoring the system console is to utilize the features of the console terminal itself. If the console is a smart terminal, then it is likely that the information stored in the terminal's memory can be read. A number of programs specific to a wide range of smart terminals have been written and are available on numerous hacker bulletin boards and electronic periodicals.

You may be able to reduce the risk of a smart terminal attack by configuring your terminal to emulate an older, dumber terminal. Another approach is to remove the read and write permissions to the terminal when no one is logged on. The use of the console terminal should be limited to only those activities which require system console access.

System Logs

System logs are a system manager's best friend. If activated and properly configured, they can record most things of interest that happen on the system. There are logs for accounting, auditing, network traffic, logins and logouts, and dozens more. Most systems come out of the box without the logging turned on, so as the system administrator you have to start logging. The hacker will attempt to find these logs so he can avoid the actions that will cause log entries, disable the logs, or falsify the log entries.

It is common for hackers to try to locate log files by using the `find` command to locate files which contain the characters "log" in their name or to run some commands that would be logged on a quiet system and look for files that have changed.

Since these are common procedures for hackers to locate logs, it is a good idea to create log files that do not contain the word "log" in their names and to put them in a protected and possibly hidden directory to make locating them as difficult as possible. It would be best if the system were to log to another system, a very secure system, or to a nonerasable media such as a printer or a WORM device.

It is also advisable to have a process that logs a heartbeat, that is, an entry in the log at regular intervals, so that the health of the logging process can be monitored.

Increasing Security

Why would a hacker want to beef up security on a system that he has broken into? Well, there is nothing worse for a skilled hacker than being found out because some neophyte hacker broke into a system that the skilled hacker was using. Once a hacker is on a system, he won't want to share it with other hackers. Each system that he can control gives him greater capabilities to get elsewhere. So he will want to close all the easy holes, add a few new ones just for himself, and keep the system manager happy, thinking that nothing is happening on the system.

It is not advisable to let hackers on your system to help you beef up your security. However, a number of security professionals got their expertise on the ins and outs of security while hacking.

Not Making Tracks

If the hacker plans to consume resources that your system possesses, he will try to become invisible, so he can stay undetected on your system and use the system at his discretion. The resources the hacker wants to access could be the strategic location of the system on the network for network snooping, or it could simply be one more CPU on which to collect and analyze data.

This can be accomplished by connecting with a method that does not leave evidence of the connection, or by leaving evidence that would misdirect anyone to the source of the connection, or by removing the evidence after the fact. A hacker's success at connection hiding is dependent on both the hacker's knowledge and skill and the skill and knowledge of the system administrator.

Anonymous Connections

Anonymous connections allow access to systems without providing an identity for the connection. These connections can be logged which can indicate the source location of the connection and the activities performed while connected. The tracks that are left by hackers via anonymous connections are often of limited value. Hackers will often use an intermediary site to hide the actual origin of the connection. Anonymous services usually provide only specific, limited services and are widely utilized externally, so any specific instance will be buried among an overwhelming amount of legitimate uses. The volume of use of an anonymous service, and thereby the size of the logs, often lead to organizations not logging or minimally logging an anonymous service.

Stealth Connections

Most of the connection monitoring and reporting programs use accounting log files: `/etc/utmp` for currently logged on users, `/etc/wtmp` for historic logins, and `/etc/btmp` for bad login attempts on those systems that support the `btmp` file. There are a few ways to connect to a system and avoid this logging environment, thus leaving very little evidence.

The first is to use the noninteractive C shell. A noninteractive shell is a shell that does not have a tty device attached to it. It is generally used to run background jobs, although it can be used to run foreground jobs. However, since it does not have a tty, it cannot run processes that require tty control, like editors and other screen-based applications. It is invoked with the command `csh -i`. Since it does not associate a tty, it does not create an entry in the `utmp` log file.

Another method is to execute the `xterm` program with the utmpInhibit resource set to TRUE. This can be done with the `-ut` command-line option or by setting the X resource to TRUE in either the system-wide X resources file or your local X resources file, usually `.Xdefaults`. These options exist to simplify the connection information from users on X terminals. Generally, the login process from the X terminal will create an entry in the utmp log file and then, without the "utmpinhibit" option, each `xterm` window creates another "user" on the system, causing a misrepresentation in reporting information and licensing problems on some systems.

These methods only hide the connection to the system. Anything that is run on that system is open to monitoring while the process is executing or logging when the process has completed.

For the system manager to overcome this approach, all connections to a system should be logged through appropriate auditing procedures. All programs that create an interactive shell should be audited. As for network connections, both the network sockets should be logged and the daemons that use the sockets should be audited. The socket log will indicate from where the system receives connections while the daemon audit trail will indicate the activities of the service that was using the socket. It may be worthwhile to invoke some countermeasures to determine the origins of the connections.

Connection Hiding

Connection hiding is the process of keeping the system from reporting the connection. Connection hiding requires the insertion of tools (software) which either keep the connection from being logged or prevent the connection from being reported. These can be in the form of libraries which have been altered to do this or "Trojan" utilities which perform as the utility they replace but without reporting the hacker's activities. Many hacker toolkits include versions of system utilities that do not report the hacker's presence.

Another method is to alter the information in the utmp log so that the standard commands that report connection information will report incorrect information. This file can be altered to show a connection by someone else or to show no connection at all.

The hacker software "uthide," which is available on the included CD-ROM, removes all references to the given user ID from the `/etc/wtmp` file, effectively hiding the user's connections. This is, of course, not the only log file which can be recording these actions. However, it does illustrate how simple it is to remove tracks from logs.

However, the process of altering this log with uthide, under close examination, will reveal that someone was logged on to the system and that the utmp file has been altered. The log will not indicate who it was that was logged on or who altered the system log.

Process Hiding

Process hiding is the process of using system resources without leaving records of that use. The information about what is currently running on your system is available through commands which get their information from reading the structures directly from memory. How processes are started will alter how they are reported. The reporting commands may have limited command length and will truncate the options and parameters that were passed to the command that goes beyond this limit. A system administrator needs to understand how his auditing reports the commands and if there are any limitations to these commands. A skilled hacker understands this and is very careful to keep his activities secret.

The information about what is currently running on your system is available through the `ps` command. This command gets its information from reading the structures directly from memory.

You also need to be aware that the way a command is issued will affect the amount of information that is visible in the process status. If the command is invoked with a parameter, the command and the parameters will appear on the program status list. However, if the input is redirected into the command, only the command will appear on the program status list. For example, running the command

```
cat /etc/passwd
```

will be seen with the `ps` command as

```
cat /etc/passwd
```

where the command

```
cat </etc/passwd
```

will be seen as

```
cat
```

Even though each of these commands does the same thing, using redirection will report less information.

A skilled hacker understands this and is very careful to keep his activities secret. He will also understand that "exec"ing a child process will replace the parent process in the process table with the child process, thereby removing the parent process from the system. So "exec"ing a shell over a setUID program will disguise the fact that it is running with an effective UID of 0.

Hackers will also name their hacking tools something that does not look threatening, or the same name as a standard UNIX command, so that if it is seen running, no one will think twice about it.

Some hackers will install a modified version of the process status command, ps, that will not report the processes that are being run by the hacker's purloined account. The system manager should monitor the attributes of the executable programs on the system to detect programs that have been changed.

Removing Tracks

It is impossible for a hacker to spend much time on a system without leaving some tracks. These tracks will appear in system logs and on system backups. These two areas are very important because this captured information can be used as evidence in any criminal charges that might be brought.

It is quite common for hackers to attempt to modify, falsify, or eradicate these tracks. Some of these logs are well-known in both location and format.

Changing Logs

All systems do some logging; a good system administrator will turn on more than the default logging. Locating logs has been previously discussed. The question is, now that a hacker knows what logs are being kept and where they are, what can he do about them?

Some of the logs are simple text files. A hacker can edit these with a text editor to remove the evidence of his existence from them. Other logs are encoded binary files that cannot be edited with a text editor. To modify these files, the hacker must know the format of the information in the file. Some of the standard log files have well-known formats and there are programs that will allow them to be edited.

The system manager may be able to tell that the logs have been altered, but he will not be able to tell what information has been altered or removed. Some of these tools leave fingerprints in the log where the entry was altered. The hacker may decide to take the easy path and delete log files. This will remove the information from the file; however, it will also be evident that someone is tampering with the system.

The program "invis," which is available on the included CD-ROM, allows the hacker to change the login name and the associated terminal of his current session in the /etc/utmp file. This will effectively remove his session and replace it with another user login name and terminal. A hacker could use such a tool to misdirect an investigation or to attempt to lay blame elsewhere.

If the system's auditing allows for auditing of events to a specific file, you should audit all activities that pertain to the log files. If you are saving the log files to another machine, the connection to that machine should be audited.

Destroying Evidence

If the hacker has completely finished using of the system, with no expectations of returning, he may opt to delete everything. This will guarantee that the system manager will want to hunt him to the ends of the earth. However, few system administrators have the time to do this; they have systems to repair and users and managers to appease.

You must remember that you can never lose more information than what has changed since your last backup, unless you leave your backups online, or your procedures allow a hacker to request that an operator mount the backup tape. In this case, a hacker can delete your backups. There is one case of an intruder who erased all the tapes in an automated tape silo and then deleted all the files on the system, thereby deleting all the backup for that system.

During the recovery process, you must also remember that your system has been compromised. Until you can identify the time that the hacker first entered your system and recover your system to that point, the system will still be suspect.

Misdirection

Misdirection is a common tactic used by malicious hackers to lead investigators down the wrong path. False leads will consume investigation resources and the good will of those whose assistance is needed.

Masquerading

The hacker will find masquerading very useful in an environment where there is a light to moderate amount of monitoring. He will be able to keep from becoming visible by consuming too many computer resources or too much connect time. He will do this to buy some time in case his activities are discovered, while the system manager chases after the person he is masquerading. The problem for the hacker with masquerading is that the person as whom he is masquerading may notice that someone is using his account and alert security of the hacker's presence. So an experienced hacker will select someone who is not using the system, or someone who is not very sophisticated in his use of the system. A security awareness program will reduce this threat.

IP Spoofing

IP spoofing is a process by which a hacker can convince another computer that he is on a system other than the one he is actually on. This can be accomplished through a number of methods, including altering the ARP or DNS cache, altering router information, intercepting or guessing IP sequence numbers, or by manipulating IP-routing and using a false IP source address.

Every machine has a cache of addresses, both link level, MAC, in its ARP cache, and network level, IP, in its DNS cache, so it does not have to request from a remote system for these frequently used addresses. Since these caches are maintained on each local machine, altering the contents of these caches can alter where the packets of information from that machine are sent.

Another method used to misroute messages is to corrupt the routing information contained in the network equipment itself, such as bridges and routers. Many of the protocols that were developed for these network devices to communicate with each other have limited security. Most of the remote configuration protocols are also lacking in security. However, newer protocols with better security are being introduced and are replacing the older, nonsecure protocols. You should contact your network vendor to determine the status of the security of your network devices.

A new method of misrouting packets has recently come to light. TCP utilizes sequence numbers as its base level of authentication. Each packet contains a sender and a recipient packet number with each system incrementing its respective packet number for each packet sent in this specific connection. This allows packets to arrive out of order and be reassembled and to give some level of authentication if the numbers match. However, with the current speed of computers and networks, it is possible to eavesdrop on a connection and steal the sequence numbers and then to masquerade as one end of the communication. Hacker tools such as "hijack" have been created to do just this. Currently, improved authentication methods are being evaluated to secure network connections better. In the meantime, data encryption is the only safe way to send information over an untrusted network.

For the system manager to overcome this approach, all connections to a system should be logged through appropriate auditing procedures. All programs that create an interactive shell should be audited. As for network connections, both the network sockets should be logged and the daemons that use the sockets should be audited. The socket log will indicate from where the system receives connections while the daemon audit trail will indicate the activities of the service that was using the socket. It may be worthwhile to invoke some countermeasures to determine the origins of the connections.

Changing Time

When it comes to reconstructing what has been happening on a system, time is very important. The ability to construct a consistent linear time line is paramount to understanding the sequence of events that occurred on the system. If the time on the system is inconsistent, it increases the complexity of this analysis. The inability to build a creditable time line can greatly reduce the ability to prosecute the case. The inconsistencies in time reduce credibility and confuse juries. Therefore, if a hacker changes the time of the system, or timestamps in logs or timestamps of files, he can create a great barrier to the system administrators in their attempts to track down the hacker at work.

If a system is auditing or running sufficient logging, the system manager will be able to reconstruct this type of tampering. However, the process is time-consuming.

System Time

Every computer system and most network devices have a locally stored time. This time is used whenever the system needs to know the time for timestamps, or logging. On any single system, time is consistent unless the system clock is changed, and this activity, which requires specific privileges, will be reported and logged. However, when logs from multiple systems are compared or consolidated, then the differences in the system clocks of those systems are an issue. The timestamps in the logs from each system are different. This leads to increasing the work in being able to reliably reconstruct a time line of the hacking activities. The clocks on systems on a network should be synchronized. A system should use an auditable time service to set all the clocks to the same time.

Timestamps on Files

Every file has three timestamps: creation time, last access time, and last modified time. Anyone with permission can alter the timestamp on a file with the touch command or program-matically. Hackers will often change the timestamps on files to make tracking their activities more difficult and to help disguise what files have been altered.

There may be certain files for which altering their timestamps may affect the operation of the system. For example, some systems use the timestamp of a specific file to indicate the time of the last backup, which is compared to the timestamps of all the files on the system when an incremental backup is performed. Altering this timestamp will alter what files are backed up. A hacker may do this to keep his activities from being recorded on a backup.

Time Zone

The time zone variable is an environment variable and is used by some programs to display and calculate the time. E-mail is the most prevalent of these programs. The e-mail client sending the mail will timestamp the time which it is sent. A system with an incorrect or altered clock will misreport the time when the mail was sent.

The format of the time zone variable is three or more characters that designate the standard time zone, followed by a numeric offset that must be added to the local time to arrive at Coordinated Universal Time, followed by three or more characters that designate the summer or daylight-savings time zone. For example, the Pacific Time zone would be represented by "PST8PDT."

If a hacker resets this variable so that the time zone designations do not correspond to the same time zone as the offset listed, such as "EST8EDT," it can cause the calculated time and the displayed time to differ. He can utilize this fact to make it appear as if something happened at a different time than it actually did.

## CHAPTER 14

Increasing Monitoring

Τhe system manager has an advantage when it comes to monitoring the system. He can run processes that can watch for suspicious activities around the clock. These can be dynamic real-time alerts to an operation center or network management system to notify someone that an attack is in progress. A hacker will raise his chances of getting caught if he leaves processes running while he is not on the system. The system manager also knows what should be running on the system, while the hacker may not have this insight into the system.

All the logging, monitoring activities, log analysis software, and countermeasures do no good if someone does not review the output. It still requires time and effort for someone to monitor the system. Log analysis software will make the job easier since it reduces the volume of information to be reviewed. Expert systems that respond to specific types of attacks also reduce the amount of work. But the bottom line is that someone has to look for, or be notified about, the unexpected occurrences.

Increased monitoring enables accountability by having the information necessary to show who was responsible for a specific action. This is needed by an organization to enforce disciplinary actions and is required for criminal prosecution.

Install and enable as much logging as possible and automate log monitoring with a data reduction application to eliminate the normal events. Someone must still look at the remaining unusual events and follow policy and procedures when these events occur.

Many network management or operations center tools make it easy to forward alerts to a central site for management. These systems will allow you to set severity levels for each type of alert, and then based on the severity level, issue appropriate notification or an automated response.

Monitoring Files

A computer system, at its simplest, is a collection of files which contain the information on what the system is to do and for whom. The information the system contains is held within files, the configuration information which controls the system is held within files, and on UNIX systems the devices themselves appear on the system as files. The controlling of these files is critical to the security of the system. Monitoring these files is equally important to maintaining the security. Hackers alter and replace files to change the behavior of the system or to gain access to information.

Tripwire

Tripwire is a tool that checks to see what has changed on your system. The program monitors key attributes of files that should not change. Tripwire was developed by Dr. Eugene Spafford and Gene Kim of Purdue University in 1992. It has become a basic technology in monitoring systems for unauthorized changes.

Tripwire software can help to ensure the integrity of critical system files and directories by identifying when they are changed. Tripwire configuration options include the ability to receive alerts via e-mail if particular files are altered and automated integrity checking via a cron job. Using tripwire for intrusion detection and damage assessment helps you keep track of system changes and can speed the recovery from a break-in by reducing the number of files you must restore to repair the system.

Tripwire compares files and directories against a base-line database of file locations, dates modified, and other data. It generates the base line by taking a snapshot of specified files and directories in a known secure state. (For maximum security, tripwire should be installed and the base line created before the system is at risk from intrusion.) After creating the base-line database, tripwire compares the current system to the base line and reports any modifications, additions, or deletions.

The tripwire policy file is a text file containing comments, rules, directives, and variables. This file dictates the way tripwire checks your system. Each rule in the policy file specifies a system object to be monitored. Rules also describe which changes to the object to report and which to ignore.

System objects are the files and directories you want to monitor. Each object is identified by an object name. A property refers to a single characteristic of an object that tripwire software can monitor. Directives control conditional processing of sets of rules in a policy file. During installation, the text policy file (/etc/tripwire/twpol.txt) is encrypted and renamed, becoming the active policy file (/etc/tripwire/tw.pol).

When first initialized, tripwire uses the signed policy file rules to create the database file, /var/lib/tripwire/host_name.twd. The database file is a base-line snapshot of the system in a known secure state. Tripwire compares this base line against the current system to determine what changes have occurred. This comparison is called an integrity check.

When you perform an integrity check, tripwire produces report files in the /var/lib/tripwire/report directory. The report files summarize any file changes that violated the policy file rules during the integrity check.

The tripwire configuration file (/etc/tripwire/tw.cfg) stores system-specific information, such as the location of tripwire data files. Tripwire generates the necessary configuration file information during installation, but the system administrator can change parameters in the configuration file at any time after that point. Note that the altered configuration file must be signed in the same way as the policy file in order for it to be used by default.

The configuration file variables POLFILE, DBFILE, REPORTFILE, SITEKEYFILE, and LOCALKEYFILE specify the locations of the policy file, database file, report files, and site and local key files. These variables are defined by default at the time of installation. If you edit the configuration file and leave any of them undefined, the configuration file will be considered invalid by tripwire. This causes an error on the execution of tripwire, making the program exit.

Note that the altered configuration file must be signed in the same way as the policy file in order for it to be used by tripwire.

Tripwire can e-mail someone if a specific type of rule in the policy file is violated. To configure tripwire to do this, you first have to know the e-mail address of the person to be contacted if a particular integrity violation occurs, plus the name of the rule you would like to monitor. Note that on large systems with multiple administrators, you can have different sets of people notified for certain violations and no one notified for minor violations.

Tripwire is supplied with Red Hat Linux and the Tripwire Open Source code is available from tripwire.org and is on the CD-ROM.

Monitoring Users

There are many commands that can be used to monitor user connections. The simplest way to see who is logged onto the system is with the who command. The -u option will report all the users on the system and from where they are connected. The -w option of the who command will list all active users and their current process. This will give some idea of what the user is doing. You can tell who has been logged on recently by using the last command.

All the commands that monitor connections use the accounting log files, the "utmp" file, usually /var/adm/utmp or /etc/utmp, for current connection, and the "wtmp" file, usually /var/adm/wtmp or /etc/wtmp, for historic connections, to extract the information. These files are very important in reporting user activities accurately. It is common for hackers to modify these files to hide their activities. An extra layer of monitoring should be applied to these files.

Keystroke Monitoring

Keystroke monitoring is the process of capturing the user inputs, usually key presses and mouse clicks, to be able to record and reconstruct the activities of that user. Keystroke monitoring can be used by computer systems administrators, as a method of protecting computer systems from unauthorized access. Keystroke monitoring should be limited to only those whose activities are suspected of breaching security and in compliance with company policy. Sites not covered by U.S. law should consult their legal counsel before implementing keystroke monitoring.

Sites which will be using keystroke monitoring must give notice to those who would be subject to monitoring that, by using the system, they are expressly consenting to such monitoring. Since it is important that unauthorized intruders be given notice, some form of banner notice at the time of signing on to the system is required. Notification of only authorized users will not be sufficient to place outside hackers on notice.

The banner should give clear and unequivocal notice to intruders that by signing onto the system they are expressly consenting to such monitoring. The banner should also indicate to authorized users that they may be monitored during the effort to monitor the intruder even if they are not the subject of the investigation. We also understand that system administrators may in some cases monitor authorized users in the course of routine system maintenance. If this is the case, the banner should indicate this fact. An example of an appropriate banner might be as follows:

> This system is for the use of authorized users only. Individuals using this computer system without authority, or in excess of their authority, are subject to having all of their activities on this system monitored and recorded by system personnel.
>
> In the course of monitoring individuals improperly using this system, or in the course of system maintenance, the activities of authorized users may also be monitored.
>
> Anyone using this system expressly consents to such monitoring and is advised that if such monitoring reveals possible evidence of criminal activity, system personnel may provide the evidence of such monitoring to law enforcement officials. [56]

Monitoring Resources

Today's client server architecture minimizes the number of users who actually log in to a system. They access the information over the network, utilizing services provided by software on the server. Monitoring the resources being utilized by the system will give a more accurate view of what is happening on a system. There are many utilities which report on the use of system resources. The two main systems which report consolidated use information are the accounting and auditing packages.

---

[56]   "CERT® Advisory CA-1992-19 Keystroke Logging Banner," 7 December 1992.

Accounting

The accounting package was built for UNIX systems to provide usage information to bill-back resource consumption on timesharing systems. Accounting software is structured as a set of tools (consisting of both C programs and shell procedures) that can be used to build accounting systems. The accounting system reports connect time, which is handled by various programs that write records into /etc/utmp, disk usage, file input and output, printer usage, CPU consumption, and memory utilization. This information can be reported by user or process. Per process accounting is performed by the HP-UX system kernel. Upon termination of a process, one record per process is written to a file, normally /var/adm/pacct.

HP-UX Auditing

The purpose of the auditing system is to record instances of access by subjects to objects and to allow detection of any attempts to bypass the protection mechanism and any misuses of privileges, thus acting as a deterrent against system abuses and exposing potential security weaknesses in the system.

- **User and Event Selection** — The auditing system provides administrators with a mechanism to select users and activities to be audited. Users are assigned unique identifiers called audit IDs by the administrator which remain unchanged throughout a user's history. The audusr command is used to specify those users who are to be audited. The audevent command is used to specify system activities (auditable events) that are to be audited. Auditable events are classified into several categories, illustrated by the event category list at the end. (An event category consists of a set of operations that affects a particular aspect of the system.)

- **Self-auditing Programs** — To reduce the amount of log data and to provide a higher-level recording of some typical system operations, a collection of privileged programs are given capabilities to perform self-auditing. This means that the programs can suspend the currently specified auditing on themselves and produce a high-level description of the operations they perform. These self-auditing programs include: at, chfn, chsh, crontab, login, newgrp, passwd, audevent, audisp, audsys, audusr, cron, init, lpsched, pwck, and sam. Note that only these privileged programs are allowed to do self-auditing, and that the audit suspension they perform affects only these programs and does not affect any other processes on the system.

The Logging System

Information logging is key to a properly secured system. Most systems have a great deal of system logging capabilities. However, they often have to be configured or enabled. UNIX systems have a number of standard logging facilities which are common to all UNIX systems.

Table 14-1 HP-UX Audit Events and Categories

Event	Categories
create	Log all creations of objects
delete	Log all deletions of objects
readdac	Log reads of discretionary access control (DAC) information
moddac	Log all modifications of object's Discretionary Access Control (DAC) information
modaccess	Log all modifications other than DAC
open	Log all openings of objects
close	Log all closings of objects
process	Log all operations on processes
removable	Log all removable media events (mounting and unmounting events)
login	Log all logins and logouts
admin	Log all administrative and privileged events
ipccreat	Log all IPC create events
ipcopen	Log all IPC open events
ipcclose	Log all IPC close events
uevent1	Log user-defined event
uevent2	Log user-defined event
uevent3	Log user-defined event

However, logs by themselves offer little security if they are not being reviewed. Logs are a tool and must be use effectively by scanning through them regularly. Unfortunately, logs are often used only in a reactionary way because of a lack of time and because of the sheer size of the logs. Consolidation of logs and automated scanning can reduce this task to a reasonable task.

On UNIX systems, the primary logging service is syslog for system messages and klog for kernel messages. These logs are usually consolidated with the syslog facility, along with any system utilities or applications which utilize logging.

The syslog service parses and separates log messages based on a system of "Facility" and "Level." The "Facility" is the software or subsystem which is generating the log message, and the "Level" is a setting indicating criticalness. Table 14-2 lists the "Levels" recognized by syslog.

Table 14-2 Syslog Levels

Level	Meaning
emerg	A panic condition. This is normally broadcast to all users.
alert	A condition that should be corrected immediately, such as a corrupted system database.
crit	Critical conditions, such as hard device errors.
err	Errors.
warning	Warning messages.
notice	Conditions that are not error conditions, but should possibly be handled specially.
info	Informational messages.
debug	Messages that contain information normally of use only when debugging a program.

Application Logging

Most applications have very little, if any, logging. When an application has logging, it is either because of legal requirements or to aid in the development or debugging of the software. Daemons and servers are somewhat more likely to provide some level of logging.

Logging from a software standpoint is very simple. An application API is provided to the syslog facility. It provides the ability for applications to put logging messages into the system's standard logging facility. Using this facility allows the system administrator to set the level of logging needed and how the logs are to be stored. Syslog APIs are widely available for C. Linux provides a Perl interface to syslog and HP-UX provides a command interface, logger. The following is a description of the C language API for the syslog service.

void openlog(const char *ident, int logopt, int facility)

> *openlog* is called to initialize communication to the log file.

> *ident* is the identification string that precedes every message.

> *logopt* is a mask of bits, indicating logging options.

> The values for logopt are:

LOG_PID — Log the process ID with each message; useful for identifying instances of daemons.

LOG_CONS — Force writing messages to the console if unable to send it to syslogd. This option is safe to use in daemon processes that have no controlling terminal because syslog() forks before opening the console.

LOG_NDELAY — Open the connection to syslogd immediately. Normally, the open is delayed until the first message is logged. This is useful for programs that need to manage the order in which file descriptors are allocated.

LOG_NOWAIT — Do not wait for children forked to log messages on the console. This option should be used by processes that enable notification of child termination via SIGCLD, because syslog() might otherwise block, waiting for a child whose exit status has already been collected.

void syslog(int priority, const char *message, ...)

syslog writes the message onto the system log maintained by syslogd. It does not log a message that does not have a level set. If it cannot pass the message to syslogd, it attempts to write the message on /dev/console if the LOG_CONS option is set.

priority is encoded as the logical OR of a level and a facility. The level signifies the urgency of the message, and facility signifies the subsystem generating the message. Facility can be encoded explicitly in priority, or a default facility can be set with openlog.

message is tagged with priority. A trailing newline is added if needed. This message is read by syslogd and is written to the system console, log files, selected users' terminals, or forwarded to syslogd on another host as appropriate.

void closelog(void)

closelog closes the log file.

The logger command provides a program interface to the syslog system log module. With this, a message can be given on the command line, which is logged immediately, or a file is read and each line is logged. If no file or message is specified, the contents of the standard input are logged. The logger command recognizes the following command-line options and arguments:

-t Defines the tag.

-p Defines the priority. The priority can be specified numerically or as a facility.level pair. The default is user.notice.

-i Logs the process ID of the logger process with each line.

-f Logs the contents of the specified file.

To send the message "System going down immediately!!!" to the syslog daemon, at the emerg level and user facility, the logger command would be:

```
logger -p user.emerg "System going down immediately!!!"
```

Kernel Logging

On HP-UX, kernel logging is a high-availability feature that gives system administrators the ability to collect the information necessary to diagnose problems with the HP-UX kernel while the system is running. `/usr/sbin/kl` is used to specify the levels of events to be logged and the kernel subsystems that will write messages to memory or disk. It also provides for managing the contents of the logfile in memory and on disk.

At start-up, kernel logging determines its default configuration by reading the file `/etc/nettlgen.conf`. The `kl` command permits only temporary changes to the default kernel logging configuration without having to stop and restart the kernel logging facility. To make permanent changes to the values in the `/etc/nettlgen.conf` file, run `nettlconf`.

Mission critical systems should always enable kernel logging. Failing to enable kernel logging causes diagnostic information about any suspicious events that might occur on the system to be lost. The recommended classes to capture are Disaster, Error, and Warning. Use the `kl -l w all` command to do so. To minimize kernel logging's impact on a running system, use the `kl -l e all` command to set all kernel subsystems to capture error-level log messages only. Only users with appropriate privileges (root) can invoke the `kl` command to control the kernel logging facility.

Enabling Logging

The main starting point to enable logging on a UNIX system is to ensure that the inet daemon is logging. This is done by starting the daemon with the "-l" option. The internet daemon will then log every time a service under its control is used and from where the connection came. Many of the services which the internet daemon starts have their own logging which can provide more information. For example, ftpd, the file transfer protocol daemon, will log connections with the (-l) option. The newest release will also log the commands sent to the ftp server, (-L) and the files received (-i) and transmitted (-o). One should consult the man page for each service which is running on the system to be sure its logging is enabled.

Any system utility which is not started by inetd should provide its own logging. Some of these utilities log by default, others require enabling the logging features. Most of the utilities utilize the syslog service. The HP-UX environmental daemon (envd), the password and group daemon (pwgrd) and ups_mond, and the HP PowerTrust Uninterruptible Power System monitor daemon are examples of utilities on HP-UX which are not started by inetd and are running on most systems.

Configuring syslog for Local Logging

The syslog daemon can redirect the logged information into separate log files based on the combination of "Facility" and "Level." Only the "Facility" and "Level" combinations listed, or indicated by wildcards, will be logged. The following is a example default `/etc/syslog.conf` file:

```
mail.debug              /var/adm/maillog
mail.none               /var/adm/maillog
auth.notice             /var/adm/authlog
lpr.debug               /var/adm/lpd-errs
kern.debug              /var/adm/messages
*.emerg;*.alert;
*.crit;*.warning;*.err;
*.notice;*.info         /var/adm/messages
```

When logging locally, a compromised system's logs have to be considered suspect. Any local files on a compromised system could have been altered. It is not possible to tell if the logs have been altered with the standard syslog system. There are no integrity checks within the syslog facility.

Configuring syslog for Remote Logging

Remote logging reduces the risk that a compromised system's logs will be altered to hide the attack. Since the logs are on a remote logging server, that server too would have to have been compromised to change the logs. Configuring a system to use a remote logging server is a simple task. All the logs can be redirected to that logging server by placing the following entry into /etc/syslog.conf:

```
*.*       @logging-host
```

Consolidated Logging Server

The remote log server should be a completely hardened system with only syslog, port 514, open. It should not depend on any external services except a secured time source. The syslog server, syslogd, should be configured to accept remote logging requests, the "-r" switch on Linux systems, and adding the syslog entry in the /etc/services file.

All network services should be disabled. This is done by disabling the internet daemon, inetd, the rpc daemon, portmap or rpcbind, and any other network service.

If remote administration is required, it should be enabled with a secure and auditable connection.

Log File Monitoring

The ability to detect malicious activities is dependent upon adequate monitoring. Enabling logging does no good if the logs are not reviewed. The problem, of course, is that there is a great wealth of data produced from all of the logging activities. A centralized logging server provides a single location for log data and consolidates the work of examining the information. It also provides a good location for an intrusion detection system which analyzes log entries to determine malicious activities.

Possibly the most important aspect of log monitoring is the ability to automate the process and reduce the amount of information which a person has to examine. There are many tools and products which help in this endeavor.

Swatch

Swatch, Simple WATCHer, is a tool written in Perl by Todd Atkins to actively monitor messages as they are written to a log file via the UNIX syslog utility. Swatch monitors your logs for specific triggers; when those triggers are matched, swatch notifies you in a predetermined manner.

It gives an administrator the ability to process the enormous amounts of logged data without being overwhelmed. The program is simple to install, administer, and expand to perform actions defined by the administrator. It can be used as a simple intrusion detection system or can front-end other systems, reducing the volume of data for them to process.

The configuration file, called swatchrc, is the heart of the swatch program. This text file tells swatch what logs to monitor, what triggers to look for, and what to do if triggered. Swatch works by looking for regular expressions that match the triggers defined in swatchrc. When it finds a match, it executes the notification procedure defined in swatchrc.

The swatchrc file consists of four fields — the first two fields are required, and the last two fields are optional. The first field is the regular expression for which swatch is looking. This is the trigger. The second is a list of actions to be performed if the pattern is matched. Swatch has various options for actions, including e-mail, paging, or executing any file you select. The third field "throttle" (which is optional) is a time interval. This time interval is the amount of time swatch will ignore identical matched patterns that repeat themselves. The fourth field (required if you are using the third field) is a timestamp.

```
#
# Personal Swatch configuration file
#
# Alert me of bad login attempts and find out who is on that system
watchfor   /INVALID|REPEATED|INCOMPLETE/
    echo inverse
    bell 3
# Important program errors
watchfor   /LOGIN/
    echo inverse
    bell 3
watchfor   /passwd/
    echo bold
    bell 3
watchfor   /ruserok/
    echo bold
```

```
  bell 3
# Ignore this stuff
ignore   /sendmail/,/nntp/,/xntp|ntpd/,/faxspooler/
# Report unusual tftp info
ignore   /tftpd.*(ncd|kfps|normal exit)/
watchfor   /tftpd/
  echo
  bell 3

# Kernel problems
watchfor   /(panic|halt|SunOS Release)/
  echo bold
  bell
watchfor   /file system full/
  echo bold
  bell 3
ignore   /vmunix.*(at|on)/
watchfor   /vmunix/
  echo
  bell

watchfor   /fingerd.*(root|[Tt]ip|guest)/
  echo
  bell 3

watchfor   /su:/
  echo bold
watchfor   /.*/
  echo
```

Part III

Legal Recourse

Even though there are big headlines about computer crime, nearly everyone who works in the computer industry knows that the crimes making these headlines are a tiny fraction of the crimes that are committed. Many companies resist pursuing legal recourse for fear of the damage that the publicity of the crime might cause the company. They understand that there is an inequity between how physically committed crimes and computer crimes are prosecuted. Companies also know that successful prosecution is difficult and time-consuming and they often feel that the perpetrators get a mere slap on the wrist, given the damages they cause.

It has been noted that if a bank is robbed by someone with a gun, the criminal will be hunted to the ends of the earth with whatever means necessary. But if a bank is robbed by someone with a computer, it is likely that the bank will not even acknowledge that a crime has been committed in order to avoid the publicity. Here are some statistics that illustrate the point.[56]

- The average armed robber will get $2,500 to $7,500 with the risk of being shot and killed.

- Fifty to 60 percent of armed robbers will be caught and 80 percent of those will be convicted and sentenced to an average of five years of hard time.

- The average computer criminal will get $50,000 to $500,000 with a risk of being fired or going to jail.

- Ten percent of those computer criminals that are *discovered* are caught, with only 15 percent of those caught being reported to authorities.

- Over 50 percent of these reported never go to trial due to a lack of evidence or a desire to avoid publicity.

---

[56] Tartaglia, John, "Introduction to Network Security," Computer Security Institute's Conference, 9 November 1993.

- Fifty percent of those who do go to trial are convicted and sentenced to five years of easy time.

However, things are changing. More laws are being written which address computer crime directly. Law enforcement agencies are becoming trained in the processes necessary to investigate computer crimes. The punishment for computer crimes is increasing. Companies are realizing that the publicity from prosecuting a computer crime, if handled correctly, can be very positive. It provides a forum for the company to show that it is being proactive and protecting its customers. It is improving its security — activities which its competitors may not be doing — and saving its customers money, by reducing losses due to crime.

It is imperative that we, as an industry, and you, as a corporate representative, be willing to prosecute computer criminals. Today, very few computer criminals pay for their crimes and most of them know the chances of punishment are slim. Increased prosecution and its surrounding publicity may make some potential computer criminals drop their plans.

If you are interested in pursuing any type of investigation or legal prosecution, you should first discuss the activity with your organization's management and legal counsel and notify any appropriate law enforcement agencies (in accordance with any policies or guidelines at your site) to see if they want to pursue an investigation.

Keep in mind that unless one of the parties involved contacts law enforcement, any efforts to trap or trace the intruder may be to no avail. You should contact law enforcement before attempting to set a trap or tracing an intruder.

For legal advice, it is recommended that you consult with your legal counsel. Your legal counsel can provide you with legal options (both civil and criminal) and courses of action based on your organization's needs.

Before you get started in your recovery, your organization needs to decide if pursuing a legal investigation is an option.

Criminal Charges

Criminal courts deal with issues of violations of the law. In the U.S., there are federal, state, and local courts to address federal, state, and local laws. Computer crime laws exist in each of these jurisdictions. Cooperation between the organizations which investigate and prosecute at each of these levels is required for smooth legal recourse.

It is up to you how you want to pursue this incident. You may want to secure your systems or to contact law enforcement to investigate the case.

U.S. sites interested in an investigation can contact their local Federal Bureau of Investigation (FBI) field office. Non-U.S. sites may want to discuss the activity with their local law enforcement agency to determine the appropriate steps that should be taken with regard to pursuing an investigation.

Civil Remedies

Civil courts address issues where financial harm has been done. If the victim is able to show to the satisfaction of juries and judges that he or she was financially damaged, then the judge or jury may settle their claim from the resources of the defendant, which may include future resources. If the jurisdiction allows, the judge may demand that the defendant pay actual restitution to the victim, recovering his or her losses. In the case of a civil suit, damages may be more than actual, with the court ordering the defendant to pay punitive damages to the victim as a means of punishment. In a case where damage is done to an individual or company, even if the person is criminally charged, it is still possible to proceed with civil processes. Although sometimes it requires more legal involvement, both tracks may be pursued with the victims receiving restitution from a criminal's sentence and a financial settlement as part of a civil suit.

## CHAPTER 15

Computer Crimes

Computer crime is any illegal act which involves a computer system, whether the computer is the object of a crime, an instrument used to commit a crime, or a repository of evidence related to a crime. Computer crimes are growing at a rate which is matched only by the growth of the Internet. These crimes are becoming as diverse as the Internet itself. As all types of commerce are moving to cyberspace, so are the commercial crimes. Financial fraud and economic espionage are only two of the many types of computer-related crimes perpetrated around the world. Financial institutions, such as banks and credit card companies, absorb large losses due to financial fraud. With worldwide online accessibility, organized criminal groups now accomplish illegal money transfers from across the globe. This new style of crime is forcing businesses large and small to take a closer look into Internet security. It is also challenging current laws and enforcement to adapt to this rapidly changing environment. Computer-specific crimes require updates of the definitions of crimes in national criminal codes, and the traditional crimes performed with the aid of computers call for improved cooperation and procedural measures.

It's obvious that using computers to facilitate a crime and unauthorized network penetration are unlawful. But less obvious is the possession of a hacker's computer that stores tools related to that network penetration or which contains proprietary information which was taken through some unlawful act. Is only the hacker responsible, or is there some level of responsibility for the owner and operator of the system? Does this responsibility include the owners and operators of the networks which were used to commit the crimes? Does it matter if any of these individuals were aware that their systems were being used by hackers?

The definition of what constitutes computer crimes varies among countries. Computer crime laws encompass intellectual property, telecommunication, and electronic trespass. These issues are not uniformly valued around the globe and have diverse levels of protection.

Many countries have passed legislation to address computer-related crime. The Council of Europe is working on treaties to consolidate the disparate laws within Europe. Even with this broad scope of the laws, there are common classifications found in most of these bodies of law.

Traditional Offenses Using Computers

Computers are an essential component of most businesses, and criminals have also taken up computers as their tool of choice. Criminals are using computers in all sorts of ways. Illegal drug manufacturers have used computers to keep track of their inventories and their transactions with customers. Computers have been used to create fake IDs and counterfeit money. Computerized communications are used by criminals to communicate with other criminals or to manipulate their victims.

Financial Fraud

The computer and the communications it provides have been used often to commit fraud. The Internet is inundated with financial scams and get-rich-quick schemes. Other schemes which use a more direct attempt to deceive people for financial gain are also abundant. There have been many cases of attempting to manipulate stocks using the Internet. Some schemes have posted false news stories, and others have faked e-mail from company executives about earnings. Below is an account of one of the most successful.

> A California man was indicted on charges that he fabricated a press release that led a publicly traded company to temporarily lose more then $2 billion in market value.
>
> A former employee of Internet Wire, Mark Jakob, sent out a bogus press release which Internet Wire distributed and a number of news organizations, including CBS Market Watch, Bloomberg, and CNBC, reported as "news." As a result of the inaccurate reports, the stock price of Emulex plummeted from more than $110 a share to about $43 a share in less than an hour.
>
> Jakob himself traded in the stock, through which he realized approximately $240,000 in profits. The SEC obtained records which showed that an account in the name of Mark Jakob was used to trade Emulex stock for the five months preceding the hoax and that there had been a series of suspicious transactions involving the stock starting about one week prior to the hoax. Specifically, the record showed that the account was used to execute short sale purchases; short sales involve selling shares of stock that a trader does not own, usually in anticipation that the price of the stock will decline. After Emulex's stock dropped, Jakob covered his short sale position and realized tens of thousands in profits. He also purchased shares while the stock was at $50 a share, after the

> false press release, and sold them when the stock had recovered most of its value.[58]

Credit Card Theft

The theft of credit card information has become a major practice on the Internet and among hackers. Credit card numbers are easily acquired from e-commerce sites which have not provided adequate security. Trafficking, the transmission of the stolen numbers from the hacker who stole them to the individuals who want to use them, has grown into a large business. The high rewards, ease of handling, and low expectations of being caught have brought traditional crime organizations into this arena.

Organized crime has become a major player in the trafficking of stolen credit card numbers. The ease of sending credit card numbers over the Internet to anywhere in the world has attracted international crime syndicates, who use stolen credit cards and the profits of selling these numbers to finance their other activities.

> More than one million credit card numbers have been stolen by several organized hacker groups from Eastern Europe, specifically Russia and the Ukraine, that have penetrated U.S. e-commerce computer systems by exploiting vulnerabilities in unpatched Microsoft Windows NT operating systems. In some instances the credit card information is being sold to organized crime groups.
>
> Once the hackers gain access, they download proprietary information, customer databases, and credit card information, then subsequently contact the victim company notifying them of the intrusion and theft of information. The hackers attempt to extort the victims by offering services to patch the system against other hackers.[59]

Hundreds of thousands of credit card numbers are stolen and sold annually. Only the largest of these thefts make their way to the newspapers.

---

[58] "Emulex Hoaxer Indicted for Using Bogus Press Release and Internet Service to Drive Down Price of Stock," *Department of Justice Press Release*, 28 September 2000.

[69] "NIPC Advisory 01-003," *FBI Press Office*, 8 March 2001.

Identity Theft

Identity theft is the malicious misuse of someone's identity. Someone can steal your name and social security number or gather enough of your identity information to be able to gain access to your financial resources. Incidents of these types of identity theft are on the rise.

Generally, this is an attempt to use the victim's good credit history to secure a line of credit that is then run up to the limit and the perpetrator disappears. Much of the information needed to steal someone's identity is often available through electronic methods: name, social security number, driver's license number, mother's maiden name, bank information, etc.

> Donald McNeese was arrested on identity theft, credit card fraud, and money laundering charges stemming from his theft of a computer database containing personnel records for as many as 60,000 employees of the Prudential Insurance Company. He worked at Prudential's Jacksonville, Florida, office until June 2000, as the administrator of a database that contained personnel records for approximately 60,000 Prudential employees throughout the United States. After stealing the database, McNeese solicited bids for the sale of that information over the Internet.
>
> Using an undercover identity, a detective from the Nassau County Police Department assigned to the New York Electronic Crimes Task Force engaged in a series of communications with McNeese, who sent the detective approximately 20 of the employees' identities via the Internet as "samples." He urged the detective to obtain credit cards in the names of the employees and send a portion of the proceeds from the fraudulent use of those cards to him in Florida. McNeese stated his intention to sell all the stolen identities he possessed to the highest bidder.
>
> Using e-mail screen names that were stolen from his victims, he posted personal information and credit card numbers belonging to Prudential employees so that the readers could use the information to obtain fraudulent credit cards in the employees' names. He also engaged in a scheme to obtain money from fraudulent credit cards through a money-remitting businesses.
>
> He allegedly sent e-mails to the victims of his credit card fraud scheme, falsely incriminating his former boss as the perpetrator of the fraud. At the time of his arrest, McNeese admitted to downloading Prudential's database.[60]

---

[60]   "New York Electronic Crimes Task Force Arrests Defendant for One of the Largest Identity Theft Cases in U.S. History," *U.S. Department of Justice Press Release*, 1 March 2001.

Simple "identity theft" is generally no more than someone misrepresenting himself or herself as you in order to gain a financial return by forging a check or passing a credit card. Your identification may be stolen by physically taking your wallet or purse, or by misusing the information that comprises your identification. Most law enforcement professionals would not even consider this as identity theft, especially if the use of the identity is a one-time or very short-lived occurrence. To be classified as identity theft they would require that the theft of the identity be more in-depth or that the misrepresentation continues over a longer period of time.

In any case, most cases are short-lived, thirty to ninety days, and are performed for financial gain. However, there have been a few cases where identities have been stolen and used for years.

But the practice is far from uncommon. The real problem for consumers isn't monetary losses, but trying to repair a wrecked credit record. And as more information becomes available through the Internet, either for free or a low price, identity theft is expected to grow.

Consumers should try to keep personal information private, but there's little one can do to ward off a determined thief — sometimes the theft isn't detected until it complicates the life of the victim.

Attorney General John Ashcroft announced 500,000 to 700,000 Americans have their identity stolen each year; yet only 86,000 complaints of identity theft were reported to the Federal Trade Commission's Identity Theft Data Clearinghouse.

In Indianapolis, two men were convicted of identity theft. Olasegun O. Ojomo, a 28-year-old Nigerian, was sentenced to 37 months in prison for stealing $224,000 by applying for student loans, purchasing telephone services, and credit card charges.

Michael A. Lee, 18, was sentenced to 10 months in a community correction center for helping an older friend steal mail from 240 homes in Marion and Hamilton counties. While Lee insisted he didn't know what he was doing, Judge David F. Hamilton noted the potential harm that could have resulted from identity theft.[61]

---

[61]   Horne, Terry, "Erasing ID Theft Takes Time, Effort," *The Indianapolis Star/News*, 6 June 2002.

Computer-specific Offenses

Many countries have passed laws that address computer-specific crime, defining new offenses related to unauthorized access to computer systems (e.g., hacking, computer sabotage and distribution of viruses, computer espionage, computer forgery, and computer fraud) and new forms of committing the offences. Computer-specific offenses also includes the theft of computer equipment as well as unauthorized utilization of resources, such as CPU, disk, memory, network, and access. The object of the crime is often intangible, e.g., consumption of computer resources, or computer source code or passwords, or running up a company's telephone bill by using its modems to dial long distance.

There is a wealth of valuable information inside computers and they are generally easier to break into than a building. Criminals can perform their crimes from a distance with a level of anonymity and without detection. Even if they are caught, computer crimes are far less likely to be successfully prosecuted and often result in a lesser penalty.

Denial of Service

Denial-of-service attacks are always ongoing on the Internet. Most attacks are too small to make headlines. Small companies, who have little recourse, are often the victims of denial-of-service attacks. Most ISPs are unable or unwilling to assist in stopping an attack. If a single site is targeted, the traffic may not be enough to impact the ISP directly. It the attack is coming from outside your ISP, which it usually is, your ISP will usually help locate the apparent source of the attack, but little more. The ISP at the source has little incentive to help you with the problem since you are not a customer. Falsified addresses in the packets which are causing the flood make tracking and stopping the attack even more difficult.

Hackers can deny services to valid users by altering access permissions, altering network configurations, overloading services, or sending invalid data to a server. Merely filling a system's disk or memory to capacity may be enough to deny service to the system. Some security procedures that were created to keep hackers from gaining access to the system may keep authorized users from accessing the system.

In any case, these outages mean the loss of productivity to a company and loss of business, either directly or indirectly. They cost time and money to fix and can damage a company's image irreparably.

Denial-of-service attacks may be due to consuming system resources, as mentioned above, or a direct attack that makes it difficult to access the computer. This may be disabling all of the users' accounts, or changing their passwords, or disabling all the terminal ports to a system, or just shutting the system down.

Police in Surrey (UK) suspect local computer hackers may have played a role in orchestrating attacks on popular IRC (Internet Relay Chat) servers in Europe and the U.S.

Two major IRC channel networks in particular, Undernet and EFnet, have come under attack in recent months. This has affected servers based in the UK, the U.S. and elsewhere in Europe. The attack involves taking over numerous machines — often located in different countries — in order to bombard a server with an avalanche of fake information, rendering it inoperable. It is particularly hard to combat.

Surrey police say that numerous servers hosting IRC channels have become the focus of distributed denial of service (DDoS) attacks apparently in retribution after hackers were removed from certain channels for promoting illegal activity. [62]

Can your business survive without access to its computer? How much lost business and lost revenue will your business experience from a computer outage? Disaster plans usually address these issues if the computer system is destroyed by fire or flood. Your disaster plan must also address computer outages caused by hackers.

A system may be compromised so that it can be used to attack other sites. The use of an intermediary increases the difficulty in tracking the attack back to its originator. Numerous compromised sites can be used to attack another site simultaneously, creating a distributed attack which is under the control of a single individual.

Denial of Access to Information

There have been a number of cases where the information was not destroyed, it was only made unavailable, sometimes through the use of encryption, other times by the destruction of the indexing method on the storage media. In any case, the owner of the information was deprived of the ability to gain access to the information.

Norway's Ivar Aasen Centre of Language and Culture called for a hacker's help after the creator of its database died without passing on his password. It took a 25-year-old Swedish hacker just five hours to succeed in getting into the system.

[62]   Knight, Will, "UK Police Crack Down on Local Hackers," *ZDNet UK (www.zdnet.co.uk)*, 24 January 2001.

> With more than 11,000 titles it would have taken the Centre about four years to recreate the catalogue if it had failed to find the password.
>
> The incident sparked a serious debate among computer experts about how passwords should be taken care of. [62]

Cases such as this, along with the difficulty in defining what constitutes the theft or destruction of information, have lead a number of laws which address "denial of access" as a crime. They have been used in cases where access was denied to either services or information.

Viruses

E-mail viruses have become the most costly area of computer attacks, even though the full destructive capabilities of sending unknown code from untrusted sources has not yet been utilized. With active content, the ability to automatically run a program or macro without any intervention by the recipient, every e-mail message can be a threat. Viruses can live in the e-mail attachments or can utilize the macro capability of your e-mail program. E-mail attacks not only attack your site, but they can also use your address book to send themselves to your friends with your return address. The ability to widely distribute dangerous code so rapidly has led to specific laws addressing e-mail viruses.

> A New Jersey man was sentenced to 20 months in prison for unleashing the "Melissa" virus in 1999, causing millions of dollars in damage and infecting untold numbers of computers and computer networks.
>
> In a cooperating federal plea agreement, David L. Smith acknowledged that the Melissa virus caused more than $80 million in damage by disrupting personal computers and computer networks in business and government.[64]

---

63   Farrell, Nick, "Hacker Cracks "Dead" Password," *Computing*, 12 June 2002.
64   "Creator of Melissa Computer Virus Sentenced to 20 Months in Federal Prison," *U.S. Department of Justice Press Release*, 1 May 2001.

Intellectual Property Offenses

Intellectual property has specific protections based on copyright and related rights. The intangible nature of this property makes the theft and redistribution easy. It also makes it more difficult to prosecute these offenses under traditional laws.

There are now laws addressing the violation of copyright and related rights as well as the circumvention of technological measures designed to protect these rights. Software counterfeiting and piracy laws have attempted to slow these activities, but better methods for the software to protect itself have to become more effective.

As the Internet becomes increasinglyimportant commercially, we are beginning to see new disputes around domain names related to cyber-squatting, warehousing, and reverse hijacking, and, naturally, there are also calls for rules and procedures to help deal with these problems.

Theft of Information

Information theft is different from physical theft since the electronic theft of information does not deny the owner's access to it — only a copy of the information is stolen. However, this information could be valuable company secrets, expensive computer software, or private information about clients or partners. Information, if released, can cost the company in lost revenue, consumer confidence, and punitive damages. The theft of the information can have devastating effects on the owner of the information or on the entity which the information is about.

Trade secrets are some of the most valuable information to competitors of your company. This is what gives companies their competitive advantage. Sometimes the information is stolen not from the company itself but from a related company.

> Cut-throat competition between two Japanese companies was the cause of a hacking attack at the National Space Development Agency of Japan.
>
> NASDA confirmed that an employee at NEC Toshiba Space Systems, a joint venture set up by NEC and Toshiba, gained access to classified plans for satellite development drawn up by rival Mitsubishi Electric. The joint venture and Mitsubishi Electric were working together at NASDA's behest to develop a super-high-speed internet satellite due to be launched in 2005.
>
> NASDA said it had barred NEC Toshiba Space Systems from tendering bids for one month and insisted that the employee be transferred to a different position. The spokesman said there were no plans to file criminal charges against the unidentified employee.[65]

---

[65] Farrell, Nick, "Japanese Space Agency Hacked by Rival," *vnunet.com*, 18 February 2002.

Trafficking in Pirated Information

Stealing software to use personally or to sell to someone else is illegal. The software may be either commercial software or in-house developed software. It can even include software created by the hacker for the company while employed by the company. You do not have to profit from the theft of the software for it to be a crime; only the act of taking it is required.

Often, the pirates trade their illegal software all over the world.

> John Sankus, the leader of an online software piracy group known as DrinkOrDie, was sentenced to 46 months in federal prison on charges of violating criminal copyright law.
>
> Known by his screen nickname of "eriFlleH" (HellFire spelled backwards), Sankus supervised and managed the daily operations of the approximately 65 group members from more than 12 countries as they specialized in acquiring new software, stripping or circumventing its copyright protections and releasing it over the Internet.
>
> DrinkorDie concealed its illegal activities using an array of technology and security measures. Members sent e-mails via the group's private mailserver using PGP encryption, identified themselves only by screenname, and communicated about group business only in private IRC channels. The group's FTP sites, which contained tens of thousands of pirated software, game and movie titles, were password-protected and secured by a combination of user ID and IP address authentication mechanisms.
>
> The organization had a clear structure of member importance and responsibility, which allowed for very rapid distribution of cracked software.
>
> "This is stealing, plain and simple," said U.S. Customs Commissioner Robert C. Bonner, "and those engaged in the theft of intellectual property deserve to be prosecuted and punished. The unprecedented penalty issued today should serve as a wake-up call to other cyber thieves." [66]

---

[66]   "U.S. Customs Dismantles One of the World's Most Sophisticated Internet Piracy Networks," *U.S. Customs Service Press Release*, 11 December 2001.

Storing Pirated Information

System owners and operators may well be legally at risk if their system is being used for the trafficking of stolen software. The courts continue to determine that the owners and operators of a computer system can be responsible for the activities on that system.

Compromised sites will often be used as a way station for information. Sites with lots of storage space or high-speed networks are often targeted to be used as these way stations. Using compromised systems reduces the communication between those who stole the software and those who want it and it reduces the risk that the hackers will be caught.

Federal law enforcement agents conducted raids at several U.S. universities and software companies in an apparently successful attempt to break up a software piracy ring. According to the *Boston Globe*, a systems analyst at the Massachusetts Institute of Technology, one of the schools raided, is alleged to have been operating near the top level of the piracy ring, dubbed DrinkOrDie. As a result of his involvement, several MIT computers were seized, including at least one server.

Think about that for a minute. Imagine federal law enforcement agents one day burst into your data center, disconnect a server or two, no telling which ones, and walk away with them. Then think about having the name of your organization splashed all over the headlines of your local metropolitan newspaper in connection with such a scandal, not to mention national news vehicles. That's exactly what happened to not only MIT, but Duke University, the University of California at Los Angeles, and the Rochester Institute of Technology.

In this particular case, authorities allege the culprit was using MIT computers to conduct at least some of his illegal activies. What was he supposed to be doing? Maintaining the security systems for MIT's Economics Department.[67]

There is another situation where a company may find the tables turned when it comes to theft of software. A company may find itself under the point of the law if it is unable to produce licenses for every copy of every piece of software it is using. These licenses can be a piece of paper or the original installation media.

---

[67]   Desmond, Paul, "The Threat From Within," Copyright 2001 INT Media Group, Inc. All Rights Reserved. Republished with permission from http://www.internet.com.

Policies and procedures and a good software inventory system can go a long way to protect a company from a lengthy inventory process under detailed scrutiny.

Compromising Information

The hacker may want to plant false information to damage the company or an individual. If the hacker has intimate knowledge of the data, as is the case with many inside hackers, he can make subtle changes that could go undetected for a long time and have disastrous effects.

Once a system has been compromised, all the information that flows through that system can also be compromised. This could be as simple as making copies of the information for the hacker, or it could be as sinister as changing the information as it flows through the system.

> Hackers broke into USA Today's Web site and replaced legitimate news stories with phony articles, lampooning newsmakers and religions but also claiming Israel was under missile attack. The bogus pages were viewable to USAToday.com readers for about 15 minutes before being discovered and taken offline, said company spokesman Steve Anderson. The entire site was shut down for three hours to upgrade security, he said, adding that the intruders appeared to have penetrated the Web server computers from outside company firewalls. There was no overt claim of responsibility, but at the end of one fake story the intruder indicated he or she planned to attend the H2K2 hacker convention in New York City .[68]

Destroying Information

The destruction of information denies everyone the use of the information. Usually, destroying information makes it unavailable only temporarily, until it can be restored. The impact of this type of attack is measured in downtime and man-hours to recover the information. A well-designed backup and recovery program can minimize the impact.

Some attacks which destroy information are more thorough than others. Information exists online, off-line and near-line. Attackers have been able to access near-line storage devices, such as automated tape silos, and delete the information which was stored on them. There have even been cases where off-line media has been successfully requested to be mounted by the attacker and then destroyed.

---

[68]   Krane, Jim, "Hackers Put Phony News Items on USA Today's Website," *Associated Press*, 13 July 2002, Reprinted with permission of The Associated Press.

Some attackers destroy information and then attempt to extort the company to hire them to recover the information. However, most companies are unwilling to pay for information that is acquired through illegal methods. Blackmailing the company from which the information was stolen is rarely successful, even when the blackmail is in the form of returning to the company as a consultant.

Other attacks are just malicious destruction.

Washington Leung, a former employee in the Human Resources department at Marsh Inc., an insurance company located in Manhattan, was sentenced to 18 months in prison for illegally accessing a protected computer without authorization and deleting approximately 950 files relating to employee compensation.

His sentence was based on his abuse of the trust that Marsh Inc. placed in him by "giving him access to passwords other employees were not privy to." He used a password belonging to another employee at Marsh to obtain unauthorized access to Marsh's computer database and deleted approximately 800 files relating to the compensation of managing directors at Marsh and approximately 150 files relating to compensation of other Marsh employees.

Leung was also ordered to pay $91,814.68 in restitution to Marsh Inc.[69]

Content-related Offenses

The dissemination, especially via the Internet, of pornography (in particular child pornography), racist statements, and information inciting violence raises the question as to what extent these acts could be confronted with the help of criminal law. The laws support the view that what is illegal off-line should also be illegal online. The author or the content provider may be liable under criminal law.

Hate Crimes

In most countries, hate speech does not receive the same constitutional protection as it does in the United States. In Germany, for example, it is illegal to promote Nazi ideology. In

---

[69]   "U.S. Sentences Computer Operator for Breaking into Ex-Employer's Database," *U.S. Department of Justice Press Release*, 27 March 2002.

many European countries, it is illegal to deny the reality of the Holocaust. Authorities in Denmark, France, Britain, Germany, and Canada have brought charges for crimes involving hate speech on the Internet.

While national borders have little meaning in cyberspace, Internet users who export material that is illegal in some foreign countries may be subject to prosecution under certain circumstances. An American citizen who posts material on the Internet that is illegal in a foreign country could be prosecuted if he subjected himself to the jurisdiction of that country or of another country whose extradition laws would allow for his arrest and deportation. However, under American law, the United States will not extradite a person for engaging in a constitutionally protected activity even if that activity violates a criminal law elsewhere.

> An obscenity-tinged e-mail message was received by 107 minority and international students at Manchester College in Indiana, warning them that their "days are numbered." About 700 Asian students at Indiana University in Bloomington the previous year received several e-mail messages laced with racial slurs. The number of computer-related incidents on campuses seems to be growing, but with computers becoming more prevalent in higher education, experts say, e-mail has become the tool of choice for racist activity. A former University of California-Irvine student was convicted of violating the civil rights of a group of Asian students when he sent them e-mail saying he would "kill every one of you." Police investigated but did not pursue the Manchester case because no specific threats were made. However, college president Parker Marden says he will keep searching for the culprit, thought to be a student. [70]

Harassment

Harassment is a methodical, deliberate, and persistent communication that disturbs the recipient. The communications are often constant, filled with disturbing and inappropriate content, and do not cease. There is a clear difference between the annoyance of unsolicited e-mail, instant messages, and other online communications and the consistent, personal nature of harassment.

People often don't take reports of online harassment seriously. There's a misconception that online harassment is easily ignored because it happens online. Harassment online is just as illegal as harassment off-line, and it's just as frightening. At times the harassment turns violent.

---

[70] "Police Say Hate E-Mail Didn't Break Any Laws. It Attacked Groups, Not Individuals." *The Indianapolis Star/News*, 14 March 1998.

Carl Edward Johnson, of Saskatchewan, Canada, was convicted on four felony counts of sending threatening e-mail messages via the Internet to federal judges and others. The first three charges were based on death threats posted to the Internet naming two federal judges based in Tacoma and Seattle. The fourth charge was based on an e-mail threat sent directly to Microsoft Chairman Bill Gates.

The conviction and sentence are the culmination of a two-year investigation by U.S. Treasury agents into anonymous threats posted on the Internet and a scheme to assassinate government officials known as "Assassination Politics."

The government was able to identify Johnson as the author of the threatening messages and an Internet assassination web page through a variety of technical means. In the case of the Ninth Circuit judges death threat, Treasury agents were able to link the unique characteristics of an encrypted digital signature on the threatening message to encryption "keys" found on Johnson's computer.[71]

Cyber-stalking

The rapid growth of the Internet and other telecommunications technologies are promoting advances in virtually every aspect of society and every corner of the globe. Most of these advances represent positive changes in our society. Unfortunately, many of the attributes of this technology — low cost, ease of use, and anonymous nature, among others — make it an attractive medium for fraudulent scams, child sexual exploitation, and, increasingly, a new concern known as "cyber-stalking." By the use of new technology and equipment, which cannot be policed by traditional methods, cyber-stalking has replaced traditional methods of stalking and harassment. In addition, cyber-stalking has led to offline incidents of violent crime.

There are incidents where it is the individual himself who, having become obsessed, turns violent and there are incidents where the individual has convinced others to perform the violent acts for him.

She was a young, attractive, friendly single clerk. He was an obsessive network administrator with access to the entire company's

[71] "Man Convicted of Threatening Federal Judges by Internet E-mail," *U.S. Department of Justice Press Release*, 21 April 1999.

computer systems. She turned him down; he wouldn't take no for an answer.

The side comments, e-mails and creepy looks never stopped. Eventually, he was fired, and that's when the trouble really started.

Armed with full knowledge of the company's network, he had little trouble breaking into its computer system from the outside. He assumed several identities and started firing off embarrassing e-mails about her around the firm. He took secret documents and, posing as other company employees, made veiled threats to release the secrets to the public. Meanwhile, he continued to try to get a rise out of the clerk. At one point, he "gave" her a $130,000-a-year raise.

Fortunately, he did most of his dirty work sitting behind a computer at his new employer — and with one e-mail, he made a mistake.

"He sent it from his work account rather than an assumed account," said Eric Friedberg, a former prosecutor for the U.S. attorney's office in New York. Armed with that single e-mail, Friedberg went to the suspect's new employer and got the firm's cooperation. Computer logs there provided plenty of evidence, and the suspect has now been indicted.

When a firm's internal IT people are involved in harassment, it creates a dangerous combination of skills and access, one Friedberg says he's seen repeatedly — in large part because many firms give little thought to the tremendous access computer experts have to company information. [72]

Privacy Offenses

The right to privacy varies widely across the globe. However, there is a growing number of countries which are trying to protect their citizens' right to privacy. Various countries have introduced criminal law addressing illegal collection, storage, modification, disclosure, or dissemination of personal data. The fundamental rights to privacy and data protection are included in the Charter of Fundamental Rights of the European Union. The European Union has adopted two directives that approximate the national laws on the protection of privacy with regard to the processing of personal data.

---

[72] Sullivan, Bob, "Cyber-stalking Rears Its Head in the Workplace," *ZDNet Australia* (www.zdnet.com.au), 1 May 2001.

In the U.S., only specific types of information are given protection; among these are medical and financial records. U.S. citizens, except for minors under the age of fourteen, do not have a specific right to privacy. However, other rights have created a foundation on which certain privacy precedents have been built. The terrorist acts of September 11, 2001, have shifted the government's basic views on the right of privacy, as it has become more concerned about secret organizations and the possible threat which they pose.

Child Privacy

Lots of money is spent to gather information about children. Just look at the "clubs" and the "return this form to get..." that have toys as the enticement and are available via child-oriented products. Marketers often use youthful zeal to create a demand for a product. Typical online questionnaires are much more detailed than the traditional cereal-box promotion.

Kids do not understand the issues of how their personal information may be used. Children will unknowingly or innocently give up information about themselves which can be used and sold to others.

The problem of gathering information from kids is worse when there is no parental involvement needed to supply the response. Pre-addressed, postage-paid response cards may request that the child only enter his/her name, address, and age, and drop it in a mailbox. The Internet has made this even simpler.

An FTC study of 1400 randomly selected websites found that 85% collect some form of personal information from consumers. But only 14% offered any notice about how the information is used and fewer than 2% included a so-called comprehensive privacy policy. [73]

A number of websites in the FTC report solicited information from children without telling them to ask for permission before providing the information. One such site oriented toward children asked them to give their name, address, e-mail address, age, and whether they have received gifts of stocks, cash savings bonds, or certificates of deposit.

Names, addresses, age gender, family income, and sometimes even specific information such as what kind of ice cream a child likes is available to anyone willing to pay.

> A Los Angeles reporter using the name of Richard Allen Davis, convicted killer of 12-year-old Polly Klaas, was able to buy a list with detailed information about thousands of children. The reporter cribbed Davis' name, along with a phony business name and phone number, sent in a $277 fee, and received a 5,500-name list of kids in the L.A. area. There was no screening process to prevent the information from being sent to a child molester, convicted felon, or pornographer.

[74]   "Online Privacy: A Report to Congress," *Federal Trade Commission*, June 1998.

"Most parents have no idea how much information is collected and sold about their children," says Marc Klaas, Polly's father. [74]

---

[74] "Largest Database Marketing Firm Sends Phone Numbers, Addresses of 5,000 Families with Kids to TV Reporter Using Name of Child Killer," *Business Wire*, 13 May 1996.

## CHAPTER 16

Legal Prosecution

Asecurity incident has many legal considerations. The organization's legal department should be notified early in the process so that it can provide input regarding the legal ramifications of various steps taken to protect information resources. The legal department can also provide input into the types of documentation that may be required for future legal action.

Legal recourse can be either criminal or civil. In a criminal prosecution, the value of the time and effort that it takes to restore the system to its initial condition may be a consideration as part of the penalty phase to determine restitution. In a civil case, you will have to itemize damages to be able to recover those damages.

Prosecution of a particular abuse may serve as a deterrent to future abuse. Deterrence may be particularly warranted if the method being used is already generally known by the public. The true value of deterrence is questionable. Many perpetrators act with irrational motives. Few are actually concerned with the chances of being caught, prosecuted, and incarcerated.

Prosecution is very important in deterring hacking. Not only will the hacker be aware that other hackers have been prosecuted for the same activities in which he was planning to participate, but each case helps define the scope of the laws and makes subsequent cases that much easier to prosecute.

Many companies are wary of legal prosecution. They fear the costs in time and personnel that will be involved and the public perception. These fears are not unfounded, but they may be overstated. To help understand the real scope of these fears, the MIS managers and computer security management should contact their company's legal office, if they have one, the local prosecutor's office, or the local law enforcement investigation bureau. Be sure to ask if there is a computer or hi-tech unit.

Getting to know these people before you need them is very useful. You will better understand their processes and procedures and when and how to get them involved. This will help you understand what the impact of prosecution will be on your company.

Computer Crime

Early on, computer crimes were prosecuted under a number of statutes, generally dealing with interstate communications, wire fraud, and attacks against government property. However, until very recently there has been very little legislation which was specific to computer crimes. Today, computers and the Internet have become the focus of much concern and publicity. Laws are often passed in response to a specific event. These laws are written quickly and address only the specifics of the recent event. They are commands written with a view of today, without addressing larger issues or seeing where technology is going. This leads to laws that rapidly become obsolete as technology changes.

Most countries have written, or are in the process of writing, computer crime laws. The focus of these laws varies. Some are concerned with the disruption of government operations, others are concerned with the privacy of the citizens, and a few are concerned with protecting the rights of the owners of the information. Governments must ensure that the laws are kept up to date.

Gaps in national criminal laws mean that cyber-crime is unpunished in many countries worldwide, a survey has revealed.

According to a report backed by the World Information Technology and Services Alliances (WITSA) — a worldwide consortium of 41 IT industry associations — only nine of the 52 countries analyzed in the report have extended their criminal laws into cyberspace to cover most types of cyber-crimes.

The report said the lack of updated laws means that cyber-criminals around the world believe they will not be punished for their crimes. It said the laws of most countries do not clearly prohibit cyber-crimes, and existing laws against physical acts of trespass or breaking and entering often do not cover their "virtual" counterparts.

Web pages such as the e-commerce sites recently hit by widespread distributed denial of service attacks are not covered by outdated laws as protected forms of property. "New kinds of crimes can fall between the cracks," the report warns.

Thirty-three of the countries surveyed have not yet updated their laws to address any type of cyber-crime.[75]

---

[75]   Ticehurst, Jo, "Cybercriminals are Getting Away With It," *Computing*, 8 December 2000.

U.S. Federal Statutes

Federal statutes address crimes against federal institutions, interstate crimes, and acts against the security of the country, such as terrorism. Due to the nature of computer networks, interstate commerce and federal telecommunications laws are often used to prosecute hackers. Early on, laws written for telephone fraud were applied to computer crime; more recently, computer-specific crime laws have been enacted, as well as new sentencing guidelines for computer criminals. The following are a sample of some of the laws which are used in prosecuting computer crimes:

- **Computer Fraud and Abuse Act of 1984**

  This is the first federal computer crime statute adopted in 1984 and amended in 1986 and 1994. It makes it a crime to knowingly access a federal interest computer without authorization to obtain certain defense, foreign relations, financial information, or atomic secrets. It is also a criminal offense to use a computer to commit fraud, to "trespass" on a computer, and to traffic in unauthorized passwords.

- **Electronic Communications Privacy Act of 1986**

  This updated the Federal Wiretap Act to apply to the illegal interception of electronic (i.e., computer) communications or the intentional, unauthorized access of electronically stored data.

- **U.S. Communications Assistance for Law Enforcement Act of 1994**

  This law amended the Electronic Communications Privacy Act and requires all communications carriers to make wiretaps possible.

- **Economic and Protection of Proprietary Information Act of 1996**

  This law extends the definition of property to include proprietary economic information so that the theft of this information can be considered industrial or corporate espionage.

- **Health Insurance Portability and Accountability Act of 1996**

  HIPAA requires that all healthcare organizations that transfer records and information electronically must follow certain standards for ensuring that the records remain secure and confidential.

- **National Information Infrastructure Protection Act of 1996**

  This law amends the Computer Fraud and Abuse Act to provide more protection to computerized information and systems by defining new computer crimes and by extending protection to computer systems used in foreign or interstate commerce or communications.

- **The Grahm-Leach-Bliley Act of 1999**

  This law limits the instances when a financial institution may disclose nonpublic personal information of a consumer to nonaffiliated third parties. It requires a financial institution to disclose its privacy polices and practices with respect to information shared with affiliates and nonaffiliated third parties.

State Computer Crime Laws

Each state has different laws and procedures that pertain to the investigation and prosecution of computer crimes. By the mid-1990s, nearly every state had enacted a computer crime statute. State computer crime laws are widely varied. Some are very narrowly drafted, while others are quite broad. The language of the law is often open to interpretation. It is difficult to adequately define the scope of the law so that it covers the behavior that it intends to control, but not so broadly as to be applied to unrelated activities. In addition to this, lawmakers are not computer experts, yet they are tasked with creating laws that address technologies that they do not fully understand and which require the use of a technical language which is not understood. This often creates laws that are not well-constructed. Many states claim jurisdiction on any electronic transaction that crosses its border. Contact your local law enforcement department or district attorney's office for guidance.

The Texas Computer Crimes Act, which is not substantially different from that of any other state, defines that "a person commits an offense if the person knowingly accesses a computer system without the effective consent of the owner." The offense is a felony if the person's intent is to obtain a benefit from the action. A computer system is defined by statute as a "data processing device that functions by the manipulation of electronic or magnetic impulses" and access is "make use of." By this definition looking at someone's digital watch without permission could be a felony. [76]

Law Enforcement Agencies

Internet-related crime, like any other crime, should be reported to appropriate law enforcement investigative authorities at the local, state, federal, or international levels, depending on the scope of the crime. Certain law enforcement agencies focus on particular kinds of crime. Citizens who are aware of federal crimes should report them to local offices of federal law enforcement.

---

[76]   "Computer Crime — Defined," *$USR/News,* May 1994.

Law enforcement authorities are tasked with the collection of physical evidence, interviewing witnesses, and preparing reports that are presented to prosecutors, magistrates, judges, and juries. In effect, this means that it serves their purposes to conduct themselves as professionally as possible. In their case preparation, interviews are conducted by officers, prosecutors, and, at times, magistrates, that are subsequently compiled into reports that eventually find their way into the hands of litigating attorneys and the courts.

Computer forensics is a relative new field which requires different skills and has different challenges from traditional forensics. In many jurisdictions, there is a shortage of trained computer forensics experts and the forensics labs, which analyze the information, often have a significant backlog of work, lengthening the investigation process.

Military Law Enforcement Agencies

Military law enforcement agencies have the longest history of involvement with computer crime. They have been addressing the issues of attacks against military (.mil) computer systems and networks from the very beginning of the ARPAnet. Generally, they focus on investigating attacks which either originate from or target military computer systems, involve military personnel, or encompass confidential military information.

Each branch of the military has a criminal investigation and law enforcement organization which will lead the investigation. The Army Criminal Investigative Division, CID, and the Air Force Office of Special Investigations, OSI, are made up predominantly of military members, whereas the Naval Criminal Investigative Service, NCIS, and the Department of Defense Information Systems Agency, DISA, are not. All of the branches have a counterintelligence mission which is coordinated with the criminal investigation activities.

U.S. Federal Law Enforcement

Some federal law enforcement agencies that investigate domestic crime on the Internet include: the Federal Bureau of Investigation (FBI), the United States Secret Service, the United States Customs Service, the United States Postal Inspection Service, and the Bureau of Alcohol, Tobacco, and Firearms (ATF). Each law enforcement agency has a headquarters in Washington, D.C., and regional offices. In general, federal crime may be reported to the local office of an appropriate law enforcement agency. Federal law enforcement officers may be called in to track a hacker if the hacker gains unauthorized access to a Federal Government computer or to a computer system protected by federal law. Other federal agencies with investigative authority are the Federal Trade Commission and the U.S. Securities and Exchange Commission.

- The **Federal Bureau of Investigation,** FBI, generally investigates violations of federal criminal law. The FBI uses a number of federal statutes to investigate computer crimes. The FBI is sensitive to the victim's concerns about public exposure, so any decision to investigate is jointly made between the FBI and the United States Attorney and takes the victim's needs into account. The focus is on national matters, such as terrorism, espionage, attacks on the nation's critical infrastructures (i.e., communications, banking systems, and transportation systems), interstate crimes (e.g., organized crime, drug trafficking, bank fraud, environmental crimes, telemarketing fraud, kidnapping, sexual exploitation of children, and consumer product tampering), crimes against federal organizations (e.g., bank robbery, postal fraud, and threats against federal officials), and crimes committed on Indian reservations.

Investigations are conducted within the Attorney General's Guidelines. The Guidelines afford centralized direction, which allows for greater uniformity and control of national and international law enforcement efforts. These investigations provide evidence for the Department of Justice, which determines the viability of prosecuting the case.

• The **U.S. Secret Service** investigates threats against the President and Vice President, and crimes associated with financial institutions (e.g., bank fraud, telecommunication and computer crimes, securities fraud, and electronic funds transfer fraud), counterfeiting, and other currency fraud.

Computers are being used extensively in financial crimes, not only as an instrument of the crime, but to "hack" into databases to retrieve account information; store account information; clone microchips for cellular telephones; and scan corporate checks, bonds, and negotiable instruments that are later counterfeited using desktop publishing methods.

State and Local Law Enforcement

Many state and local entities also investigate and prosecute computer-related crimes under the direction of the state's attorney general's office. The amount of resources put into the computer crime investigations varies from state to state. Resources are usually allocated in response to a need, so until there are a number of computer crimes needing investigation, the state may not be willing to fund the organization.

Local law enforcement is also constrained by its jurisdiction. Many computer crimes occur over the Internet and rapidly go beyond the boundaries of local law enforcement.

To report a crime, or to seek assistance relating to the investigation or prosecution of a computer crime, contact the law enforcement department within the county, state, or other jurisdiction where the criminal activity is occurring.

RCMP

The Royal Canadian Mounted Police is responsible for the investigation of all computer crime offenses within its jurisdiction. It also investigates such crimes where the government of

Canada is the victim, regardless of primary jurisdiction. In addition, the RCMP can investigate offenses involving organized crime or offenses related to the national interests of Canada.

There are RCMP Commercial Crime Sections is every major city in Canada. Each one of these units has at least one investigator who has received specialized training in the investigation of computer crimes. These investigators are supported by the RCMP High Tech Crime Forensics Unit (HTCFU) located at RCMP Headquarters in Ottawa. HTCFU can provide technical guidance and expertise to all Canadian police departments and federal government agencies in relation to computer and telecommunication crime investigation.

## CHAPTER 17

Obstacles to Prosecution

There are many obstacles to the successful prosecution of computer crimes. Cyber-crimes bring with them an environment and a set of circumstances which often make the prosecuting of the crimes more difficult. Crimes where computers are the targets are unlike traditional types of crimes. Technology has made it more difficult to answer the questions of who, what, where, when, and how. Therefore, in an electronic or digital environment, evidence is now collected and handled differently from how it was in the past.

It is common that many systems operators do not share information when they are victimized by hackers. They don't contact law enforcement officers when their computer systems are invaded, preferring instead to fix the damage and take action to keep hackers from gaining access again — with as little public attention as possible.

Identifying the Hacker

One of the primary goals of any investigation is to identify the person or persons who committed the criminal acts. The Internet adds levels of complexity to the process of establishing their identity. Because of the makeup of the Internet, it is sometimes difficult for law enforcement officers to discover the identity of a hacker. There are a variety of anonymous applications which, by their nature, obscure the identity of the user, and there are many tools which can be used by a hacker to intentionally hide or alter his or her identity. Tracking a hacker may call for a combination of Internet research skills, subpoenas, court orders, search warrants, electronic surveillance, and traditional investigative techniques.

A hacker might hide or "spoof" his Internet Protocol (IP) address or might intentionally bounce his communications through many intermediate computers scattered throughout the world before arriving at a target computer. The investigator must then identify all of the bounce points to find the location of the hacker, but usually can trace the hacker back only one bounce point at a time. Subpoenas and court orders to each bounce point may be necessary to identify the hacker.

U.S. government contractor Exigent Software Technology has admitted that unidentified hackers broke into a restricted military computer system and stole the source codes controlling satellite and missile guidance systems. Hackers got away with two thirds of the code when the target computer at the Naval Research Lab in Washington was attacked on Christmas Eve. The military detected the break-in three days later.

The theft was made public when Swedish police searched the servers of Internet service provider Carbonide on suspicion that hackers used the company's Freebox Web e-mail service to distribute the code to others. The hacker used the name "Leeif," which was a stolen account, on the system. Carbonide was able to trace the attack on its network to a server at the University of Kaiserslautern in Germany. The German federal office for criminal affairs said that an investigation is underway.[77]

Network Tracking

A computer on a network has a number of addresses. Originally, these addresses were assigned to specific machines and identified the machine. Today, that is not so. The unprecedented growth of the Internet has made the Internet numbering scheme inadequate to handle the number of users from the number of access providers. To help allow the numbering scheme to go further, and to help provide mobile computer, reusable numbering methods have been deployed.

IP addresses are issued by various organizations under the direction of the Internet Assigned Numbers Authority, IANA. DHCP became the normal method for setting addresses as Internet Service Providers were requesting and trying to manage addresses for an explosively growing market. An ISP could have one IP address for each modem and ten times as many customers. IP addresses are no longer a identifier of a system; rather, they are an identification of the location where a system gains Internet access. A machine may have a specific address for only one session, and not necessarily even that, because a machine can release an address and renegotiate for another.

Network Address Translation, NAT, is a process which allows multiple computers to share a single, or group of, IPs. It allows a company or a home network to connect multiple computers to the Internet through a service which provides only a single network address. This can provide security, since the systems do not provide their address to external networks. NAT is built into most router and firewall devices and is used extensively throughout the Internet.

---

[77]   White, Aoife, "Hackers Steal Military Source Code," *vnunet.com*, 15 March 2001.

Every network connection is to have a unique machine address. This machine address is usually part of the network interface card, and is suppose to be unique, but it is required to be unique only on a physical network. These original machine addresses were issued to the manufactures of network interfaces. However, with the explosive growth of networks, machine addresses have become assignable and configurable so that a machine can easily change its machine address.

Address spoofing is a common hacking technique whereby the source address in a packet is changed so that the actual address is not available to the system which is being attacked. This can be a nonexistent address, or an address which will lead the investigation down the wrong path.

Inadequate Logs

Computer systems of interest to hackers usually keep track of all authorized and unauthorized access attempts. These computer logs provide records which are useful and often critical clues that can be used as the starting point to trace the route taken from computer to computer through the Internet, to discover the source of the attack. However, some victims don't keep logs or don't keep them long enough so that, when a hacker's activities are discovered, the logs are no longer available. Some ISPs don't keep records, or don't keep them long enough to be of help to law enforcement officers. A victim who has no record of the IP address of the computer from which unauthorized access was gained limits the ability to track the attack and may be unable to identify the hacker.

Identifying an Individual

Determining the specific individual or individuals who are responsible can be a very difficult task. Often it will be possible to determine what was done, how it was done, when it was done, and from where it was done, but not who did it. The address, which is the usual identity found in an investigation, belongs to a machine, not an individual. The search will lead to the point where the attacker accesses the Internet, possibly the machine. You will probably be able to tell what account was used, even those accounts on other systems that were used during the attack. However, the information from the computer itself will rarely be able to prove who the person was who compromised the system. Without stronger authentication methods, there is no proof that this person was the user on the system. It generally takes physical evidence to prove that a specific person was the hacker. It could be his possession of the information that was taken or his bragging of his conquest that is the conclusive evidence.

In cases when the guilty party is found, it is important to prosecute the hacker as a deterrent to this hacker, as well as to others.

Jurisdiction

Information travels over networks which cross geopolitical boundaries, each of which may have its own regulations on information security. A single incident may cross many jurisdictions and require the involvement of different law enforcement agencies. These agencies may all have different requirements and procedures for getting involved with a security incident and may lead to issues of positioning on who is in charge of the investigation.

A computer crime may violate a number of laws at both the federal and local levels that could have either civil or criminal remedies. This will create a variety of options when it comes to prosecuting the attacker. However, it may also cause a great deal of confusion about the direction to take during the investigation. This issue is compounded by the international nature of the Internet.

A user may use a computer which is remote — at another location — accessing data from yet another location. The data, in the process of being sent over a network, could cross many boundaries on its way to a server which, in turn, could utilize multiple back-end servers which could be located elsewhere. So often the question of jurisdiction is a question of where the transaction takes place. Every transaction can cross several different boundaries and many different organizations. Even in the simplest of jurisdiction issues — when there are multiple computers involved in a transaction, where the transaction took place — is still debated, case by case.

With the explosive growth of the Internet worldwide, computer crimes are increasingly prone to have international dimensions. Some of the challenges faced by law enforcement on the international front include: harmonization of countries' criminal laws, locating and identifying perpetrators across borders, and securing electronic evidence of their crimes so that they may be brought to justice. Complex jurisdictional issues arise at each step.

> A Paris Superior Court found Yahoo liable under French law for permitting the auction of Nazi memorabilia, and ordered the service to prevent any further display of Nazi memorabilia or "any other site or service which constitute an apology of Nazism or which contest the Nazi crimes" to French citizens. Yahoo then sought a declaratory judgment in a California federal court that the French court orders were unenforceable. On November 7, Judge Jeremy Fogel ruled that the first amendment to the U.S. Constitution precludes enforcement of the French court orders.[78]

---

[78]   "Yahoo v. LICRA," *U.S. District Court, Northern District of California, San Jose*, case C-0021275, 7 November 2001.

International Issues

Due to worldwide networking, computer attacks can come from anywhere in the world. This can severely complicate the process of prosecution. In the process of tracing an attack, it may travel through many foreign countries, not all of which consider hacking a crime. Treaties, conventions, and agreements are in place with some countries, which simplifies the ability to get help and find the correct contacts.

Internet globalization has opened doors to criminal activities which are unprecedented, even in the most technologically developed countries. Furthermore, high-speed telecommunications make it easier for organized criminal groups to engage in multiple activities at the same time, spreading thin the attempt by law enforcement to fight crime. Computer-related fraud has become an international security threat, but the real toll will come when such financial damage threatens the economies of developing countries. It is widely presumed that financial fraud will continue to rise, thus giving the need for security a new sense of urgency.

The global Internet has opened the door to attacks from around the world. The FBI reports that some 122 countries around the world have the infrastructure to support hacker attacks on U.S. networks. International laws and treaties make it difficult to locate and prosecute these attacks that cross borders. Many countries still do not have criminal statutes concerning hacking.

When adjudicating cases involving foreign nationals, the courts must balance several factors. On a case-by-case basis, the courts must consider the procedural and substantive policies of other countries whose interests are affected by the court's assertion of jurisdiction. Keeping these policies in mind, the court must then consider the reasonableness of assertion of jurisdiction examined in the light of the interest of the federal government in its foreign relation policies. When extending jurisdiction into the international field, great care and reserve must be exercised. Because of these sovereignty concerns, there is a higher jurisdictional barrier when litigating against a foreign national.

Extradition

The ability to bring a computer criminal to justice is often as difficult as finding the hacker in the first place. Many jurisdictions are involved and extradition from one jurisdiction to another can be difficult, especially across national boundaries, since extradition is based on treaties between countries. This requires a certain level of cooperation between countries and their law enforcement organizations. In addition, the computer crime laws vary dramatically between countries; what is criminal in one country may not be elsewhere.

Authorities in Argentina arrested Julio Cesar Ardita, better known as "El Griton," in the computer underground. He was accused of systematic and major unauthorized intrusions into systems at a number of major U.S. universities, the U.S. Navy, NASA, and also computer systems in Brazil, Chile, Korea, Mexico, and Taiwan. Government officials in Argentina seized his computer and modem in January. Despite close cooperation between authorities in Argentina and the U.S., the man was released without charge because Argentina has no law criminalizing unauthorized intrusion in computer systems. In addition, because of the requirement for "dual criminality" in international law, it was not possible for Argentinian authorities to extradite Ardita to the United States (the requirement states that an action must be defined as criminal in both countries before a person can be extradited).[79]

Evidence

Clues to the identity of a hacker often exist in cyberspace and in the real world if the investigator knows where to look. Finding these clues is often difficult. They may be scattered across the Internet. Hackers often attempt to cover their tracks, making it more difficult to find evidence.

In cyberspace, evidence is often fleeting. The records of online events, which are important in solving a crime, are often not retained long enough to be available when someone finally realizes that the information is needed. The information which is maintained often has limited value as evidence.

The hackers that brought down UK Internet Service Provider Cloud Nine with a distributed-denial-of-service attack are almost certain to avoid prosecution. The attackers managed to cover their tracks by deleting data that could have been used to trace them, making it unlikely that they will be found.

The hackers managed to delete the logs that would have recorded exactly what happened during the attacks. Without that information, it's impossible to show that someone carried out a particular act and caused specific damage.[80]

---

[79]   "Argentine Computer Hacker Agrees to Waive Extradition and Returns to Plead Guilty to Felony Charges in Boston," *U.S. Department of Justice Press Release,* 19 May 1998.
[80]   "UK Web Host Downed by DDoS Attack," *The Register,* 30 January 2002.

Records Collection

Any information that is collected under normal operations or in accordance with written policy and procedures can be used as evidence. Evidence is often contained on backups and system and security logs. It is important that a written log detailing when and by whom backups are taken is kept. You may be able to collect information that the police cannot. You may, in compliance with policy, capture keystroke information which is admissible as evidence, but a law officer may not be able to tell you to collect this information due to Fourth Amendment (due process) issues. This is why it is important to consult an attorney and law officers to determine when to bring law officers into a security incident.

Records as Evidence

Electronic records are, for the most part, acceptable and on a par with their paper counterparts. Federal, state, and local laws and regulations specifically allow for the use of records stored electronically. State and Federal rules of evidence and civil procedure allow "non-original" Records to be admitted into evidence as if they were originals. In fact, recent passage of the Electronic Signatures in National and Global E-Commerce Act at the Federal level and the Uniform Electronic Transactions Act in various states makes clear that e-records are here to stay and cannot be denied their legal legitimacy.

For any business record to be admissible hearsay, it has to pass the Business Records Exemption. This requires that records be created in the ordinary course of business documenting an activity that is usually memorialized in a record, at about the same time that the event, documented in the record, took place.

Collection of Evidence

You should make it a practice to sufficiently identify and secure your backups. This will not only help in the prosecution, but it will also increase your confidence that when you recover from your backup, it is the correct one and has not been tampered with. Some states have passed laws providing for the protection of proprietary information from being revealed in open court.

When you are collecting evidence during and after an attack, you need to date and sign all printouts and keep a detailed log describing where, when, and how the information was found. Generally, online evidence by itself will not be sufficient to prosecute. However, it will be sufficient to get a search warrant which may uncover other evidence.

In contrast, corporations must be careful of the way in which they interview suspected wrongdoers. If corporate officials conduct interviews of employees under threatening or coercive conditions, it is possible these interviews may not be valuable to a future legal action. Additionally, many jurisdictions have whistle-blower statutes which protect the informing employee from reprisals from his or her employer for providing information to authorities. Forceful interviews may also be construed as witness tampering, thereby constituting a criminal act on the part of the interviewers. It's a good idea to consult with your company's legal and human resources departments before interviewing an employee about suspected unlawful behavior.

Chain of Custody

Central to evidentiary trustworthiness and credibility is that the record can be accounted for during its life — a record sometimes referred to as the Chain of Custody. Records that are out of the control (and, practically speaking, incapable of being altered) of the person with an interest in changing its content are less likely to be intentionally altered. Therefore, records have greater potential evidentiary benefit because they are less likely to be successfully attacked as fabricated. Simply put, a record that could be changed at any time, by any person, for any reason, is easier to attack as lacking credibility than a record that is stored at about the time the underlying transaction took place and is retained on a medium designed to minimize intentional or accidental alteration.

In one case, the Court considered excluding electronic records because the testimony "demonstrated a weakness in the security measures" taken by a bank to control access to computer terminals. There is a need to have security procedures in place for all records, including those stored on WORM. However, the fact that records are stored on a medium that promotes record security tends to decrease the likelihood of an attack to record integrity based upon lax record control.

Trustworthiness of Evidence

It goes without saying that all companies that retain records want to be able to use them for whatever purpose may be needed in the future. That should not be an issue for most business uses.

To the extent a record is not capable of being altered after it is stored (or alteration is very difficult, as is the case with WORM), that tends to provide confidence that the record will be trustworthy when accessed in the future. However, records lacking trustworthiness may be an issue when used in any formal proceeding such as an audit, investigation, or lawsuit. While an attack on record trustworthiness will not occur in every case, there is a need to maximize the likelihood that records are acceptable and usable for whatever purpose, whenever they are needed. If companies go through the trouble of methodically retaining records, they should be confident in their ability to use them to protect or support the company's business activities and legal positions.

Data Reduction

The amount of information collected by information systems, especially during an attack, is often overwhelming. Information is logged by computer systems, applications, network devices, and security systems. Most of these systems log information at a very detailed level. A simple connection to a system may generate dozens of log entries in a number of different logs.

Some of these details may be needed to illustrate exactly how a vulnerability was compromised, but the log information will have to be reduced to be able to show the larger picture of what happened during the attack.

To create a complete picture, it is usually necessary to compare and correlate information from a number of sources. It is likely that the information from these sources may have discrepancies in the way that it identifies individual or system — inconsistent naming, inconsistent time, etc.

It is likely that someone will have to prepare reports summarizing information extracted from logs and other resources of online information into a form that is understandable to a layman. Most law enforcement officers, lawyers, judges, and jurors are not necessarily going to be very computer-literate, so the evidence will have to be presented in a way that is understandable and explainable. The procedures used to reduce the data will also have to be well-documented to show that the report is accurate and complete.

Presentation of Evidence

During the process of examining various types of computer evidence, the examiner may well have to explain how specific evidentiary items arrived as found in their current condition or status. The examiner will sooner or later find himself explaining a process to an attorney, or even in court.

Cost of Prosecution

Computer crime cases are expensive to prosecute. Technical experts are required to explain the details of the information presented — how it was collected and derived. Often evidence is collected from many network service providers across the country or around the globe. It may be required that people from these companies be brought to court to testify. It may well be that the case goes to trial in a court which is remote to your location. Long-distance cases increase the expense with travel, lodging, and time away from work.

Corporate Concerns

Companies are often reluctant to prosecute the hacker. Corporations fear embarrassment or ridicule. They are concerned about the loss of control of the situation when law enforcement get involved. At times, there are some barriers to communication and understanding between IT professionals and law enforcement. The former realize that there will be more disruption of operations with the collection of evidence and interviews with law enforcement and legal counsel.

Often companies are unsure of how the information gathered during the investigation which is needed for prosecution will be handled. They are concerned about the use of proprietary information in a public trial and whether the stolen information which is recovered can be kept confidential. There are concerns about counter-suits, legal embarrassment, and liability to the company and its officers.

Public Relations

Companies are very concerned with the public's reaction to the publicity of a security incident. There are concerns for sales, stock price, customer retention, and legal actions. Usually these concerns are greater than the reality of the situation.

A security incident can be used by a company to show that it is on top of the situation. It can illustrate that the company is doing everything possible to protect the customer's information, prevent fraud, and reduce computer crime. They can be seen working with law enforcement to bring the perpetrator to justice.

Impact on Operations

All responses to a security incident will impact the operation of the system. Additional backups may have to be made, and personnel will have to assist in the prosecution. Minimally, some personnel will be called as witnesses. It is likely that the prosecution will require the involvement of personnel who will assist in the investigation and trial by identifying the property and who will act as technical advisors. It is best to assign a specific person to be a liaison between the company and the police during the investigation. This will help limit the impact of the investigation on the day-to-day operation of the company. This person can help manage the scheduling of people for meetings with the police and the courts.

Many cases are never prosecuted because the business has evaluated the cost of prosecution including legal costs, operational disruption, and publicity and has decided it is not worth it, especially if the hacker is an employee whom the company can then discipline. However, you may not be able to recover the stolen information if you decide not to prosecute.

Law Enforcement

In the case where legal prosecution is desired or required, there will be extensive interaction with law enforcement. It is also prudent to have the organization's legal department or even outside legal counsel involved. The laws that cover intellectual property and computer crime are quite new and relatively untested. The interpretation of these laws are still being defined, so legal professionals are a necessity.

Management must evaluate and prioritize efforts to identify the individual or individuals who were responsible for the security incident (even though in most cases it is not possible to identify the actual individual) and determine the level and type of punishment to pursue, which may include disciplinary actions or legal remedies, either civil or criminal.

Releasing Proprietary Data

Investigators build their cases by collecting relevant items, by requesting their surrender, by search warrant, by summons, or by court order. However, not all collected items may be incorporated into an investigator's case. These exempted items are known as privileged communications. Privileged communications may be oral, written, or electronic and their unique status is recognized by most jurisdictions. They are generally defined as communications between a lawyer and his/her client, and communications between a member of the clergy and a parishioner. There may be others, but these two are the most universally recognized. If privileged items are found to be part of a case, hearings are held, often resulting in their exclusion from the case.

Requirements to Report

What are your legal responsibilities if your site is aware of the activity and does not take steps to prevent it? Many countries have statutes that allow for a person to be prosecuted for having knowledge of a crime and for withholding this information from authorities. Actually, under the laws of the United States, it is a felony, a major crime, to have knowledge of a criminal act and fail to report it. Title 18 United States Code, Section 4 states that: "Whoever, having knowledge of the actual commission of a felony cognizable by a court of the United States, conceals and does not as soon as possible make known the same to some judge or other person in civil or military authority under the United States, shall be fined under this title or imprisoned not more than three years, or both." Many states and local jurisdictions have similar statutes requiring persons to report crimes to civil and military authorities. With this in mind, timely reporting of computer crimes is probably something most professionals will want to give serious consideration.

Personal Concerns

As a system manager, security manager, or a corporate officer, you face issues of personal risk. More and more corporate officers are being held liable for the failure of their organizations to adequately protect the integrity, confidentiality, and availability of automated information systems. If you are not actively taking steps to protect your data, you are not protecting yourself from lawsuits.

These suits are generally from three sources: violations of the law (criminal charges), violations of due care (stockholder suits), and violations of privacy (employee suits). The risk of all of these can be reduced by appropriate policies and procedures. These policies must include the topics of software piracy, appropriate use of licensed software, disaster plans containing security-based disasters — the greatest cause of data unavailability — and personnel policies concerning appropriate use of corporate computer resources, specifically addressing e-mail and usage monitoring. These policies must be adhered to by the corporation on a consistent and continual basis.

Violations of the Law

In addition to just using the computer as a tool for committing a crime, violations of the law also include very specific computer crimes. The most common of these is software piracy. Many companies, both large and small, are guilty of software piracy. This is generally the possession and use of an unlicensed software and making illegal copies of software. Most software licenses allow for only one backup copy of the software. If you are doing automated backups and appropriate backup retention, it is likely that you have more than one backup copy of the software. You need to have a current, and preferably automated, software inventory for all your systems, PCs in particular.

Violations of Due Care

How much security is required for due care? Ultimately, that is for a court of law to decide. However, there are some things that are certain. Any of the following would be considered a lack of due care: not installing a security patch, not heeding suggestions put forth in general security advisories, or not having a security policy in place.

As in all business matters, business decisions determine how much to spend to ensure that you have taken due care with the assets of the company to reduce the risk of stockholder suits. A company should implement what are considered standards of diligence for its industry.

Violations of Privacy

There are two areas of privacy that are a concern to the information technology organization. The first is the privacy of customer information and the second is the privacy of employee information.

Customer privacy is an issue of a company's having confidential information about its customers. It may have this information because of the type of business it conducts, such as doctors having patients' medical records, or financial institutions having their customers' financial records, or companies that have relationships with their customers to the point that they share confidential information. This will often require a nondisclosure agreement that any information that is considered confidential will not be disclosed to any third party. This requires that the company do all that is prudent to keep the information confidential.

Employee privacy is a sticky situation because it is an employee relations issue. When a person becomes an employee, he or she gives up some rights to the company. However, he or she does retain certain rights. It is best that these rights be spelled out when the employee is hired.

The best defense is a good offense, that is, a good ongoing employee awareness program is important. Your employees must know what privacy they have, what privacy they do not have, and what the benefits are of giving up this privacy. The two biggest areas of concern are privacy of personal files/e-mail and electronic employee monitoring. The amount of privacy will vary depending on the years of service with the company. It is expected that new employees will be monitored more than experienced employees. This is an area where policies and procedures are most important.

Appropriate behavior, ethics, and employee privacy should be covered under current personnel policies. Just because a computer is involved does not mean there should be a difference in the employees' rights and responsibilities. If employees' paper mail is not read, their e-mail should not be any less private.

It is also likely that you have a wealth of information about your employees on your computer systems. The company has a responsibility to its employees to maintain the privacy of this information. Depending on the type of information, the company may have a legal responsibility to keep the information private.

Improving Successful Prosecution

$\mathbf{M}$any cases are never prosecuted because the business has evaluated that the cost of prosecution, including legal costs, operational disruption, and publicity is not worth it, especially if the hacker is an employee that the company can discipline. However, you may not be able to recover the stolen information if you decide not to prosecute.

In the event of a security incident, it is important to be able to prosecute the assailant. Successful prosecution of an attacker depends upon the strength of the evidence. Since most intrusions are remote, the perpetrator is virtually invisible and there is limited physical evidence. The electronic evidence will indicate when accounts are used maliciously, but will not be able to prove beyond a reasonable doubt that the specific individual was the attacker. It is imperative that this connection be firmly established. It must also be shown that the evidence was collected appropriately and handled correctly. The amount of detailed records concerning the intrusion incident that must be presented is overwhelming. Judges and juries do not normally have a technical background, so the evidence must be presented in such a way as to be understood by the jury. The evidence will need to be summarized in a clear and concise manner.

Connecting the attacker to the activities requires that once the hacker is identified, a search warrant must be obtained and his computer equipment (magnetic and other data media) and documents must be seized and examined for evidence. A forensic consultant must analyze the seized materials to establish the connection between them and the evidence collected from your computer system. The prosecution will present its findings from the computer materials seized during the search. Expert testimony is necessary to prove that the alleged hacker is the one who perpetrated the intrusion. An expert's findings, conclusions, and opinions are the underpinning of the entire case.

Enforcing Security Policy

Security policies are critical to the identification of inappropriate behavior and the collection of evidence. Policies should define what is and what is not acceptable on the part of the users of the system and also on the part of administrators of the system. Appropriate use policies and information privacy policies are two of the most common security policies.

Policies addressing the collection and use of information in the case of criminal activities are needed to adequately support the information which will be used in the prosecution of the case. Both procedures and practices have to be a matter of course and regularly performed for the evidence to be considered as part of the normal business process.

Consistent Enforcement

It is necessary to provide consistent enforcement of security policies to be able to prosecute an individual for violating those policies. Intermittent or selective enforcement makes the policy ineffective. These actions are seen not as part of regular on-going business practices; rather, they can be viewed as discriminatory or punitive. Security policies have to be enforced from the very top of the organization all the way down — executives, administrators, etc. — with no exceptions.

Fair Notice

U.S. case law has set the standard that a computer hacker has to have prior knowledge that the his activities are not allowed. When the hacker is not breaking the law, he can contend that he would have no way of knowing that his activities were not acceptable. He will probably be able to produce other environments where the activities are acceptable as a defense. So, it has become a legal imperative that a warning message be posted so that the intruder is aware that he is committing an inappropriate act. These messages should state that the system is the property of the organization, is subject to monitoring, that there is no expectation of privacy, and that unauthorized use is prohibited. The exact wording should be determined by your legal department.

Posting Warning Banners

A requirement for successfully prosecuting those unauthorized users who improperly use a government computer is that the computer must have a warning banner displayed at all access points. That banner must warn both authorized and unauthorized users. The Department of Energy's Office of the General Council has approved the following banner for Federal Government computer systems:

> ### NOTICE TO USERS
>
> This is a Federal computer system and is the property of the United States Government. It is for authorized use only. Users (authorized or unauthorized) have no explicit or implicit expectation of privacy.
>
> Any or all uses of this system and all files on this system may be intercepted, monitored, recorded, copied, audited, inspected, and disclosed to authorized site, Department of Energy, and law enforcement personnel, as well as authorized officials of other agencies, both domestic and foreign. By using this system, the user consents to such interception, monitoring, recording, copying, auditing, inspection, and disclosure at the discretion of authorized site or Department of Energy personnel.
>
> Unauthorized or improper use of this system may result in administrative disciplinary action and civil and criminal penalties. By continuing to use this system you indicate your awareness of and consent to these terms and conditions of use. LOG OFF IMMEDIATELY if you do not agree to the conditions stated in this warning.[81]

Any open service needs to have a warning banner. Removing services from the system improves security and eliminates the need to have a warning banner for that service. The details of implementing warning banners for UNIX machines depend on the particular vendor and service. For machines that do not use these methods for displaying banners, consult the man pages for each service to see if there is a banner mechanism available.

Terminal Access

For many recent systems (Sun, Linux), creating the file `/etc/issue` containing the banner text causes the banner text to be displayed before the console login and before all interactive logins such as `telnet`, `rsh`, and `rlogin`. Linux systems use two such files, `/etc/issue` for console logins and `/etc/issue.net` for telnet logins, so be sure to place the banner text in both.

For other systems and for services that do not respond to the `/etc/issue` file, put the banner text in the file /etc/motd. The contents of this file are displayed by the global `/etc/.login` and the `/etc/profile` files, depending on which shell you start (sh or `csh`), immediately after a successful login. Displaying the `/etc/motd` file immediately after login is also an option for the Secure Shell daemon, `sshd,` and is set in the `/usr/local/etc/sshd_config` file.

---

[81] J-043g: Creating Login Banners, CIAC, 9 May 2000.

FTP Access

Newer versions of the FTP daemon provide for a banner message to be displayed prior to the remote user entering his username and password. This is configured in the /etc/ftpaccess file. The following entry displays the file /etc/ftpbanner to anyone who connects to the ftp daemon:

```
banner /etc/ftpbanner
```

Web Access

Add a JavaScript program to your home page that is executed whenever the page is loaded. No matter which initial banner you use, each page should contain a button in the header or footer labeled "Notice To Users" that takes the user to a page that displays the banner or that runs the JavaScript banner.

The following JavaScript program is run whenever the page containing it is loaded and displays the banner in a dialog box with an OK button. To add it to a web page, copy everything between the two SCRIPT tags, including the tags, into the HEAD of the web page. To make it run whenever the page is loaded, add the onLoad="do_banner()" attribute to the BODY tag. Note that if the users have JavaScript turned off for their browser, this JavaScript banner will not be displayed.

```
<HTML>
<HEAD>
<TITLE>Home Page</TITLE>
<SCRIPT LANGUAGE="JavaScript">
function do_banner() {
var msg = "<HTML><HEAD><TITLE>NOTICE TO USERS</TITLE></HEAD>\n"+
"<BODY BGCOLOR=white><FONT FACE='Times' SIZE=2>\n"+
"<CENTER>NOTICE TO USERS</CENTER>\n"+
"THE HTML FOR THE TEXT OF THE BANNER GOES HERE "+
"<CENTER>\n"+
"<FORM>\n"+
"<INPUT TYPE=button VALUE='OK' onClick=window.close()>\n"+
"</FORM>\n"+
"</CENTER>"+
"</FONT></BODY></HTML>";
win1 = window.open("", "messageWindow",
"toolbar=no,scrollbars=yes,width=600,height=500")
win1.document.write(msg)
}
</SCRIPT>
</HEAD>
<BR>
<!--The following line starts the body of the web page and runs
the JavaScript banner program whenever the page is loaded. -->
```

```
<BODY onLoad="do_banner()">
 .
 . <!---body of the home page--->
 .
</BODY>
</HTML>
```

Marking Information

When information is recovered from an intruder's system, it will be necessary to be able to identify that the information came from your site. Identification of digital information requires that what makes it uniquely identifiable has to be part of the data. In some cases, it can be the data themselves, in other cases it may need to be an imbedded signature.

Visible Signatures

Visible signatures are information which are added to the data, as part of the data, which identifies the data. Including visible contact information in files that are likely targets of hackers will increase the likelihood that you will be contacted if the files are found on other systems. There have been many cases where hackers have been apprehended with password files and other information where the origin of the files could not be determined, so no one was able to notify the owners of the information that they had been compromised or to get their assistance in supplying evidence. The password is the most common file to be taken by hackers so that they can crack the passwords on another machine.

Imbedded Signature

An imbedded signature is created by placing data within the information in a manner in which they are not visible in a casual inspection. It is often used for the protection of creative material, by imbedding copyright notices. There are a number of methods which can be used to imbed signatures, including encryption which can be used to make the information presented unintelligible except to those who have the decryption key.

Digital Signatures

Digitally signing the evidence adds a level of credibility to the evidence when it comes to trial. The digital signature freezes the information at a point in time with a high level of assurance that it has not be altered. This credibility greatly increases the likelihood that the evidence will be admitted in a court of law.

Proper Evidence Preservation

The proper collection, recording, storage, and handling of information which will be used as evidence are crucial to an effective prosecution. Information about the processes used in each of these steps will have to be supplied to show that they were done in a manner which would properly insure the quality of the information. For information to be admissable as evidence, it has to pass a number of tests.

Chain of Custody

Proper handling of evidence is required to prove that the evidence has not been tampered with. In the case of computer-related crimes, physical evidence consists of hardware, software, and, most importantly, storage media. Whether the matter is civil, criminal, or administrative, these items are the mother-lode of physical evidence in supporting legal actions. For this reason, it is imperative that these items remain unaltered and undisturbed until they are delivered to investigators. Facilitating the structure of a case, it is very important that a written chain of custody is maintained relative to those who had access to the evidence. A chain of custody schedule is simply a list identifying all the persons possessing evidence, and the times and dates on which they held the evidence. Some jurisdictions require that all persons are listed who had access to the evidence during the time of its custody. Extreme care must be exercised in completing a chain of custody. More than one piece of critical evidence has been thrown out because of an incomplete chain-of-custody schedule.

Proper Timestamps

Timestamps on logs at the time of the event which show the events of the incident are necessary to provide a strong evidence of the activities which were part of the incident. Timestamps show when files were created and last modified. They are important in showing that the file containing information which is to be used as evidence was collected at the time of the incident and that has not been altered after the incident. Timestamps used in conjunction with digital signatures provide strong support to the proper handling of evidence.

Trusted Time

When it comes to reconstructing what has been happening on a system, time is very important. The ability to construct a consistent linear time line is paramount to understanding the sequence of events that occurred on the system. If the time on the system is inconsistent, it increases the complexity of this analysis.

Therefore, if a hacker changes the time of the system, or timestamps in logs or timestamps of files, he can create a great barrier to the system administrators in their attempts to track down the hacker at work. Inconsistent time can be enough to prevent the prosecution of an incident.

System Clock

System time is critical to the appropriate running and monitoring of a system. All time information is retrieved from the system clock. Altering the system clock will alter the perception of time throughout the entire system. The date command can be used to change the system time. This command is generally restricted so that only the superuser can execute it. All processes that can change the system clock should be audited and any changes to the system time should be logged to the system log file.

Some systems are more restrictive on changing the time. The restrictions may be different on setting the clock backwards than forwards. Changing the clock might be restricted to only during the start-up process. The system may not allow the clock to be changed at all if it is using a trusted time source.

Network Time Protocol

Network Time Protocol (NTP) is a method of getting the time from an external source. It is used to synchronize the system clocks on a number of systems.

Traditionally, NTP is implemented only when the synchronization of system clocks is very important. However, it is usually implemented without enough security to keep a compromised time service from affecting the systems that are dependent on that service. A hacker can compromise the system time by compromising the system that is the source of the time for the other systems or by compromising the communication between the systems. This is especially true when your NTP is obtained from an unsecured host on the Internet.

If system synchronization is critical to the running of your business, then the time sources must be extremely well-secured and the NTP data communication must be secured.

Time Server

A time server is a system which supplies a consistent and accurate time to other systems with NTP. This system should have a secure time source. Common time sources include GPS, the global positioning system, and the National Institute of Standards radio broadcast from Colorado Springs. These sources use atomic clocks to maintain correct time.

It is suggested that the time server and the log server should be hosted on the same system. This configuration will aid in maintaining consistent time within the different systems logs. This will help facilitate correlation of events on these different systems. As far as prosecution goes, accurate time for evidence collection is critical.

## PART IV

Halting the Hacker

Halting the hacker is no easy task. First, it is not a level playing field. A hacker needs only to find a single flaw one time to penetrate security, but a security manager has to have the security completely correct all of the time so that it cannot be penetrated. Second, security is everyone's responsibility. Users must select good passwords and not share information with people. System administrators must keep the system current and install security patches, as well as keep aware of current security issues. System vendors must start shipping systems with an operating system that is more secure out of the box and software suppliers must design their products with security in mind. Finally, security is a balancing act. You have to balance the cost and effort of securing and monitoring a system against the possible losses if the system is compromised. You have to balance the cost and effort to restrict users and systems against the ease of use and productivity of those users. And you have to balance the value of prosecuting a hacker against the publicity that such a prosecution would bring. Historically, the imbalance has been that honest users have paid the cost of more monitoring and more restrictions for the activities of a few hackers, who do not pay for their crimes because of the company's fear of bad publicity.

Proactive Security Measures

Proactive security measures are processes that look for security issues before they become problems. Proactive security tools test for known security problems — configuration problems used by standard attack scenarios. They also include software that assists users in keeping the systems secure, whether a tool to help users select good passwords or one that encrypts network traffic to keep hackers from snooping on the network. Most security tools are proactive security measures.

Any tool that compares the system to a checklist of configurations is this type of tool. These tools can be very effective if they are run on a frequent basis and their reports monitored. It is best to run these tools on an irregular schedule so the hacker is not certain of the size of the window between the tests. If these programs are scheduled to run each day at a given time, the hacker will know he will have a 24-hour window where he can clean up after his hacking and go undetected.

Reactive Security Measures

Reactive security measures will report attacks that have already taken place or are currently taking place. These measures are generally either processes that monitor the system and report any anomalous behavior or processes that are looking for activities that correspond to defined attack profiles.

These can be real-time monitors and alarms that will immediately report suspicious activities or they can be batch processes that run at scheduled times and review and correlate logged information to determine and report suspicious activities. Real-time monitors require that there be someone to notify immediately who can take action while the attack is underway. Otherwise, they provide the same features as batch-processed security reports. These reports are used to locate attacks and determine how they were perpetrated to know how to close the holes or where to set real-time traps to catch the hacker during a later attack.

Preparation

The quality of any project is built upon the quality of its preparation. For computer systems, preparation is the definition of the function of that system. It must include what services the system will provide and what software will be used to provide those services. It will define what communications to other systems are required, who the users are, and what data will be contained or manipulated.

Define What Needs Protection

An organization's assets are those things that add value to the organization or whose loss would remove value from the organization. Information resources are those resources that either store information, transport information, create information, use information, or are information.

One must adequately identify the organization's resources that are to be protected to appropriately evaluate risks and apply proper security measures.

The following types of losses are commonplace:

- Denial of service is the **loss of availability** and is the most visible of all losses. The loss of availability is immediately apparent to any entity that needs access and is unable to get access. Availability is often considered the most important attribute in service-oriented businesses that depend on information (e.g., airline schedules and online inventory systems).

- Disclosure is the **loss of confidentiality** and indicates that the resource has the potential to release information to unauthorized entities. For some types of information, confidentiality is a very important attribute. Examples include research data, medical and insurance records, new product specifications, and corporate investment strategies. In some locations, there may be a legal obligation to protect the privacy of individuals. This is particularly true for banks and loan companies; debt collectors; businesses that extend credit to their customers or issue credit cards; hospitals, doctors' offices, and medical testing laboratories; individuals or agencies that offer services such as psychological counseling or drug treatment; and agencies that collect taxes. Information disclosure is generally the area of greatest concern to an organization.

- Destruction or corruption is the **loss of integrity** and indicates that unauthorized changes have been made to information, whether by human error or intentional tampering. Integrity is particularly important for critical safety and financial data used in activities such as electronic funds transfers, air traffic control, and financial accounting. If the quality of the resource is in question, then all the decisions that utilize that resource must also be in question. Information corruption may be the most devastating type of loss to an organization.

Define How Much Protection Is Required

The environment in which the organization operates can make a huge difference in what is the appropriate level of security. The business environment will indicate the level of threat to the organization. An organization can become a target if its customers are targets. An organization which caters to a famous or highly visible clientele will be of more interest to a hacker than another organization.

Compliance with Legal Requirements

Certain industries are regulated and have specific laws which define the level of protection required for the information entrusted to a company. In the United States, the financial services and health care industries have the most regulations on the proper handling of information and security procedures to prevent disclosure of private information. Protection of information has been the primary focus of the information security regulations.

In the wake of terrorist activities in the United States, and numerous reports detailing the country's dependency on infrastructure which is in the control of private industry, it is expected that these providers of critical infrastructure will be required to meet specific security requirements. These industries include communications, transportation, and energy. Cyber-attacks against these industries which would cause a loss of service could be a matter of national security.

Compliance with Industry Standards

Industries which are not as regulated depend on standards within the industry to set the level of protection which is appropriate for the information which is common to the industry. Professional organizations within each industry are the common place to find information on best practices. These practices describe how the leaders and the longtime players in the industry handle the process of security. These can be used as a model or a baseline to build the organization's specific security environment.

Compliance to Security Policy

Each organization has unique needs which have to be addressed by policy. Most companies have defined their specific critical resources which need protecting. These specifics will dictate the specific details of the security environment. The organization's existing policies and procedures must be inspected to determine what is the correct level of security for the organization.

Corporate culture has a large impact on the security practices which are put in place. How a company conducts itself in business transactions and with its employees will mold how its security will be implemented.

Decide How Much Protection Is Afforded

A risk analysis is needed to quantify the proper level of security based on the value of the information assets, the threats to the system and information, and the amount of harm that can be caused if they are lost, altered, or disclosed. This process should include some indication of the size and type of investment that the asset represents, the impact on the organization that the loss of the asset would represent, and the ease with which the asset may be replaced. The type and size of the threat must be evaluated, as well as the availability and effectiveness of security precautions and countermeasures. Once the whole picture is understood, then informed decisions can be made.

A risk analysis is required to understand the potential impact on operations and to justify the expenditures on security. This analysis should include a thorough information resource inventory and threat assessment. Security reduces risk. To determine the level of security required, one must understand the probability of a security incident and the scope of the damage that the incident could cause.

An enterprise-wide risk analysis is required to collect all of this information. This is by no means a small task. Since everyone in the organization handles information, it requires significant support from management and involvement from individuals throughout the organization.

Value of Information Assets

Information is an important corporate asset. A company's information represents its competitive advantage. It is this intellectual property which differentiates a company from all other companies. IT deserves a level of protection second only to the company's employees.

Not all information is viewed by the law as needing the same level of protection. However, much of a company's proprietary information can be just as valuable to the organization. Next to your employees, information is your most valuable resource. It is more valuable by far than the computer systems that contain it. This is the target of the professional corporate hacker.

An organization which has private information about its customers is a more likely target. This private information can be as common as credit card information or as specific as personal itineraries. Credit card theft is one of the most common types of information theft. However, the theft of more personal information — where one will be or personal or family information is much more alarming.

Company information comes in a variety of categories. Here are some general categories, each with its own security issues.

- **Public information**: Information about the company that is readily available from a number of sources.

- **Company confidential information**: Information that is not to be shared with anyone outside the company.

- **Proprietary information**: Information that gives the company a competitive advantage. This could be the secret recipe or business plans.

- **Personnel information**: Information about employees. This could include payroll information, names, addresses, or birth dates.

You must define what the appropriate categories are for your business and then you must classify all your data by these categories. Once these categories are defined, you should develop security policies for each classification. These policies should define what is required for access, modification, and deletion, and what level and cost of security measures are required for each classification. Data classification is the first step toward data security.

Threats to Information Assets

Threats are those things that have the potential to cause losses. Threats are always present. They are outside the direct control of the organization. The threats themselves cannot be eliminated, only anticipated, but safeguards can be put in place to minimize their impact. The threats to assets should be assessed (denial of service, destruction, disclosure of information, theft, and unauthorized access). The examination of threats must include a discussion of both the probable and maximum possible impact of the realization of the threat, including both direct impact and flow-on consequences.

The size and type of threats are based in part on the type of business the organization conducts and the level of technology embraced. To fully understand the threats, not only do the sources of the threats need to be examined, but one must also examine the organization as a prospective target. The malicious threat to an organization is often based on the organization's image or perceived image, or the organization's business activities and associations. Good employee and public relations can be the greatest tool to minimize malicious threats. In this area, perception is truth. That is, the truth is not as important as the perception, since it is this perception that the attacker is responding to, whether it is a disgruntled employee or an external attacker. These threats need to be recognized and understood so that appropriate security measures can be implemented to minimize the potential losses.

Information systems face a variety of threats including computer-based fraud, espionage, vandalism, accidents, natural disasters, computer viruses, and computer hackers. As the world's dependence on information continues to increase, threats become more widespread, more ambitious, and increasingly sophisticated.

Losses

The severity of loss of a specific resource depends on the importance of the resource to the organization and the timing of the loss. Information can be valuable because of what it is worth to the organization. The timing of the loss can have a dramatic impact on the cost of the loss — such as information disclosure just before important decisions are to be made, or the inability to access information systems when the information is needed.

Unauthorized access to information may represent the loss of an asset, even though the information is still available to the organization. Security requirements should vary, depending upon the importance of the particular resource. Security cannot make it impossible to suffer a loss. What it can do is reduce the likelihood and make the cost of a malicious attack prohibitive for the information gained.

To completely understand the impact that a loss will have on a business, a business impact analysis should be performed. Often there are significant downstream effects that may not be initially apparent. This information is not maintained in a vacuum. It is used for business decisions that affect the organization and its employees, partners, creditors, and competitors. Poor business decisions can have significant, far-reaching implications. There are also issues of collateral damage: the impact on things that were thought to be unrelated but, due to location or other circumstances, are affected by the incident or the response to the incident.

Define What You Have

Most organizations have some basic security measures, even if they are only informal activities. The current status of the security procedures must be evaluated, not only for their effectiveness but also for their applicability to the areas that the risk analysis has determined to be important. It needs to be determined if they appropriately address the areas of security that are most important to the organization. Evaluation of the effectiveness of current processes requires analysis of the procedures and testing of the practices.

Policies and Procedures

All organizations have security policies and procedures, even if they have no *written* security policies and procedures. There are policies in other groups outside the information technology group, such as human resources, which have security aspects. They will define acceptable and unacceptable behavior and how to handle employees who are in violation of the policies. These are a great starting point in developing security-specific policies.

The information technology department will have procedures which pertain to security. It will have data handling procedures for backup and recovery and processes for adding new users and other activities which involve security. These practices will need to be evaluated and incorporated into written security policy and procedures.

The organization's policies which are already in place will need to be examined to determine how they can be applied to information security or how to draft new policies that follow them. Often an organization's employee personnel policies and physical security policies can directly apply or be broadened to encompass information security.

Define How to Protect It

Defining the protection process creates a framework in which to build security processes and evaluate security products. This foundation should define the attributes of the system (availability, confidentiality, integrity) which need protection, the priorities in protecting them, and the processes to be used to protect them. A number of security principles should be utilized.

Defense in Depth

No single security measure will stop all attacks against a resource's availability, confidentiality, and integrity, so multiple measures have to be used. Defense in depth says that there should be layers of security, each addressing specific security issues. This layering creates a more comprehensive security solution. It also require's that an attacker penetrate layer them to get access to the resources.

Isolation

Isolation protects processes from the side effects of other processes. The further isolated a system is from an untrusted area, the less likely it is to be compromised. Physical separation provides isolation. This can be applied to isolating networks, or power sources.

Separation of Duties

Separation of duties provides accountability by requiring different people to perform the different steps in a process. This increases the complexity of committing fraud by requiring that multiple people be involved. Having more people required to commit fraud increases opportunities for mistakes or the likelihood that someone will talk.

Least Privileges

The principle of least privilege is that a person should be given no more than the very least privileges needed, for the minimum amount of time required to perform his or her duties. This minimizes the opportunity to abuse these privileges and the possibility of accidental abuse of privileges.

The level of privileges granted should be based on a business need and justification. This exercise will help clarify the business processes and the security issues with them.

Set Minimum Security Requirements

Minimum security requirements should be defined. These will set a base line of security which must be met. Document all exceptions with a business justification and a definition of what is being done instead to mitigate the specific risk.

Implement Change Control

Most vulnerabilities are a result of inadequate management of change — changes to source code, changes to system configuration, or changes in personnel. A controlled change-management procedure can help eliminate the mistakes and improve the likelihood that malicious changes will be caught.

## CHAPTER 20

Installation

Given the opportunity, starting from scratch with a system is the best way to ensure the security of the system. A cold install creates a controlled environment which provides the opportunity to select exactly what software is on the system and what is not.

A careful evaluation of precisely what is needed on the system should be performed, to determine what software is required to support the server's operation. Install the minimum amount of software necessary to support the services which the system is to provide. The less software on the system, the fewer opportunities for vulnerabilities.

It is better to not install software than to remove it after it has been installed. Removing software leaves remnants which have to be cleaned. The cleaning process is rarely completely effective.

Software Structure

Today, system software is structured in a manner to assist the administrator in installing all the software necessary to create a working system. Software dependencies are known by the installer, so that installing a software product will in turn install all the software required by the selected software. The installers will perform hardware scans and select the software needed to support the attached hardware. However, these processes may lead to installing unwanted or unexpected software. Understanding the organization of the system software will help in selecting the software to load and what is required to secure it.

Linux

Red Hat Linux uses rpm, Red Hat Package Manager, to install software. The files which make up a software system are grouped into packages. The rpm command installs this software into the appropriate location and checks for dependencies. It checks those packages on which the new package depends and it also makes sure the addition of this package will not interfere with the dependencies of any package already installed. It performs a number of checks during this phase. These checks verify that the command is not attempting to install an already installed package or attempting to install an older package over a newer version. The rpm command performs tasks which are required before the software is installed and those tasks which are needed after the installation.

Packages are organized into groups based on their function, for example, C Development, Networked Workstation, or Web Server.

HP-UX

HP-UX systems use the *swinstall* command to install software. The files which make up a software system are grouped into filesets. These filesets are independent autonomous units. Dependencies can be defined between filesets so that any fileset which depends on another fileset cannot be installed until the correct version of that fileset is installed.

Filesets are grouped into products. These groupings are used to contain everything which is included in a single purchasable product. Products can be grouped into bundles. These are groups of products which are sold together, like a workstation bundle or an e-business bundle.

Install Minimum Base Operating System

Even if your system comes with a preinstalled operating system, the security benefits of starting with a clean operating system install, and knowing exactly what you have, far exceed the minor cost in your time to install it. During the initial installation, configuration, and testing, make sure that your system is not connected to any untrusted networks. The system may need to be connected to a network, even if it is only a local hub, so that the network interfaces can initialize appropriately. Document your configuration steps as you perform them — you may discover later that a change that was made causes unforeseen problems. And it may take several install iterations to get everything working correctly.

Boot the system from the installation media. These systems will proceed to a menu offering you the chance to select the option of installing a new system or repairing an existing system. There will also be the ability to configure some basic settings which may be required before the operating system is installed.

Installing Linux

Before the actual install starts, there are a number of questions and options to select concerning language, keyboard layout, and mouse type. Then you will be prompted for the type of install you want — Workstation, Server, Laptop, or Custom. The custom installation gives you the most flexibility, but requires the most knowledge of the system on which you are installing. The Linux installation leads you directly through the process — partitioning the disk, boot loader installation, network configuration (if you plan to install over the network), language selection, time zone, authentication model, and finally, selection of the software packages to be installed.

All the packages should be evaluated for their need before installing them on the system. Installing too few packages during the installation is preferable to installing too many. The `rpm` command can be used later to install any additional packages which were overlooked.

Installing HP-UX 11i

With the 11i release of HP-UX, the installation process groups the filesets into "operating environment" bundles. These bundles are not alterable during the installation, so an entire bundle has to be loaded onto the system. "HP-UX 11i Base OS" is the smallest of these environments and contains over 600 filesets. It should be the selected environment to be installed.

Interrupt the boot sequence and boot from the CD-ROM.

```
BO ALT
```

Allow the system to load with the default settings.

```
Interact with IPL (Y, N, or Cancel)?> N
```

Select the default configuration with the minimum environment.

```
Configurations: HP-UX Bundle B11.11 Default
Environment:    HP-UX 11i OE-32bit
```

Remove Any Unneeded Software

Unnecessary software provides an opportunity to be exploited. If a piece of software is not being used, it is likely that it will not be patched, so unused software is more likely to be vulnerable. Any software which was included with the installation bundles which is not needed should be removed. This includes manuals, examples, and software for hardware which the system does not have.

Linux

Red Hat uses the `rpm` command to remove, as well as to install, software. The granularity and the ease of selecting the software offered make it unlikely that you will have to install something you do not want to if care is taken when installing the software in the first place. The command used to remove software is:

```
rpm -ev packages
```

HP-UX 11i

Uninstalling software from the base environment is somewhat tricky, given the dependencies defined. However, one can patiently start at the bottom of the dependency tree and prune his way up to remove many of the unnecessary filesets. Use swlist with the "-l product" and "-l fileset" options to determine what is on the system which needs to be removed. The following are suggestions on removing software after the initial install:

- The X windows system is not generally needed on servers. Its network model makes it a prime target of hackers to gather information and gain access. It can be removed with the following command:

```
swremove -x "autoreboot=true" AudioSubsystem CDE DigitalVideo \
ImagingSubsystem VUEtoCDE X11 Xserver Sup-Tool-Mgr.STM-UI-RUN
```

- NFS has a long history of security issues. All of the NFS filesets can be removed except for NFS-CORE NFS-KRN and NFS-SHLIBS. To remove them, run swremove interactively selecting NFS and unselecting these filesets.

```
swremove -i NFS
```

- To remove the software programming environment, start swremove interactively with the following command, and then *un-select* ProgSupport.C-INC. This fileset is needed to rebuild the kernel.

```
swremove -i CPS Perl5 ProgSupport SourceControl Judy-lib \
KernDevKit Networking.NET-PRG InternetSrvcs.INETSVCS-INC \
Networking.LAN-PRG
```

- Many of the serial data communication products have been exploited. They should be removed if not needed.

```
swremove UUCP SystemComm TerminalMngr NonHP-Terminfo KeyShell \
Curses-Color
```

- Other user facilities can be removed if the server will not be supporting logged-in users. These facilities include e-mail, printing, text editors, and formatters.

```
swremove MailUtilities
swremove TechPrintServ PrinterMgmt DistributedPrint
swremove TextEditors TextFormatters Spelling
```

Removing user messaging and native language support will save space on the server.

- The international language support is dependent upon a number of message libraries which are loaded in a number of other products, so before the "International" product can be removed, all of the message libraries have to be removed with the following command:

```
for i in `swlist -l fileset | grep '\-MSG' | awk '{print $1}'`
do
  swremove $i
done
swremove International
```

- To remove all the man pages from the system, use the following command:

```
for i in `swlist -l fileset | grep '\-MAN' | awk '{print $1}'`
do
  swremove $i

done
```

Install Additional Products

If there are any additional products which need to be loaded to support the services which the server is to support, they should be loaded at this point so that they can be secured along with the base operating system. Careful evaluation should be done to assure that only necessary software is installed.

HP-UX 11i

At this point, install any additional software which is needed. `swinstall` provides the ability to install software from local media or over the network from a software depot. Install whatever software which is needed for the applications which the server will be running and any additional security software which will be used.

HP-UX provides encrypted communication with IPSec and SSL, access control with IPFilter and TCPWrapper, system hardening with Bastille/UX, and intrusion detection with IDS/9000.

Linux

The Red Hat package manager, `rpm`, provides the ability to install software from local sources or over the network using a variety of protocols, including *nfs, ftp,* and *http*. This provides tremendous flexibility in software distribution but it increases the need to enforce using only trusted software sources. A secure system should load only software from local media or over a secure network from a known and trusted source.

Install Standard Patches

Even the most current version of an operating systems has patches. These patches can address flaws in software, support for new hardware, and enhancements which are not significant enough to warrant a new release of the software. Patches apply to specific sets of hardware or software, so not all patches are needed on all machines. You should install only the patches which are pertinent to the system.

HP-UX Support Plus Bundle

The Support Plus CD contains the General Release patches. This is an accumulation of the patches which have been released since the latest HP-UX release. The install CD contained a recent set of patches from when the media was produced. Mount the Support Plus CD and use `swinstall` to install the GR bundle XSWGR1100.

Linux

The Red Hat Update Agent, `up2date`, can retrieve the latest software packages directly from Red Hat. This tool can be used to keep the system up-to-date with all security patches, bug fixes, and software package enhancements. Your system will have to be configured with the current Red Hat GNU Privacy Guard (GPG) key to verify the authenticity and integrity of the software being downloaded.

Install Security Patches

A security patch review should be performed to determine if any security patches should be installed. Each patch for a product currently installed on the system should be analyzed to determine if it needs to be installed. First, you should check to see if it's already installed from either the install media or the patch bundle. If not, you can look at the patch .text file for details about the patch, including dependencies, filesets effected, and files patched. You can determine filesets installed on the system by executing `swlist -l fileset`.

Just because a patch exists doesn't mean that you need to install it, though it is usually safe to do so. Some patches may fix buffer overrun defects or other attack channels in set-uid root commands or root processes. If you plan to remove the set-uid bits you may choose not to install them. You may also not have a program configured (for example, `rlogind` listening on the network), but sometimes it can be difficult to determine if a defect is remotely or locally exploitable.

Security Patch Check for HP-UX (B6834AA)

Security patch check is a Perl script that runs on HP-UX 11.X systems. It performs an analysis of the filesets and patches installed on an HP-UX machine, and generates a listing (report) of recommended security patches. In order to determine which patches are missing from a system, security_patch_check must have access to a listing, or catalog, of security-related patches. The following command will download the patch catalog from the HP site:

```
security_patch_check -r
```

Since new security patches can be released at any time, security_patch_check depends on a patch catalog stored on an HP server. This catalog is updated nightly. To help automate the process of checking for security patches missing from a system, security_patch_check is able to download the most recently generated catalog from an HP FTP site. To download a catalog from an HP ftp site, you must have ftp access to the public Internet, either directly or through a proxy server. Define the proxy by setting the *ftp_proxy* environment variable.

```
export ftp_proxy=<protocol of proxy>://address:port
```

Once security_patch_check has access to a security patch catalog, it will create a list of the patches which are both applicable and not installed. Note that although the security patch catalog contains the most recent and highest rated patches, security_patch_check will recommend a patch only if it addresses a security problem not already addressed by an installed patch.

If you do not want to install Perl on the system, securty_patch_check can be run on another system using a swlist from the original system as input. The tool can be run remotely from a management system, pointing to a production system. For this to work the "Perl" and "Security Patch Check" filesets must be installed on the management system. You must also consider appropriate swacl settings to allow yourself remote swlist access but not others (default is open).

There is another method which does not require enabling swlist access to the system. You can copy the swlist output of a production system to a management server and point security_patch_check to the swlist output.

Remove Software Remnants

During the process of installing and removing software and patches, software remnants are sometimes left behind. This can include empty directories, unused start-up scripts, and modules which were replaced by patches.

HP-UX — Remove saved patches.

By default during patch installation, rollback copies of all patch files modified are saved in /var/adm/sw/save/. After verifying the operation of the patched systems, the disk space being used by the before-image can be reclaimed by marking the patches "committed."

However, once a patch is committed, there is no way to uninstall the patch with `swremove`. The following command will commit all the patches.

```
swmodify -x patch_commit=true '*.*'
```

## CHAPTER 21

Proactive Protection

Proactive protection is the processes taken to keep an attack from occurring. This is done by making the system difficult to locate, uninteresting to hackers, and difficult to compromise. The goal is to reduce both the number of total attacks and the number of successful attacks.

There is a great deal of information, research, and tools to help a system prevent successful attacks. Unfortunately, vendors continue to be slow to provide systems which are secure out-of-the-box.

Remove What Is Not Needed

As a general rule, if you are not using it, take it off the system. This applies to programs, data, accounts, files, everything. Removing these things will not only make it more difficult for the hacker to probe and compromise your system, it will also free up resources, disk space, and processor cycles, which in turn will allow you to back up your system more quickly and on fewer removable media, saving you both time and money.

Information gathering and reporting tools should be restricted so that only the superuser can run them. If reports are left on the system, they should be encrypted. This may slow down the speed at which a hacker can infiltrate your system. Security auditing tools should be removed from the system. Keeping them on a removable disk, mounting them on the machine you are monitoring, and removing them when you are not using them, can make a convenient and secure process for the security administrator. This will also force the hacker to bring his own tools.

Remove Unused Accounts

Unused accounts are a vulnerability because hackers will use them as a place to hide. They are viewed as safe since there is no one using them, and therefore no one to notice their being used. Compromising one of these accounts can give a hacker access to a system that may go undetected for a long time.

Unused accounts should be removed from the system. An unused account can be defined as an account which does not own files and does not run processes The following commands will determine if there are any files owned by the user or group specified. If there are none then the file can be removed.

```
find / -user  username -exec ls -ls {} \;
userdel username
find / -group groupname-exec ls -ls {} \;
groupdel groupname
```

On HP-UX, default users can include: uucp, lp, nuucp, hpdb, www, and daemon; and default groups can include: lp, nuucp, and daemon. Red Hat Linux can include the default users of: bin, daemon, adm, operator, and rpc; and groups of: root, bin, daemon, sys, adm, tty, disk, mem, and wheel. However, the exact list is dependent on the software installed on the system.

Remove Unneeded Set-ID Programs

Many of the methods used to compromise UNIX systems utilize set-ID programs. So it is somewhat surprising to see the number of set-ID files which are installed by default, especially, when most of these programs do not actually need the privilege. Administrative commands, which are expected to be executed by privileged users, have no need to be set-ID. Some commands which have privileges to enable regular users to use some of their features may be deemed unnecessary in a secure environment, particularly on a server where no one other than administrators are expected to be logged in.

The security of the system can be improved by removing programs with set-ID privileges, or by removing the set-ID privilege. To obtain a list of all files with either the set-uid or set-gid bit set on the system, execute this command:

```
find / \( -perm -4000 -o -perm -2000 \) -type f -exec ls -ld {} \;
```

On HP-UX, removing the set-uid bit from the following software distributer and logical volume manager commands will greatly reduce the number of files with set-ID privileges, because of the number of links each file has.

```
chmod u-s /usr/sbin/swinstall
chmod u-s /usr/sbin/vgcreate
chmod u-s /sbin/vgcreate
```

Some of the set-ID commands will function fine without the privilege using default or commonly used options. However, some of the functionality may be lost for non-privileged users. This may well be acceptable for most server installations.

One strategy is to remove the set-id bits from all files, then selectively add them back to just a few programs that need to be run by non-root users. The following commands will remove the set-uid and set-gid bit from all files, then add it back to su and the shared lib PAM version of the passwd command:

```
find / -perm -4000 -type f -exec chmod u-s {} \;
find / -perm -2000 -type f -exec chmod g-s {} \;
chmod u+s /usr/bin/su
chmod u+s /usr/bin/passwd
```

If the system does not expect to have any login access, except for administrators, then the su command may be the only set-uid program needed.

Disable What Is Not Used

There are some features of the system which you will not use which cannot be removed. It may be that something you do want to use is dependent upon the feature, or that it is so integrated into the system that removing it is more difficult than disabling it and monitoring it.

Disable Needed Pseudo-Accounts

Pseudo-accounts which are needed for proper operation of the system should be configured so that no individual can gain access with the account. The remaining pseudo-accounts should be disabled. The password entry should have an invalid shell program and an invalid home directory. This will disable remote connections.

On HP-UX , the needed pseudo-accounts are: bin, sys, and adm.

```
bin:*:2:2:NO LOGIN:/bin/false:/dev/null
sys:*:2:2:NO LOGIN:/bin/false:/dev/null
adm:*:2:2:NO LOGIN:/bin/false:/dev/null
```

Red Hat Linux 7.2 contain the following pseudo-accounts.

```
bin:x:1:1:bin:/bin:/sbin/nologin
daemon:x:2:2:daemon:/sbin:/sbin/nologin
adm:x:3:4:adm:/var/adm:/sbin/nologin
sync:x:5:0:sync:/sbin:/bin/sync
shutdown:x:6:0:shutdown:/sbin:/sbin/shutdown
halt:x:7:0:halt:/sbin:/sbin/halt
operator:x:11:0:operator:/root:/sbin/nologin
rpm:x:37:37::/var/lib/rpm:/bin/bash
```

Disable Internet Services

Misuse of network services is the most common method of attack; therefore, only required network services should be enabled. All nonessential services should be disabled. It is rare that a system will not require some network services, so it is unlikely that internet daemon can be removed from the system. All services, except for those specifically required, should be disabled.

On **HP-UX** the internet services are controlled by the inetd daemon. These services are disabled by de-configuring them in the `inetd` configuration file (`/etc/inetd.conf`). The default `inetd.conf` file for HP-UX 11i has the following services enabled:

```
ftp       stream tcp nowait root /usr/lbin/ftpd ftpd -l
telnet    stream tcp nowait root /usr/lbin/telnetd telnetd
shell     stream tcp nowait root /usr/lbin/remshd   remshd
exec      stream tcp nowait root /usr/lbin/rexecd   rexecd
ntalk     dgram  udp wait    root /usr/lbin/ntalkd   ntalkd
ident     stream tcp wait    bin  /usr/lbin/identd   identd
printer   stream tcp nowait root /usr/sbin/rlpdaemon  rlpdaemon -i
daytime   stream tcp nowait root internal
daytime   dgram  udp nowait root internal
time      stream tcp nowait root internal
echo      stream tcp nowait root internal
echo      dgram  udp nowait root internal
discard   stream tcp nowait root internal
discard   dgram  udp nowait root internal
chargen   stream tcp nowait root internal
chargen   dgram  udp nowait root internal
kshell    stream tcp nowait root /usr/lbin/remshd remshd -K
klogin    stream tcp nowait root /usr/lbin/rlogind rlogind -K
```

Red Hat Linux 7.2 has replaced the `inetd` daemon with `xinetd`. The processes which are controlled by `xinetd` are listed in the directory `/etc/xinetd.d`. In this directory, there is a configuration file for each service which xinetd is to service. These files contain information about the programs which service the protocol.

To enumerate the services and their start-up state, the following `grep` command can be used.

```
grep disable /etc/xinetd.d/*
```

This lists the files and the lines containing the disable directive:

```
/etc/xinetd.d/chargen:       disable = yes
/etc/xinetd.d/chargen-udp:   disable = yes
/etc/xinetd.d/daytime:       disable = yes
/etc/xinetd.d/daytime-udp:   disable = yes
/etc/xinetd.d/echo:          disable = yes
/etc/xinetd.d/echo-udp:      disable = yes
/etc/xinetd.d/rsync:         disable = yes
/etc/xinetd.d/time:          disable = yes
/etc/xinetd.d/time-udp:      disable = yes
```

To disable the service, there should be a disable=yes directive set in the file. However, for compatibility, the /etc/inetd.conf file is also used by xinetd, so both have to be examined to see what processes are enabled.

Disable RPC Services

RPC services are the basis for the network services from SUN which include NIS and NFS. These services are not usually used on a system on which security is a concern. On HP-UX 11, rpcbind provides the RPC services; prior to this, the services were provided by portmapd. Linux runs portmap for managing RPC services. On Red Hat-based systems, the following command will shut down portmap and prevent it from restarting.

```
/etc/rc.d/ini.d/portmap stop
chkconfig --del portmap
```

On HP-UX 11, rpcbind is started from the nfs.core script. These scripts can be disabled by either removing them or setting their permissions to 0. Setting the permissions of the rpcbind program to 0 helps ensure that it does not get started accidentally.

```
chmod 0 /sbin/rc1.d/K600nfs.core
chmod 0 /sbin/rc2.d/S400nfs.core
chmod 0 /usr/sbin/rpcbind
```

Disable SNMP Daemons

On HP-UX, many of the filesets are dependent on SNMP, so that they cannot be removed. Therefore, you need to disable the services. This is done by changing the "START" variables in the start-up configuration files to prevent the services from starting. This is done by editing the following lines in the SNMP start-up configuration files:

In /etc/rc.config.d/SnmpHpunix.

```
SNMP_HPUNIX_START=0
```

In /etc/rc.config.d/SnmpMaster

```
SNMP_MASTER_START=0
```

In /etc/rc.config.d/SnmpMib2

```
SNMP_MIB2_START=0
```

In `/etc/rc.config.d/SnmpTrpDst`

`SNMP_TRAPDEST_START=0`

Disable swagentd (SD-UX) Daemon

The swagentd script is run twice in the bootup start sequence. When it is run from `S120swconfig` it will complete any cleanup work from an install which required a reboot, such as remove the files listed in `/var/adm/sw/cleanupfile`. It is run again as `S870swagentd`. This start-up file, `/etc/rc2.d/S870swagentd`, should be removed to keep the daemon from running on the system.

Disable Password and Group Caching Daemon

HP-UX has introduced a password and group caching daemon, pwgrd, to improve the performance of accessing user and group IDs. It utilizes a UNIX domain socket for client requests, so the daemon should be disabled. Edit the following line in the file `/etc/rc.config.d/pwgr`:

`PWGR=0`

The sockets used by the password and group caching daemon should be removed.

```
rm /var/spool/pwgr/*
rm /var/spool/sockets/pwgr/*
```

Disable pty Daemon

The ptydaemon is a carry-over from the proprietary networking days at HP. It supports the `vt` and `dscopy` commands. It is unnecessary since `dscopy` is unsupported and `vt`, an unsecure MAC level terminal connection, is rarely used. Edit the following line in the file `/etc/rc.config.d/ptydaemon`:

`PTYDAEMON_START=0`

Environment Daemon

The environment daemon, envd, logs messages and can perform actions when over-temperature and chassis fan failure conditions are detected by the hardware. This feature is available only on specific hardware systems. For example, it will perform an orderly shutdown when an over-temperature condition occurs. It is probably best to leave this daemon running, but it can be disabled by editing its configuration file: `/etc/rc.config.d/envd`:

```
ENVD = 0
```

Network Tracing and Logging

The network tracing and logging system in the system default configuration starts three daemons: `ntl_reader`, `nktl_daemon` and `netfmt`. These are easily disabled by editing `/etc/rc.config.d/nettl`; however, you will lose potentially valuable log data, such as link down messages. However, `netfmt` is the console filter formatter which sends the log messages to the system console. If this is not needed, then the following commands will stop the system from sending network logging to the console and will not start the `netfmt` daemon:

```
nettlconf -L -console 0
nettl -stop
nettl -start
```

The `nettlconf` command modifies the network tracing and logging configuration file, `/etc/nettlgen.conf`, so this change will persist across system starts.

Restrict the Rest

Anything which is left on the system at this point should be restricted as much as possible to allow appropriate use and deny inappropriate use. Use of host-based firewalls is suggested to limit the services at a low level. Services which can in themselves restrict access should employ this application level security.

Restrict syslogd

The system logger, syslog, records kernel, system, and application log messages. It also will accept messages from other systems on the network. This network feature should be disabled so that other systems cannot utilize local resources.

- **Linux**, Red Hat 6, by default does not accept remote syslog messages. To enable this feature, edit /etc/rc.d/init.d/syslog and add the "-r" option so that the system logging deamon is started as:

```
daemon syslogd -r
```

- **HP-UX** accepts remote syslog messages by default. To disable this feature, add the "-N" option to `/sbin/init.d/syslogd` so that the line which starts the system logging deamon is:

```
/usr/sbin/syslogd -DN
```

Earlier versions of HP-UX require patch PHCO_21023, which adds this feature to the system logging deamon.

Restrict the Privileged Group

Hackers can change the ownership of files to misdirect investigations or to let another user pay for resources which are not his in a bill-back environment. Non-privileged users really don't need to be able to change the ownership of files to other users.

Linux allows only the superuser to change the owner of a file.

HP-UX restricts the access to changing ownership through the privileged group mechanism. By default the "CHOWN" privilege is a global privilege and applies to all groups. To disable this privilege, the file `/etc/privgroup` should be created with permissions set at 400 and containing "-n". This will disable any privileged group.

Privileged groups is a process in HP-UX by which certain privileges can be delegated to specific groups of users. Manipulation of these privileged groups is controlled with the `getprivgrp` and `setprivgrp` commands. Table 21-1 lists the system capabilities which can be granted to groups.

Table 21-1 HP-UX Privileged Group

CHOWN	Can use chown to change file ownerships.
LOCKRDONLY	Can use lockf to set locks on files that are open for reading only.
MLOCK	Can use plock to lock process text and data into memory and the shmctl function to lock shared memory setments.
RTPRIO	Can use rtprio to set real-time priorities.
RTSCHED	Can use sched_setparam and sched_setscheduler to set real-time priorities.
SERIALIZE	Can use serialize to force the target process to run serially with other processes that are also marked by this system call.
SETRUGID	Can use setuid and setgid to change, respectively, the real user ID and real group ID of a process.

The default setting for privileged groups is to allow the "CHOWN" privilege to all groups. To change the default setting, the configuration file, /etc/privgroup, must be created and contain lines indicating which privilege is assigned to which group.

Convert to a Trusted System

HP-UX provides a facility called Trusted Systems, which implements "C2" level security. This includes password shadowing — the process of removing the password hash from the /etc/password file and enhanced user access restrictions, and system auditing.

```
/usr/lbin/tsconvert
passwd root
```

Passwords on existing accounts will expire as a result of the conversion, which is why the password for root has to be changed after converting to a trusted system.

Restrict the Root User

On UNIX systems, the root user is all powerful. The root user, or any user with UID=0, bypasses all of the security policies which are enforced by the kernel and the file system. However, there are some things which can be done to help limit the root user and help track his activities.

- **Restrict root login to the console** — By using the secure terminal facility, securetty, login access for the root user can be restricted to a specific list of terminals. If the root user is restricted to be able to log in only at the console, then physical security measures can be employed to provide more security. Administrators who know the root user password, can still su to root to perform their administrative functions, and this provides a log of who actually is performing these privileged activities. Put the following entry in /etc/securetty:

```
console
```

and set the permissions:

```
chown bin:bin /etc/securetty
chmod 400 /etc/securetty
```

- **Change root home directory to /root** — Moving the home directory for root to something other than /, helps eliminate unintentional security problems from files being accidentally placed in the root, /, directory. It also allows the permissions of the root user's home directory to be set more restrictively. This is accomplished by editing the password file entry to:

```
root:*:0:3::/root:/sbin/sh
```

Then build the directory:

```
mkdir /root
chown root:root /root
chmod 700 /root
mv /.profile /root
pwconv
```

Restrict File Permissions

File permissions should be as restrictive as possible while still allowing the system to operate properly. This minimizes the scope of the damage which an unprivileged user or program can cause. Generally, this means that there should not be any files which are world-writable, except a very few temporary files. A freshly installed system will contain a number of files which are world-writable. These files can be listed with the following command:

```
find / -perm -002 ! -type l -exec ls -ld {} \;
```

Symbolic links are excluded from the search since the permission bits are not used.

One approach is to remove the world-write bit from all files, then selectively add it back to those files and directories where it is necessary. The following can be executed to remove the world-write bit from all files with it set:

```
find / -perm -002 ! -type l -exec chmod o-w {} \;
```

Now we open up the permissions of files that need to be writable by the world:

```
chmod 1777 /tmp /var/tmp /var/preserve
chmod 666 /dev/null
```

The sticky bit should be set in publicly writable directories to prevent unprivileged users from removing or renaming files in the directory that they do not own.

The umask command sets the default permissions bits to be used when creating a file. For system start-up processes, the umask has to be set in a start-up script. The default umask for users has to be set in the user's session start-up scripts. One side-effect of converting to a trusted system is the default mask of 0 is changed to 07077, so nothing needs to be performed to tighten up the mask.

Security NetworkTuning

Network tunable parameters can have a significant effect on the security of a system. Default parameters are generally set to optimize performance or to increase functionality, usually without concern for security.

On Linux, /proc is a pseudo-file system which is used as an interface to kernel data structures rather than reading and interpreting /dev/kmem. Most of it is read-only, but some files allow kernel variables to be changed.

```
# Defend against SYN attacks
/sbin/sysctl -w net.ipv4.tcp_max_syn_backlog=1280
/sbin/sysctl -w net.ipv4.tcp_syn_cookies=1
# Don't send IP redirects
/sbin/sysctl -w net.ipv4.conf.all.send_redirects=0
/sbin/sysctl -w net.ipv4.conf.all.accept_redirects=0
# No source routing
/sbin/sysctl -w net.ipv4.conf.all.accept_source_route=0
/sbin/sysctl -w net.ipv4.conf.all.forwarding=0
/sbin/sysctl -w net.ipv4.conf.all.ms_forwarding=0
# Set the TIME_WAIT timeout
/sbin/sysctl -w net.ipv4.conf.vs.timeout_timewait=60
# Defend against SMURF attacks
/sbin/sysctl -w net.ipv4.icmp_echo_ignore_broadcasts=1
```

HP-UX 11 introduces the ndd command to perform network tuning. Start-up scripts read /etc/rc.config.d/nddconfig and set initial values for the network parameters. ndd -h produces a list of help text for each supported and unsupported tunable parameter that can be changed. This output should be examined to determine what is best for your environment. The following is an example /etc/rc.config.d/nddconf file.

```
# Defend against SMURF attacks
# Don't forward directed broadcasts
TRANSPORT_NAME[0]=ip
NDD_NAME[0]=ip_forward_directed_broadcasts
NDD_VALUE[0]=0
# Don't respond to ICMP echo request broadcasts
TRANSPORT_NAME[1]=ip
NDD_NAME[1]=ip_respond_to_echo_broadcast
NDD_VALUE[1]=0
# Don't respond to ICMP address mask request broadcasts
TRANSPORT_NAME[2]=ip
NDD_NAME[2]=ip_respond_to_address_mask_broadcast
NDD_VALUE[2]=0
```

```
# Don't respond to ICMP timestamp request broadcasts
TRANSPORT_NAME[3]=ip
NDD_NAME[3]=ip_respond_to_timestamp_broadcast
NDD_VALUE[3]=0
# Don't respond to other broadcasts
# Don't forward packets with source route options
TRANSPORT_NAME[4]=ip
NDD_NAME[4]=ip_forward_src_routed
NDD_VALUE[4]=0
# Don't forward or redirect packets
# Disable IP forwarding
TRANSPORT_NAME[5]=ip
NDD_NAME[5]=ip_forwarding
NDD_VALUE[5]=0
# Don't send IP redirects
TRANSPORT_NAME[6]=ip
NDD_NAME[6]=ip_send_redirects
NDD_VALUE[6]=0
# Defend against SYN attacks
# Increase TCP listen queue maximum
TRANSPORT_NAME[7]=tcp
NDD_NAME[7]=tcp_conn_request_max
NDD_VALUE[7]=500
TRANSPORT_NAME[8]=tcp
NDD_NAME[8]=tcp_syn_rcvd_max
NDD_VALUE[8]=1024
# Shorten the TIME_WAIT state timeout
TRANSPORT_NAME[9]=tcp
NDD_NAME[9]=tcp_time_wait_interval
NDD_VALUE[9]=60000
# Don't send text messages in TCP RST segments
TRANSPORT_NAME[10]=tcp
NDD_NAME[10]=tcp_text_in_resets
NDD_VALUE[10]=0
```

Host Hardening Systems

Proactive protection is all about making a system more resistant to security failures.

A great number of the items which are used to proactively protect a system are applicable to all hosts in all environments. To help simplify and standardize how these processes are implemented, scripts have been developed by both administrators and security companies. Some of these projects have made their way to becoming products.

/etc/default/security

A centralized location (/etc/default/security) for default security parameters has been created in HP-UX 11i. Currently, the login, password and switch-user processes utilize this information. Each line in the file is treated either as a comment or as configuration information for a given system command or feature. If any parameter is not defined or is commented out in this file, the default behavior detailed below will apply. This file must be world-readable and root-writable. Parameter definitions, valid values, and defaults are defined as follows:

- ABORT_LOGIN_ON_MISSING_HOMEDIR — This parameter controls login behavior if a non-root user's home directory does not exist. If the parameter is set to one, the login session will exit if the user's home directory does not exist. If it is set to zero, the user will be allowed to log in and his home directory will be set to the root directory (/). The default value is zero.

- MIN_PASSWORD_LENGTH — This parameter controls the minimum length of new passwords. For nontrusted systems, it can be any value from 6 to 8. It is not applicable to the root user on an untrusted system. For trusted systems, it can be any value from 6 to 80. The default value is 6.

- NOLOGIN — This parameter controls whether non-root login can be disabled by the /etc/nologin file. If the value is 1, the contents of the file /etc/nologin will be displayed and the root user will not be allowed access. If the value is 0, the presence of the file is ignored. The default value is 0.

- NUMBER_OF_LOGINS_ALLOWED — This parameter controls the number of logins allowed per user. This is applicable only for non-root users. A value of zero allows unlimited logins. The default value is 0.

- PASSWORD_HISTORY_DEPTH — This parameter controls the password history depth. A new password is checked only against the number of most recently used passwords stored in password history for a particular user. A user is not allowed to reuse a previously used password. The password history depth configuration is on a system basis and is supported in a trusted system. This feature does not support the users in NIS or NISPLUS repositories. Once the feature is enabled, all the users on the system are subject to the same check. If this parameter is not configured, the password history check feature is automatically disabled. When the feature is disabled, the password history check depth is set to 1. A password change is subject to all of the other rules for a new password, including a check with the current password. The default value is 1.

- SU_ROOT_GROUP — This parameter defines the root group name for the su command. The root group name is set to the specified symbolic group name. The su command enforces the restriction that a non-superuser must be a member of the specified root group in order to be allowed to switch-user to root. This does not alter password checking. If this parameter is not defined or if it is commented out, there is no default value. In this case, a non-superuser is allowed to switch-user to root without being bound by root group restrictions.

- SU_DEFAULT_PATH — This parameter defines a new default PATH environment value to be set when one uses the `su` command. The PATH environment variable is set to the new PATH when the `su` command is invoked. Other environment values are not changed. The path value is not validated. This is applicable only when the "-" option is not used along with the `su` command. By default, the path is not changed.

Bastille

Bastille is a security tool which improves the security of a UNIX system by applying settings to "harden" the operating system. It utilizes a wide variety of reputable sources on UNIX security to define the appropriate settings for configuring daemons, setting operating system parameters, and more. It attempts to provide the most secure, yet usable system possible programmatically. It is available for HP-UX and a variety of Linux systems. Bastille must be run by the root user when the machine is quiet.

Bastille uses a "hands on" approach for building a more secure system by allowing the system administrator to make decisions about the security settings for his system. The interactive use of the tool is designed to educate the administrator about security issues involved in each task with online help. Each step is optional and contains a description of the security issues involved. It allows inexperienced system administrators to make appropriate security decisions and trade-offs.

From the command-line, Bastille can be run in three different modes:

- **bastille –x** starts Bastille in the interactive mode, starting the GUI and walking the user through a series of questions. Bastille must be run in this mode on the first execution to create a configuration profile.

- **bastille –b** runs Bastille in the background, applying a predefined configuration profile from the file `/etc/opt/sec_mgmt/bastille/config` to the machine. This can be used to reapply a configuration on a system or to apply a configuration onto multiple machines with the same operating system.

- **bastille –u** resets the system to the state it was in before Bastille was run on the system.

Any time a change is made to an operating system or patches are installed, the security lockdown procedure should be performed.

Security Testing

T esting is the only way to be sure that the proactive protection processes which were put in place are working appropriately. The tests should determine the quality of the implementation. This should focus on evaluating the level of compliance to the policies and the completeness of the implementation. Security procedures must be practiced throughout the organization. The evaluation will determine the effectiveness of the current security environment and may highlight areas that were not previously considered.

Evaluate Current Status

Most organizations have some basic security, even if they are only informal activities. The current status of the security procedures must be evaluated, not only for their effectiveness but also for their applicability to the areas that the risk analysis has determined to be important. It needs to be determined if they appropriately address the areas of security that are most important to the organization. Evaluation of the effectiveness of current processes requires analysis of the procedures and testing of the practices.

Assess the policies and procedures by reading them. Determine if they cover all the necessary topics and give enough detail in response to the defining and handling of infractions. Compare them to the policies and procedures of other similar organizations.

The inspection process covers a tremendous range of issues, and, like most projects, the more analysis that is done up front, the more successful the project will be. Good planning will reduce the impact of security on the efficient running of the system.

Compliance with Security Program

Security policies are technology-independent descriptions of the security precautions that are required. They are generally defined as *rules*, which define specific bounds within which the system must operate, and *guidelines*, which ensure that security measures are not overlooked, even when they can be implemented in more than one way.

Security procedures define how to implement policies in respect to a specific technology. Procedures determine how standards should be implemented. Generally, they are written to apply to a class of systems that have similar attributes or security issues. Procedures must take into account the limitations of both the systems that are implementing them and current technology. Procedures are specific steps to follow that are based on the corporate security policy. Procedures are usually organized into *standards,* which define an acceptable level of security to which every system must adhere, and *exceptions*, which indicate specific instances where the standards will not be implemented. Exceptions require a definition of how the security issues, addressed by the standard which was not implemented, will be addressed.

Integrity of Installed Software

Monitoring the integrity of the software on your system is key to maintaining the security of the system. Software is altered directly by hackers installing hacking tools or through covert software which utilizes viruses, parasites, or worms to compromise systems.

Verifying Installed Software

Verifying the integrity of the installed software is necessary to determine that none of the software has been altered.

The software management system for HP-UX, Software Distributor, provides a utility which verifies the integrity of the installed software — swverify. Unfortunately, many of the patches do not modify the integrity database which the software verification system uses to determine if the installed software has been altered. Therefore, the swverify command will often indicate packages which have been patched as suspect.

To verify all software on your system, enter:

```
/usr/sbin/swverify \*
```

After the analysis, any inconsistencies, warnings, or errors will be found in the logfile: /var/adm/sw/swagent.log.

Integrity of Configuration

The system configuration should be tested to assure that the configuration is unable to be altered by unauthorized users and that it is free of errors.

Configuration Files

The configuration files should be tested to assure that they are of the correct format and are appropriately secured. The configuration fields should be tested, where applicable, to assure that they have reasonable values.

- **pwck** scans the local password file, /etc/passwd, and reports any inconsistencies to standard error. The checks include validation of the number of fields, login name, user ID, group ID, and whether the login directory and optional program name exist.

- **grpck** verifies all entries in the local group file, /etc/group, and reports any inconsistencies to standard error. This verification includes a check of the number of fields, group name, group ID, and whether all login names appear in the password file.

- **authck** checks both the overall structure and the internal field consistency of all components of the authentication database. It reports all problems that it finds. The protected password database and /etc/passwd are checked for completeness so that neither contains entries not in the other. The cross references between the protected password database and /etc/passwd are checked to make sure that they agree. However, if NIS+ is configured in your system, the password table is also checked before reporting a discrepancy. This means that a discrepancy would not be reported for a user that does not exist in /etc/passwd but exists in the protected password database as well as in the NIS+ passwd table. Fields in the protected password database are then checked for reasonable values.

Permissions

Appropriate permissions on configuration files and directories should be checked to assure that they are not modifiable by unauthorized users.

Security Scanners

As technology and computer systems become more complex, they are more prone to have security holes. At the same time, computer hackers are becoming more knowledgeable and sophisticated. Amateur hackers and sophisticated industrial espionage will continue to proliferate. Knowledge of security holes and hacking techniques is being spread widely and quickly by highly available communication channels and networks.

Vulnerabilities which are already known are the most common source for intrusions. Hackers write tools to exploit these vulnerabilities. Administrators must keep up to date by researching known vulnerabilities for all the systems in use to avoid losses. This one step can significantly reduce loss.

Host-based Vulnerability Testing

Host-based vulnerability testing evaluates the security of a system by evaluating configuration files for errors and software for known vulnerabilities.

- Tiger, the Texas A&M system checker, is a tool that inspects security-related settings of UNIX computers. It is a set of scripts that scan a UNIX system looking for security problems, in the same fashion as Dan Farmer's COPS. Tiger was originally developed to provide a check of UNIX systems on the A&M campus that were to be accessed from off campus, so it had to be simple enough that even new system managers would be able to use it.

- TARA, Tiger Analytical Research Assistant, is a variant of the Tiger software developed by the Advanced Research Corporation. It was developed since the original had not been updated for a very long time and there were numerous changes made to the "systems" directories. Output was streamlined to provide a more readable report file. Also, minor bugs in the "scripts" directory were corrected. TARA was tested under Red Hat Version 5.x, 6.x, SGI IRIX 5.3, 6.x, and SunOS 5.x. This upgrade was performed by the Advanced Research Corporation under a contract from the United States Government.

The following example of a configuration file indicates the tests that are performed by these programs:

```
Tiger_Check_PASSWD=Y            # Fast
Tiger_Check_GROUP=Y             # Fast
Tiger_Check_ACCOUNTS=Y          # Time varies on # of users
Tiger_Check_RHOSTS=Y            # Time varies on # of users
Tiger_Check_NETRC=Y             # Time varies on # of users
Tiger_Check_ALIASES=Y           # Fast
Tiger_Check_CRON=Y              # Fast
Tiger_Check_ANONFTP=Y           # Fast
Tiger_Check_EXPORTS=Y           # Fast
Tiger_Check_INETD=Y             # Could be faster, not bad though
Tiger_Check_KNOWN=Y             # Fast
Tiger_Check_PERMS=Y             # Could be faster, not bad though
Tiger_Check_SIGNATURES=N        # Several minutes
Tiger_Check_FILESYSTEM=Y        # Time varies on disk space...
Tiger_Check_PATH=Y              # Fast for just root... varies for all
Tiger_Check_EMBEDDED=N          # Several minutes
```

Network-based Vulnerability Testing

Network-based tools scan hosts on the network for open ports to test for general security vulnerabilities and specific exploits. They evaluate the services which are available.

- SAINT, Security Administrator's Integrated Network Tool, in its simplest mode, gathers as much information about remote hosts and networks as possible by examining such network services as finger, NFS, NIS, ftp and tftp, rexd, statd, and other services. The information gathered includes the presence of various network information services as well as potential security flaws — usually in the form of incorrectly set up or configured network services, well-known bugs in system or network utilities, or poor or ignorant policy decisions. It can then either report on this data or use a simple rule-based system to investigate any potential security problems. Users can then examine, query, and analyze the output with an HTML browser such as Mosaic, Netscape, or Lynx. While the program is primarily geared towards analyzing the security implications of the results, a great deal of general network information can be gained when using the tool — network topology, network services running, types of hardware and software being used on the network, etc.

  However, the real power of SAINT comes into play when used in exploratory mode. Based on the initial data collection and a user configurable ruleset, it will examine the avenues of trust and dependency and iterate further data collection runs over secondary hosts. This not only allows the user to analyze her or his own network or hosts, but also to examine the real implications inherent in network trust and services and help them make reasonably educated decisions about the security level of the systems involved.

- SARA, Security Auditor's Research Assistant, is a second-generation tool for examining systems over the network to determine the security of the services which it provides.

  The first generation tool, the Security Administrator's Tool for Analyzing Networks (SATAN), was developed in early 1995. It became the benchmark for network security analysis for several years. However, few updates were provided and the tool slowly became obsolete in the growing threat environment.

  The original author of SAINT (a SATAN derivative), Bob Todd, joined Advanced Research in early 1999 and has been working to evolve SATAN and the original SAINT concept to a community-oriented product (i.e, SARA).

```
# Probes by attack level.
  #
# ? Means conditional, controlled by rules.todo. * Matches anything.
  @light = (
          'dns.sara',
          'rpc.sara',
          'showmount.sara?',
          );
```

This means that a light scan will run the dns.sara and the rpc.sara scans, and the showmount.sara if SARA determines that the target is running NFS.

A bit further down shows:

```
@normal = (
              @light,
              'finger.sara',
              'tcpscan.sara 70,80,ftp,telnet,smtp,nntp,uucp',
              'udpscan.sara 53,177',
              'rusers.sara?',
              'boot.sara?',
              );

    @heavy = (
              @normal,
              $heavy_tcp_scan = 'tcpscan.sara 1-9999',
              $heavy_udp_scan = 'udpscan.sara 1-2050,32767-33500',
              '*?',
              );
```

There is nothing unusual here, except for the tcp and udp scan numbers; these refer to the port numbers that SARA examines for signs of activity.

## CHAPTER 23

Security Monitoring

Even though most resources have been spent on protection, detection is the most important part of computer security. Without detection, you will be unable to tell when you have had a security incident, and, even worse, you will be unable to determine when a security incident began. Without this information, you will be unable to rebuild your system with confidence in the integrity of the restored information.

Detection is a key component of system security. No matter how well you protect a system, there is always someone who will attempt to find a way to compromise the system. Companies can rarely afford to completely secure a system, so detection is the only way of knowing when the system has been compromised. Even worse than having a security incident is having one and not knowing it.

Detection is composed of monitoring the system and detecting anomalies or a series of activities that indicate that a break-in is occurring and reporting it. It is important that tools notify not just known attacks, but also new scenarios. Detection tools must look for the unusual and the unexpected.

Detection requires a commitment. Even though monitoring software and data reduction models can reduce the amount of information that the administrator is required to process manually, he must still look at the reports and assess the seriousness of the information.

Monitoring for New Vulnerabilities

New exploits to vulnerabilities appear every day, so it is a full-time job to keep a system without known vulnerabilities. Administrators have to monitor patches and updates to all the software on their systems. Some vendors will bundle security-related fixes into general release patches, so it is not enough to remain current with security patches; all software patches have to be managed.

Keeping Software Current

Keeping the software current is extremely important in keeping the system secure. A system that is well-managed, with a system manager who keeps current with the activities of his system and its users, is much less likely to become the victim of a successful attack.

New versions of software fix known bugs that could have been used to compromise a system, sometimes without any notification of the repair. It is more likely that older versions of software have had their behavior studied and their flaws exploited. Most security incidents are caused by exploiting known security problems, generally with older software.

The Red Hat Update Agent, `up2date`, can retrieve the latest software packages directly from Red Hat. This tool can be used to keep the system up-to-date with all security patches, bug fixes, and software package enhancements. Your system will have to be configured with the current Red Hat GPG key to verity the authenticity and integrity of the software being downloaded.

Installing Security Patches

By the time a security issue has been defined and a repair has been released for it, the hacker community also knows about the problem and how to exploit it. This is why it is imperative that you install all applicable security patches. This will protect you from known problems. Quite often it is these defects that are the basis of tools created to compromise a system that are utilized by unskilled hackers.

> Repeated intrusions of federal websites reveal that agencies are not adequately training their IT sentries to take advantage of readily available systems security solutions. In two months, hackers penetrated more than 100 federal computer systems, primarily taking advantage of a well-known weakness in the Microsoft Corp. Windows NT operating system. According to federal computer security experts, the attacks have been successful because federal systems administrators are failing to apply a software patch that has been available from Microsoft for more than a year.
>
> A 17-year-old hacker known as YTcracker, who penetrated several government and military websites (including those belonging to the Bureau of Land Management's National Training Center, NASA's Goddard Space Flight Center and the Defense Contracts Audit Agency), said he routinely sends messages to government website administrators insisting that they address vulnerabilities and adopt UNIX or other more secure systems, but the messages largely go ignored. YTcracker said in his defacement of websites that he

> "targeted the systems the government would look at and take seriously." [82]

Subscribe to security mailing lists, especially those specific to your vendor. These mailing lists will discuss current attacks that have been experienced and will announce security patches when they become available. Read these lists and heed the suggestions in them.

Obtaining HP-UX Security Bulletins

Security software patches are available via e-mail from the HP Electronic Support Center, which encompasses all aspects of support for HP products. An up-to-date security patch matrix and the Security Bulletin archives which requires registration. Follow the instructions at the following web page.

```
http://www.hp.com/security/support/notification.html
```

You should also examine the security bulletins themselves, because not all security bulletins result in a patch.

Linux Security Alerts

All Security Alerts, Bug Fix Alerts, and Enhancement Alerts (collectively known as Errata Alerts) can be retrieved directly from Red Hat. Red Hat Network (rhn.redhat.com) is an Internet service designed to aid in the managing of Red Hat Linux systems. It keeps track of when Errata Updates are released and sends you e-mail notifications, thereby reducing the time and effort required by system administrators to stay on top of the errata list, minimize security vulnerabilities in your network by providing the patches as soon as they are released and schedule automatic update delivery to selected systems.

Intrusion Methods

The next step in intrusion detection is understanding the processes used by intruders to attack an information system. There are a number of intrusion methods that are used successfully against information systems. Intrusion methods are either technical or social. These attacks have been performed by both lone individuals and by groups working a well-orchestrated script.

You should take a look at your system from the perspective of an attacker from outside the system. The log files on network equipment, like routers and bridges, can give insight into

---

[82] Frank, Diane, "Feds Leave Door Open for Hackers," *Federal Computer Week*, 20 December 1999.

activities that are unusual. Hackers will often clean up logs on systems but overlook the logs left on network devices.

Intruders tend to follow the path of least resistance, so attacks will be where it is easiest to gather the information or at the sites where information accumulates in order to give a greater return on investment from the attack. Strongly secured systems will be skipped over for easier targets. Intruders will focus on desktop and laptop computers where the security is often lax. They have a tendency to attack file servers and database systems, since these systems contain a greater amount of valuable information.

Malicious attacks on information can be either a social intrusion, when information is gathered from a person, or a technical intrusion, when information is retrieved from a computer. When the goal of the attack is information, the form of information is irrelevant.

Physical Intrusions

Physical intrusions require the attackers to come to the organization to make physical contact. They may gain access as part of a tour, or they might impersonate a delivery person or maintenance person. They might physically remove items or just be gathering information. Dumpster diving, which is pawing through trash and looking for some useful information, is a form of physical intrusion.

Technical Intrusions

Technical intrusions use a technical aspect of the information system to gain access and authorization. They will exploit vulnerabilities in technical systems to gain access to information. Computer hacking is a form of a technical intrusion.

Social Intrusions

Social intrusions utilize people to gather information. There are a number of processes used to get people to reveal information. Today, these processes are collectively called social engineering.

Determining When a Security Incident Has Occurred

This sounds deceptively simple. However, it may be very difficult to determine that a security incident has occurred. A system may be running "oddly" because the system has been compromised or it may be that the system is just running oddly.

Unless you have active system monitoring in place, it is unlikely that you, the system manager, will detect an intruder. More likely, a user who is on the system regularly will notice that the system is running slowly, or that he is unable to access something he should be able to access, or that the system is running out of free space, or some other oddity. In a large organization, these will be filtered through the help desk. It is these people who are the first to have the information needed to make a preliminary determination that the system may have been compromised. All reports should be taken seriously. Hackers have a tendency to brag. Often those they brag to or even the hacker himself may report a security problem.

This is why it takes both technology to set up detection software and procedures to define the proper time and person to notify when an incident is detected and to make an appropriate response to the security incident.

> Bibliofind, a subsidiary of Amazon.com for hard-to-find books, disclosed that customer credit card information was stolen between October 2000 and February 2001.
>
> The security breach was discovered on February 26, when the site's homepage was defaced with electronic grafitti. It took the defacement to its website to compel Bibliofind to undertake the investigation of its network logs and server, which uncovered that they had been broken into for at least five months.[83]

Determining the Severity of a Security Incident

Most information that shows up in security reports is because of harmless curiosity and honest mistakes — generally, activities that require no follow-up actions. However, all incidents should be logged and reported in a statistical summary that can indicate changes in trivial attacks or where user education is needed. Management of the volume of data from security logs requires that you classify the severity of the incident reported by the information. Incidents that are common and are stopped by regular security measures, such as an unsuccessful attempt to telnet to your firewall system which does not accept telnet access, should be recorded but not reported. However, activities that indicate that a successful attack is underway, such as the unexpected changing of an executable file, should be reported immediately.

Classification of security alarms requires experience and common sense. It is fairly easy to identify the activities that are unimportant and those that are critical. It is all those in between that have to be evaluated, and an appropriate response defined. What is unimportant on one system might be critical on another. The unsuccessful telnet attempt from an unknown host to the firewall may be unimportant whereas the same activity to a banking system server may be considered critical.

In general, it is best to over-classify the severity of an incident and, with experience, lower the classification to an appropriate level. All new or unexpected activities, those that has not been previously classified, must raise a high level of alarm so they can be investigated and

---

[83]   Elad, Barry, "Bibliofind.com Finds Out it Has Been Hacked," Copyright 2001 INT Media Group, Inc. All Rights Reserved. Republished with permission from http://www.internet.com.

classified appropriately. This is an ongoing process that requires the input of system managers, information owners, and policy makers.

System Monitoring Techniques

The system supplies a variety of monitoring tools that can be used to monitor suspicious activities on the system. The logging information from subsystems, such as networking and databases, have a lot of information about connections — where they were from and what they were doing — especially if you utilize some of the additional tools that increase the detail in the logs.

UNIX systems provide a number of facilities which enable you to monitor the systems. There are tools which can report active users (who) and processes (ps) as well as those who have been logged-on (last). More detailed information is available from systems monitoring software.

System accounting can give a picture of who is using the system and how. Auditing can give a more detailed look at the processing and data that each user is using. These can also be used as a basis for building user profiles to be used as norms to detect deviations from these norms.

The accounting system was created to monitor, accumulate, and report the activity of users and the processes they have run in order to be able to charge-back for the resources utilized. It is able to report when users use the system and how they use the system. This information is useful when building user profiles and determining when there is a change in behavior.

The audit system examines kernel structures and reports when privileges are used or system processes are invoked. Most audit systems lack enough context information to adequately limit the reported information to these invocations which indicate a security issue and not just normal operations.

User Monitoring

User monitoring provides information about what the users are doing. Changes in the behavior of a user can indicate a potential problem. This information can imply that the account is being used by someone other than the actual user or that the user is doing things that he should not be doing.

Programs should be run which report:

- Connection time
- Time of connections
- Resource utilization
- Specific programs executed

This information is useful in identifying abnormal behavior, since most users have very regular schedules and perform basically the same amount of the same type of work.

Process Monitoring

The processes which are run on a system are generally fairly consistent. Servers run specific processes to perform their tasks, as do users. Unexpected changes in the amount of processing or the type of processing being run on a system can indicate that it is being misused.

Performance analysis tools can also be useful for system security when used to report processing that is out of the normal day-to-day processing. An unexpected change in overall system utilization or an increase in a specific user's utilization, or a process that has increased its activity — any of these may indicate that the system is being used improperly.

Data Monitoring

File system monitoring is the process by which you compare all the relevant attributes of a file with a known secure version, in order to determine if the file has been altered in any manner. These attributes should include ownership, permissions, timestamps, file size, and a cryptographic checksum of the contents of the file. Using specific sets of these attributes allows files to be organized into groups based on their function.

The contents of a file can be tested with the file size and checksum. If these attributes have changed, then the contents of the file have changed. Ownership and permissions indicate the file's relationship with its environment. These two attributes are key to the security of a file. The timestamp of the file will indicate when the file was created, last modified, and last accessed. The following broad categories can be applied:

- Programs — This includes executable programs, binaries, and scripts. Programs should not change, so size, checksum, ownership, permissions, creation time, and last modified time should be tested.

- Devices — This includes all device files. Device file's major and minor numbers should not change, and all device files should be in the device directory.

- Logs — This includes all log files. Logs are regularly appended, so the contents of these files are changing, but the ownership and permissions should not change and should be tested.

- Directories — A directory's behavior is based on what is in the directory. A directory that contains files that do not change will not change, and all of the attributes should be tested. If it contains files that are modified, it will change. In all cases, the ownership and permissions should not be changed and should be tested.

Both existing files and new files need to be monitored. If a new file is created with the setUID or setGID bit set, then it may indicate a security problem. If device files are being created, this is probably a security problem.

Tripwire is a widely utilized tool which monitors the key attributes of files on a system. It can determine and report if any of these attributes change. These attributes include ownership of the file, the file size, the contents of the file, the file permission, and the last modified time of the file. These attributes can be grouped into classes, to which specific files can be assigned.

For example, log files should not have a change in ownership or permission, but are expected to grow larger as more records are written.

Comprehensive Monitoring

Comprehensive monitoring systems, often called host-based intrusion detection systems, monitor a variety of system attributes to determine when a security incident occurs. In addition to the system monitoring, they have the ability to corollate information from any of these systems and infer security breached from this data.

Detection software is key to keeping the system secure. It should monitor the integrity of the system as well as activities that could be considered suspicious. Detection software should be configurable so the level of detail can be adjusted.

You have to capture a reasonable amount of data, enough to be useful, but not so much as to be overwhelmed, and store it for a reasonable amount of time on off-line storage. The off-line storage of security logs needs its own media, separate from backups, and its own reuse cycle. Security logs have different recovery needs from other data.

You must have rapid detection to facilitate rapid notification and response. The sooner you are able to identify that your system has been compromised, the less there will be to clean up and the easier it will be to get the hackers off the system.

HP Intrusion Detection System / 9000 (J5083AA)

HP provides its intrusion detection system free of charge for HP-UX 11i. The HP Intrusion Detection System (IDS/9000) enhances local host-level security by automatically monitoring each configured host for signs of unwanted and potentially damaging intrusions. IDS/9000 concentrates on detecting and alarming the HP-UX 11 operating environment at the kernel audit data level of the operating system. IDS 9000 can monitor one or more HP-UX systems for users or applications who try to break security.

When the IDS/9000 is installed, it immediately provides intrusion detection. Pre-planned detection templates, surveillance groups, surveillance schedules, and alerts are built into the system, making basic detection and alerting available immediately. IDS/9000 continuously monitors for patterns of suspicious activities which suggest that security breaches or misuses are underway. When it detects a potential intrusion, it alerts immediately and creates audit events.

The alert also has the ability to execute any HP-UX command or program. IDS/9000 uses a variety of data sources to determine misuses, including:

- Kernel audit data which are generated by the trusted component of the operating system provide secure and robust data on the use of kernel functions.

- System logs provide information about access to the system, utilization of network services, and the use of system utilities.

- Application logs record activity and utilization, which enables detection of well-known attacks.

It detects a variety of exploits, such as: unauthorized access, modification of user resources, virus infections, privilege violations, Trojan horses, and "root" exploits. System conditions which can indicate misuse are race conditions, buffer overflows, unusual system states, and unusual daemon behavior. All communications within the IDS/9000 are secure are and built upon the Secure Socket Layer (SSL) protocol to protect the client/server messaging.

## CHAPTER 24

Reactive Security

Even though you cannot predict what kind of security incident you may fall victim to, you can prepare for the type of outage you might experience and plan your response. Your response to a security incident should be planned well in advance of any need for it. It should be a part of your information security policy or disaster plan. All business implications should have been evaluated and a policy based on business decisions should have been created. How security incidents are handled can have a profound effect on the company. No plan can handle every contingency. However, a general plan can be developed that can handle the majority of incidents.

Preparation is critical to a quick and successful response. While your system is under attack is no time to be trying to make business decisions on what you should do. And it is even a worse time to be creating policies and procedures, which is exactly what you will be doing by default.

Organizations generally spend a significant amount of time and money in the preparation of a business continuity plan that addresses natural disasters. However, it is unlikely that this plan adequately prepares for a disaster caused by a security incident, which is much more likely than a tornado, earthquake, fire, or flood. An incident response plan is a key element of the business continuity plan and requires the same level of attention. This means the same level of preparation and testing. An untested plan is only slightly better than no plan at all. If you haven't tested the plan, you have no assurance that it will be beneficial in the case of a security incident.

Review the Incident Response Plan

Regardless of the philosophy of responding to a security incident, there must be a preplanned response. An incident response plan will establish management procedures and responsibilities to ensure a quick, effective, and orderly response to security incidents. Incident response is not usually a revenue-generating activity, so this makes it difficult to obtain necessary resources. However, careful and intelligent planning and justification can be key to illustrating the scope of the issues. All of the business implications should be evaluated and a policy based on business decisions should be created.

The incident response plan should be the best-defined section of security procedures, yet it rarely is. The usual excuse is that the response will depend on the type of the attack. Specific incident handling procedures are often created for specific types of incidents. These usually evolve from best practices and address simple intrusions such as computer viruses, compromised user authentication, or system scanning or probing. This may be true for the specifics. However, in general, the response to a security incident will be the same. Even though you cannot predict the kind of security incident to which you may fall victim, you can prepare for the type of outage you could experience and plan your response accordingly. Your outage will either be a system outage or a data outage. The attack will come from either a live attacker, a programmed threat, or both. In any case, the response process will be the same.

The response plan should contain certain topics to adequately prepare the organization for responding to an incident.

Hackers come prepared with the tools and knowledge they need to do battle. It is up to the system manager to be just as well-organized with pre-planned responses and contingency plans. This ground work should be laid before the system manager finds his system under attack. When your system is going down in flames and all eyes are upon you is no time to be searching for solutions.

A good incident response plan will have defined and prioritized the response processes. It will have defined ownership of the process and contain basic check lists for each process.

Preserve the State of the Computer

Capturing the state of the system at the time of the incident by making a backup copy of logs, damaged or altered files, and files left by the intruder, will capture a picture of what has been done to the system. Any hacker tools which have been loaded on the system will be recorded. This captured data, and the information derived from it, is the evidence which will be needed to stop and prosecute the hacker.

Re-creating the activities of a hacker is a difficult and time-consuming task and deters organizations from prosecuting. Skilled hackers will employ the methods highlighted in this chapter and hop from one system to another, increasing the difficulty of synchronizing logs from many machines to create an accurate picture of the hacker's activities.

Destructive HackerTools

Today, some hacker tools monitor their environment and self-destruct if they perceive that they have been detected. Some of the ways a tool will monitor for discovery is if the system is shut down or if it is unable to access the Internet. So, to avoid alerting these smart tools, it is best to crash the system and remount the system disks onto another system so that the code has no chance to take its responsive actions. At this time, the exact images of the disks can be copied.

Reporting the Incident

Once you have determined that a security incident has taken place, you must determine the severity of the security incident so that the correct people can be notified at the appropriate time. This is very important — too soon may create undo concern, too late, embarrassment. These people will include system administrative personnel, users, management, and local, state, or federal law enforcement authorities.

Notification must be made of the security incident to the appropriate people (management, legal counsel, law enforcement) at the appropriate time. Some actions cannot be taken until authorized by the appropriate individual. The response cannot begin until those responsible for implementation are notified and mobilized.

Corporate Management

An incident should be communicated to management immediately. Computer-based communications such as e-mail, electronic notes, or instant messaging programs should not be used, since they may not be secure. Contact management using the telephone, pager, or in person. Do not use web-based or other computer services to send an alpha page. Inform the manager that you have identified a possible breach of computer security.

Affected Partners

If the affected system is known to be a trusted host of any other systems, inform the manager of this and any activity that has been performed to detect intrusion activity on the other systems. Provide them with any information they may need in order to allow others to detect any other intrusions that may be in progress on other systems.

Law Enforcement

It must be necessary or advantageous to contact law enforcement about the incident. Law enforcement may need to be involved to recover stolen information or equipment, or to get the information necessary to track the intruder. Contact law enforcement and provide incident documentation, share information about the intruder, and share any ideas about possible motives. To initiate an investigation, contact your local FBI office or the appropriate federal, state, or local law enforcement agency.

Contain the Incident

Logically, containing the incident should be the first step in responding to a security incident. However, due to the cost of having systems or data unavailable and due to the time and effort involved, this step is often postponed until services and data are restored. Restoring data and services prior to understanding the cause of the problem can result in the problem reoccurring. This may turn into a lengthy process of repeatedly restoring the system until the problem is isolated. For most system administrators, this is the most interesting part of the problem.

Isolate the System

Close the machine to outside access. Remove the network connection to the machine and any other remote connections that can be used to provide access to the intruder. Remember, if the intruders sense that you are on to them, they may try to cover their tracks by destroying the file system of the machine.

Containment involves limiting the incident to those systems and data that have already been compromised. Minimizing the impact of an incident has to be the primary goal of any response plan and should be put into motion immediately.

Secure the System

Securing the system is composed of two parts: determining the cause and repairing the problem to avoid reoccurrence. Determining the cause can take a considerable amount of time and resources. Quite often the exact cause will not be able to be determined; rather, a list of possible causes will develop. In this case, all of these possible causes need to be addressed and all the related problems repaired.

Check the system for automated processes that do not belong on the system, such as processes set up to run automatically at a certain time or upon a specific alarm condition. Lock out all accounts that will not be used in the course of the investigation. All passwords will have to changed on the system prior to resumption of normal activity. If a passworded account may have been the source of the attack, change the passwords on all the other accounts which that user has on other systems or lock out the accounts to prevent possible abuse of the password elsewhere. Identify all files that have been modified or created in the time window in which the breach occurred. Check particularly for any modifications to files that control logins, trusted host access, and file system sharing or exporting.

If you are planning to restore services or data prior to determining cause, it is best to take a complete "image" backup, including the entire disks, not just the files on the disk, so the cause can be determined at a later time.

Eradication is the removal of the cause of the incident. All systems affected must be examined for evidence of the incident. Any changes must be corrected and the system returned to its normal configuration. Additionally, any backup media of the affected systems should be examined to determine their state. Eradication involves a complete review of the system and may be time-consuming. Security tools may be used to speed the process.

Document Everything

The importance of documenting every step you take in recovery cannot be overstated. Recovering from a security incident can be a hectic and time-consuming process in which hasty decisions are often made. Documenting the steps you take in recovery will help prevent those hasty decisions and will give you a record of all the steps you took to recover, which will be useful for your future reference. Documenting the steps you take in recovery also may be useful if there is a legal investigation.

Documentation is critical to effective resolution and post-incident review of a security incident. The documentation should include the activities of the intruder as well as the activities of those who are attempting to repair the damage. Much documentation which is collected by automated systems can be very useful in the case of a security incident. However, it requires condensing and interpreting to isolate the information that is specific to the security incident and to make it comprehensible to those who need to be informed about the incident.

Gather Information

Information gathering is a critical step in responding to a security incident. Information has to be gathered to determine the extent of the damage and the source of the attack. Gather information from the sources which are available. Other sources of information should be investigated and utilized as deemed appropriate. Review access logs and audit trails to identify the intruder's identity, origin, and what activities he or she performed while on the system.

Increase Monitoring

When an incident is discovered, any additional information gathering services should be started. Enabling more logging, accounting, or auditing can provide a more detailed view of the activities of the hacker. However, this requires that the hacker's activities continue after he is discovered.

While the incident is in progress, activate auditing software and consider implementing a keystroke monitoring program if the system warning banner permits. This information is going to be vital to locating, apprehending, and prosecuting the attacker.

Gather Counterintelligence

When a system manager suspects that his system is under attack or has been compromised, it is likely he'll be trying to gather information about the hacker. There is, however, a question about how much information gathering is legal. This will vary if the system being examined is managed by the system manager or the computer is owned by the company that is gathering the information. But if the hacker is coming in from another system, gathering information from that system creates a whole new set of issues. Of course, you don't have to worry about what is admissible in a court of law until the hacker is caught and goes to trial.

Is it proper for a system manager to use counterintelligence techniques? The answer to this question may end up being defined in a court of law based on the policies and procedures you have in place. Adherence to and consistent interpretation of your policies are key to presenting a successful court case.

Collect all the information available about the intruders from your system. Your company policy should indicate that in order to diagnose problems in response to a security incident, it may be necessary to collect information and examine files that would otherwise be considered private. This can include an examination of user files and e-mail.

Remember, because the hacker is often using someone else's system to attack you, the system manager of the system from which the attack is coming may have no idea that the attack is underway. The system manager of this system may be experiencing system problems. If you are trying to gain information from counterintelligence measures in which you may use the same information-gathering commands as an attacker would use, the system manager of the system from which you're being attacked may interpret your activity as an attack. Therefore, automated counterintelligence measures should be discouraged. You should contact the system manager of the attacking system and enlist his support in tracking down the intruder.

These are just a few of the questions you and your legal staff must ask and decide upon your answers. During a successful attack in progress, is it justified to penetrate the attacker's computer system under the doctrine of immediate pursuit? Is it permissible to stage a counter-attack in order to stop an immediate and present danger to your property? These questions will also have to be answered by the courts.

The distributed and interconnected design of the Internet make it difficult to track attackers. In the wake of highly publicized Internet attacks, the FBI has created new tools to enable them to rapidly respond to intrusions and automatically determine an attacker's network entry point and collect information on the attackers activities withing the constraints of the law.

The Carnivore system is a computer-based investigative tool that is designed to allow the Federal Bureau of Investigation, in cooperation with an Internet Service Provider (ISP), to comply with court orders requiring the collection of certain information, ranging from merely "to/from" information to full content concerning e-mails or other electronic communications to or from a specific user identified as part of an investigation.

Carnivore is, in essence, a special filtering tool that can gather the information authorized by court order, and only that information. It permits law enforcement, for example, to gather only the e-mail addresses of those persons with whom the individual under investigation is communicating, without allowing any human being, either from law enforcement or the service provider, to view private

> information outside of the scope of the court's order. In other words, Carnivore is a minimization tool that permits law enforcement strictly to comply with court orders, strongly to protect privacy, and effectively to enforce the law to protect the public interest. In addition, Carnivore creates an audit trail that demonstrates exactly what it is capturing. [84]

Countermeasures

Automated responses to an incident can be extremely useful and aid in the rapid response to an incident. Automatically enabling information-gathering systems and disabling vulnerable services can reduce the impact of the attack. However, one may be tempted to take counter measures and strike back at the attacker with a denial-of-service attack or other means to disable the attacker's ability to continue the attack.

> One week before Superbowl Sunday, the nation's leading satellite TV service struck back at hackers who have been stealing its signal for up to four years by altering access card codes. DirecTV struck back at satellite pirates with a major electronic counter measure, ECM, which rendered illegal access cards useless. DirecTV satellites delivered a special signal to its millions of receiver boxes in homes across North America instructing them to shut down the unauthorized access cards.
>
> Hackers reporting on websites said it could take weeks to recover from the ECM, if they could recover at all. Not only were the illegal cards, which can connect users to DirecTV programming, deactivated, some were left unusable. Hackers dubbed the day "Black Sunday." [85]

---

[84]   ""Carnivore" and the Fourth Amendment," *Statement of Kevin V. Di Gregory, Deputy Assistant Attorney General, U.S. Department of Justice Before the Subcommittee on the Constitution of the House Committee on the Judiciary*, 24 July 2000.

[85]   "DSS Wars," *System Resource Group*, 8 May 2001.

Counterstrike

The concept of retaliation is not new. It is a basic military strategy to eliminate the opponent's ability to wage war. This appears to be the stance of a growing number of large companies that have been victimized by hacker attacks.

Countermeasures include tools that disable an attacker's browser, block TCP/IP connections, or launch debilitating countermeasures such as denial of services or flooding attacks.

> Companies are taking the law into their own hands to beat hackers who cost them millions each year. They are going on the offensive and adopting hacking tools and techniques themselves, according to a former director of information warfare for the U.S. Department of Defense.
>
> A popular tactic is hiring experts to trace the source of a hack and find weaknesses in a culprit's system. One website was offering the facility to overload a hacker's own computer with spam email. But counter-attacks could fall foul of the Computer Misuse Act or hit the wrong target.[86]

However, it is difficult to be assured that the attack is coming from the location it appears to be.

Even though the concept of counterstriking is intriguing, one problem with getting involved in a cyberspace shoot-out is being certain that you are targeting your attacker. It is common for an attacker to route the attack through other sites on the way. Hackers can also forge packet headers to make it appear that an attack is coming from a completely different location. If a company is shooting first and asking questions later, innocent people could be hurt. And the organization that returns fire may open itself up to civil, criminal, or physical risk.

The net-based counterattack described above, although minor in scope, raises important legal and political issues. Do organizations have the right to counter any of the hundreds of hacker attacks they receive everyday with counterattacks of their own? Will this depend on whether the organization is a government or military organization or a private company? Will the source of the attack, being either foreign or domestic, affect this question?

All of these questions will have to be answered in the coming digital years.

---

[86]   McCue, Andy, "Companies Hit by Hackers Fight Back," *Computing,* 27 April 2001.

## CHAPTER 25

Recovery

Incident recovery is the process of bringing the system back to a known good state, removing any damage caused by the incident, and restoring the availability and accuracy of the information. Recovering a compromised system is required to return it to normal operations. Recovery should occur after the incident is contained and there is some idea of its scope. However, it may be a business necessity to return the system to operation before the incident is fully contained. This risk needs to be carefully managed so that the system can be successfully restored. Restoring systems at the same time as containing the incident requires a great deal of coordination so that efforts do not interfere. You must be able to determine how long the security incident has existed before you can determine what may have been compromised and what has to be restored. If a security incident has been going on undetected for some time, it is often difficult to pinpoint an exact start date. It is generally best to err on the side of caution and select a date that is clearly prior to the start of the incident so you can be assured that the information recovered from that date is not compromised.

Assess the Scope

Assess the scope of the damage. This allows you to isolate the compromised systems and data and begin the process of determining the cause, nature, and extent of the attack.

Setting Priorities

In most environments, it is more important to have accurate information than availability; however, in some environments, availability is more important than accuracy. The order and importance of these must be driven by business factors. In either case, the primary concern of incident recovery is the minimization of losses. The primary method of limiting losses is to limit the length of the incident. This is achieved through focusing on rapid detection and recovery.

To adequately determine priorities, one needs to understand the costs of having the systems unavailable, the risks of enabling the service when it is not secured, and the time frame requirements for restoring the systems. The costs and requirements are based on business priorities and contractual and legal requirements.

Business Continuity Plan

Your business continuity plan should define the priorities for the system. It will define the relative importance of availability and integrity and at what point contingency plans, such as remote disaster sites, should be used. The choices made in recovering from an incident are business choices and should be based on good business decisions. The information needed to make these good decisions comes from financial impact and the relative success of mitigation options.

Secure the System

If the compromised system provides services to customers, a service recovery procedure should be started to reinstate the interrupted services in a secure fashion. Remember that it is better to interrupt a service to protect customer information from tampering or disclosure, and to prevent a system from becoming a bridge for further break-ins, than to leave it up and risk these events.

You must rigorously determine what has been compromised and what has not. If you do not thoroughly clean your system after a security incident, you probably will be doing it again. If the compromised system cannot be verified as being secure (i.e., binaries checked for modification, passwords changed, security holes patched, etc.), then the services should be recovered by some means other than returning the compromised system to production. If necessary, remove the system's media for investigation and replace it with new media for a system rebuild. Customer data which may have been compromised should also be identified. Check the system to identify any changes to customer data that may affect system operation (programs in customer areas that may run with administrative privileges, for example.) If necessary, lock out specific accounts or data areas that pose a risk. In some cases, it may be possible to resume production with a new system created from backups of the compromised system. The restored system should be checked to make sure that there are no security vulnerabilities restored that may have been in place prior to the detected incident (a back door may have been in place prior to the detected incident, allowing the intruder entry.)

Repair the Vulnerability

Logically, repairing the problem should be the first step in responding to a security incident. However, due to the cost of having the system or data unavailable and due to the time and effort involved, this step is often postponed until services and data are restored. Restoring data and services prior to understanding the cause of the problem can result in the recurrence of the problem. This may turn into a lengthy process of repeatedly restoring the system until the problem is isolated.

Once a vulnerability is discovered, it must be repaired; to do otherwise is negligent. Most of the time, vulnerabilities will be discovered by others who will report them to industry emergency response teams or to the vendor of the systems with the vulnerabilities. Then fixes to the vulnerabilities can be distributed to eliminate the problem everywhere. There is no reason that a system should be compromised because of a known vulnerability that should have been repaired. However, most successful attacks are against known vulnerabilities. Every system should apply all appropriate security patches from the appropriate vendors and keep abreast of new patches as they become available. If you have suffered a security incident the vulnerabilities that were exploited must be identified and repaired to avoid recurrence.

For many system administrators, this is the most interesting part of the problem. It can take a considerable amount of time and resources. Quite often the exact cause cannot be determined; a list of possible causes will develop instead. All of these possible causes need to be addressed and all the related problems repaired.

Repairing a vulnerability entails getting the correct resources. Process vulnerabilities can be addressed by the management responsible for the process. Administration vulnerabilities require that new administration procedures be defined and implemented. Software vulnerabilities must be repaired by those responsible, whether they are in-house or external software suppliers. These suppliers may issue a patch until the fix can be integrated into the software development cycle. If a patch is not rapidly forthcoming, then other methods of eliminating the vulnerability must be investigated. Evaluate how the vulnerability was exploited to determine if it will represent a class problem that could affect other areas of the system. Repairing the vulnerability is always the preferred methods of eliminating recurrence. Vulnerabilities can be repaired in a number of ways.

Apply a Patch

A patch is a piece of software that addresses the specific vulnerability. Generally, it is a small piece of code that has minimal impact on the software system. Patches are used because they can be quickly written, tested, and applied. However, they are usually focused on a very specific issue. They may not address other related vulnerabilities or the same vulnerability in other related software systems.

Disable the Service

Disabling the service that has a vulnerability will effectively remove the ability to exploit that vulnerability. If the service is not needed, then its software should be removed from the system so that it is not inadvertently restarted.

Change the Procedure

Changes to procedures may be able to eliminate a vulnerability if the changes in how the system is used affect how the system is misused, or if the vulnerability is a vulnerability in the procedure itself.

Security procedures require continuous review. Changes in technology, business conditions, the law, etc., all relate to the effectiveness of procedures.

Redesign

Redesigning the system indicates an acceptance of the fact that security really must be designed into the system and not bolted on after the fact. This is the most expensive way to fix a security vulnerability. However, if done correctly, it is the most likely to fix it on a long-term basis. Redesign is not generally considered until all other options are exhausted.

Redesign does become a viable alternative when new systems are being implemented. Designing a security architecture requires that all new systems and major renovations of existing systems adhere to the architecture. In time, this will increase the level of security of the information systems.

System Recovery

The company loses money every minute that the system is unavailable. This may be lost income or it may be lost productivity. However, restoring services may be of little value if the data on the system have been compromised or if the hacker still has access. Restoration of services involves bringing both the specific service and the system that supports it online. The restoration of the system may enable other services, which will also need to be verified as uncompromised.

- **Availability** — There may be cases where loss of service — user or application downtime — is more important than restoring data. These cases could include systems that control automated environments, factory floors, or where income is based on having the service available, such as service providers or network providers.

  Often in these cases, restoring services is more important than securing the system. If you restore services prior to determining the cause, you may find yourself involved in combat with an attacking hacker. This can turn into a long and painful battle.

  If you are planning to restore services or data prior to determining the cause, it is best to make a complete "image" backup, including the entire disks and not just the files on the disk, so that the cause can be determined at a later time.

- **Integrity** — Restoring the integrity of a system requires the verification of all parts of the system. Intruders will often compromise the integrity of a system by planting malicious software, such as back doors and Trojan horses. The integrity of the processes is vital to the accuracy of the results.

*   **Confidentiality** — The installation of information-gathering software is common in attacks. These programs primarily assist in gathering information that will be used to gain more access or privileges. However, they are also used to gather information from the victim organization. One such tool, a network sniffer, is able to gather information from systems that have not been compromised by monitoring all the information that travels over the network.

The information system must be sufficiently secured prior to restoring services to ensure that restarting the services will not allow more information to be compromised.

HP-UX

Ignite-UX's `make_recovery` command creates a system recovery tape. This tape can be used to boot and recover a system which has become unbootable due to corruption of the root disk or volume group. A system can be booted and installed from the tape without user intervention for configuration, customization, software selection, hostname, or IP address.

The system recovery tape consists of a boot image, followed by an archive of system files that comprises a minimum core OS. The minimum core OS consists of `/stand`, `/sbin`, `/dev`, `/etc`, and subsets of `/usr`, `/opt`, and `/var` that are required during the install process. The devices or volume groups that correspond to the file systems/directories `/`, `/dev`, `/etc`, `/sbin`, `/stand`, and `/usr` are considered core devices or volume groups. These devices or volume groups are re-created during the recovery process. All non-OS data on them would be removed and restored during the recovery process, if they were specifically appended to the recovery tape. If `/opt` or `/var` are mounted elsewhere, they would not be reinstalled during the recovery process and are fully preserved.

The `make_recovery` command provides a mechanism for you to specify your own non-system files in the archive by using the `/var/adm/makrec.append` file. These specifications are limited to files or directories that belong to file systems in the core devices or volume groups. To specify including all files from core volume groups, use the -A option.

The `make_recovery` command also provides a mechanism for you to exclude selected files from the archive via the -p and -r options. For backing up and recovering non-core file systems which are not on the core device or volume groups, you would use normal backup utilities.

Linux

Reinstallations of Linux systems are performed in the same manner as original installations. However, Red Hat provides a tool, kickstart, which allows you to build a single file containing the answers to all the questions that would normally be asked during a typical Red

Hat Linux installation. This provides administrators with an automated installation method to create a system with a specific configuration.

Kickstart installations can be performed using a local CD-ROM, a local hard drive, or via NFS, FTP, or HTTP. Normally, a kickstart file (ks.cfg) is copied to the boot disk or made available on the network. To begin a kickstart installation, you must boot the system from a Red Hat Linux boot diskette or the CD-ROM and enter a special boot command at the boot prompt. If the kickstart file is located on a boot diskette that was created from the boot.img or bootnet.img image file, the correct boot command is:

```
boot: linux ks=floppy
```

Kickstart installations can also be run interactively so that the default values will populate the input fields, but the administrator has the option to override them.

Data Recovery

It has often been said that you can lose no more information than that which has been created or changed since your last backup. This is true. However, destruction of data is only one of many goals that the hacker might have. The hacker may want to make copies of your information. Having the information compromised may be more costly to the company than the loss of that information. If the system has information that is confidential, then it should be transmitted and stored in an encrypted form. This gives you that one additional layer of security to protect the information from prying eyes. Or the hacker may just want to use the resources that the system has to offer. It may be very annoying to have a hacker using your system, but it may be less costly than having a hacker who takes or destroys your information.

Generally, the data on a system are the most valuable assets in the data center. Restoring the data on a system that has been compromised is usually of prime importance. However, it may be more important to secure the system first, which will require determining the cause and repairing the problem, so that when the data are restored, there will be some level of confidence that the restored data will be able to maintain their integrity.

The restoration of data may take any of a number of forms based on the type of attack and the business decisions on how to restore data. It may be enough to validate the integrity of the online data, or it may be more appropriate to restore the system from a backup — a known good backup — or the data may have to be re-created from processing. The level of system compromise may have to be evaluated before a determination of restoration process begins. If compromised data are not discovered and remain on the system after you have closed the security incident and have returned to business as usual, that data could affect business decisions, production processes, and people's lives for a very long time.

- **Availability** — Restoring the availability of data is usually the first step in a recovery scenario. The data must be restored to a known good state, generally from a known

good backup, or the data may have to be recreated from processing. If there are changes
to be made to make the data current, they must be applied. The data must be restored
before services can be made available to the users.

- **Integrity** — It may be enough to validate the integrity of the online data, or it may be
  more appropriate to restore the system from a backup. If the data have been changed or
  altered but not destroyed, it may be very difficult to identify the compromised data. The
  process of verifying the integrity of the data can be a lengthy one, as every data item has
  to be checked by comparison to a known good copy or by cryptographic checksum.

- **Confidentiality** — When an information system has been compromised, one must
  assume that the confidentiality of the information has also been compromised. Once the
  confidentiality of data has been compromised, it cannot be restored; only the scope of
  the damage can be controlled. Stopping the spread of the data is the prime concern. If
  the intruder can be caught, it might be possible to limit the compromise to the intruder.
  If the spread of the information cannot be stopped, then reactive measures must be
  implemented to limit the impact of the compromise.

You must test your recovery process beforehand to make sure you can fully recover data in
the event of an emergency.

Never recover in place any critical files such as `/etc/passwd`, or those in `/tcb/files`.
Instead, restore the file to a temporary directory (do not use `/tmp`) and give this directory permissions "drwx------," preventing anyone else from using it. Compare the restored files with
those to be replaced. Make any necessary changes.

Backup Strategy

The old backup theory of doing full backups weekly and incremental backups daily took
nothing into account except efficiency of tape rotation. A backup strategy should be based on
the needs of the data which are being protected. Different types of data have different requirements. Some data are very transient and have little shelf life, so there is no need for long-term
storage of this data, while other information, such as security logs, needs to be kept for a long
time since it is not known when it will be needed.

The timing of backups should take into account the flow of the information. Backups
should be scheduled directly after significant changes to the data have taken place, if possible.
Backups should minimize losses and make recovery as efficient as possible.

Media retention schedules should be determined by the retention requirements of the data
they contain. Data with similar retention needs and security requirements can be grouped on
common media for convenience. Keep archives for a minimum of six months, then recycle the
media.

Backup media deserve the highest level of security since they contain all of the system's data. Label backup tapes and store them securely. Off-site storage provides maximum security. Access to the media should be allowed only with proven need.

Examine the log file of the latest backups to identify problems occurring during backup. The backup log file should have restrictive permissions set.

Linux

One of the most used and most useful backup systems is the Advanced Maryland Automatic Network Disk Archiver, Amanda. It is a sophisticated network backup system that can back up all the systems on a network to a backup device on a single server. It supports many different type of systems.

Amanda is not actually a backup program; rather, it is a wrapper that manages other backup programs.

It has strong tape management services which help maintain a large repository of networked backups. It keeps track of which backups are on which tapes and can print out labels and directories.

HP-UX

The prescribed backup and recovery software for HP-UX is fbackup and frecover. These are the only utilities which can back up and recover files selectively and retain access control lists (ACLs).

Frecover maintains the permissions which the file had when it was backed up. An index of a backup tape can be previewed with frecover using the "-I" option, but frecover prevents you from reading the file if the permissions on the file forbid it. Frecover allows you to overwrite a file. However, the file retains the permissions and ACLs set when the file was backed up.

Fbackup is integrated into the menu-based administration interface, SAM, which allows delegation of privileges. Backup operators can be given restricted SAM access to perform backup and recovery procedures without being given full root access.

Monitor for Additional Signs of Attack

A system that has been compromised is likely to be attacked again. Monitoring the restored systems will help verify that the improvements deter future attacks and can assist in the gathering of information about the attacker if he returns. The monitoring should include the services that were compromised, the processes that were used to compromise the system originally, and the connections for other systems that were compromised. The restored system should be placed at the highest level of monitoring for a period of time after the attack to help restore confidence in the system.

Restoration of Confidence

Restoration of confidence is very difficult. Once an impression is made, it is difficult to change it. This is why you must be proactively prepared to report on the incident in a very positive light. You must show that you have always been on top of the situation and that you were able to detect the situation and respond quickly to protect the vital information assets of the organization.

This is the area where an incident plan is most useful. A good incident plan will direct what information is released when and by whom. It can prevent a loss of confidence.

There are a number of groups about whose confidence you need to be concerned.

- **Management** has control over setting priorities and allocating budgets. Management confidence is critical to all projects and departments in the organization.

  Management must be confident that the situation is being handled quickly, quietly, and in the best interest of the company. It needs to be confident in the information security organization and its ability to handle the situation.

- **Stockholders** are the ultimate owners of the corporation and, as the owners, they need to understand the financial impact of security incidents. However, due to the fact that it is a publicly held corporation, any information that is made available to the stockholders is also made public.

  Much like the message to management, the message to stockholders should indicate that everything was handled quickly and in the best financial interests of the corporation. They need to be assured that their interests are always being protected.

- **Users** are the people who are directly affected by the unavailability of data caused by a security incident. It is their work that is interrupted and they are the ones who must trust the system to use the system. Users must be confident that the systems are restored to provide rapid and accurate results.

  Without confidence in the systems they employ, users will find other methods to accomplish their work. This may include using other systems that were not designed for the task at hand or going outside the organization for their information systems needs. These choices are often not cost-effective and may reduce the overall security and efficiency of the organization.

- **Partner relationships** are created to mutually benefit both organizations. They add value to an organization by supplying something which the other organization does not have. The partner relationship is built on trust and sharing. These are two attributes that can be severely damaged by a security incident.

  Partners must be confident that their trust in another company is well-founded and that the information that is shared between the companies is given adequate care. They must believe that the partnership does not raise their exposure to danger and that the partner's systems will not be used to exploit their own systems.

- The **public** must have confidence in the quality and responsibility of the company. People must feel that the company is capable of handling any situation that arises and that it is safe to do business with the company. The public should feel that the company is doing what is best for the public good.

Public Relations

Public relations, perception management, rumor control — whatever you call it — may be more important than any other aspect of response because, even if everything is done perfectly, if the perception is that things were out of control, then the truth doesn't matter. Customer perception can ruin a company.

Letting people know at the right time will limit the rumors that may otherwise be created. All those involved with the security incident should be given the same story. Policy should state how, when, and by whom information about a security incident is disseminated to management, to employees, and to the public. Companies should limit the number of people who talk to the press, preferably leaving this to individuals who are trained in handling the press.

The same incident might be reported "Hacker Cracks Corporate Computers" or "Local Company Aids Police in Tracking Down Hackers." The only difference is perception.

Public relations is best left to the professionals who can weigh the issues of bad press from going public with the incident versus bad press if news of the incident is leaked, and can put the incident in the best light for the company.

## CHAPTER 26

Review

$\mathbf{O}$nce the chaos of the situation has subsided and all the systems are restored to a normal mode of operation, it is time to take a clear look at the incident and perform a follow-up review. This follow-up stage is one of the most important phases of a security incident, yet, since the incident is under control, it is often not done. Every incident is different and brings unexpected issues, so there is always something new to be learned.

This incident review should document the incident, determine the cost of the incident, evaluate the handling of the situation, and determine what further actions are required. The review process should include a cross-section of the organizations that were, or should have been, involved in the incident and monitored by management. This group will not only perform a postmortem of the incident, it will plan the implementation of remedies to prevent recurrence and open up communication with users and others affected by or involved with the incident. It will need to determine the business impact of the incident. All in all, it is responsible for total quality process improvement. The group should take this opportunity to develop a set of lessons learned, improve future performance, and inform management of the steps taken during the incident. Additionally, the development of postmortem improvements will provide the opportunity to organize any documentation that may be necessary should legal action be required.

The scope of a post-incident review may, on the surface, seem overwhelming. However, most of the information should have already been gathered and documented in the individual logbooks of those who were involved in the incident. Documentation from a security incident will be plentiful. Everyone involved must keep a logbook that details his or her activities during the incident. Security monitoring systems generate a tremendous amount of information that was probably utilized during the incident. Information systems can monitor and log in the most excruciating detail. It is because of this overwhelming amount of detailed and technical information that condensed and summarized documentation of the incident is required.

Determine the Cost of the Incident

Calculating the cost of an incident will give you a measurement of the importance of security for your organization. You may find calculating the cost of this incident useful in explaining to management that security is important to your organization.

The business impact analysis determines the financial impact which a security incident has on the organization. It is based on product revenues and the impact of peak seasons. It also takes into account the upstream and downstream implications and includes estimated costs associated with implementing determined recovery strategies. The comparison of actual losses to the estimates will help improve the ability to better predict the business impact of future disruptions.

Legal Reporting

In many industries, especially financial services, security incidents have to be reported to the governing body if they cause a significant financial impact.

In any case, a financial impact analysis will generally be required so that the appropriate information can be presented to the owners of the organization.

Learning from Mistakes

Document and review your lessons learned from going through the process of recovering from a root compromise. This will help you decide on the appropriate revisions necessary for your security policy.

Evaluate the Response Process

A security incident tests the procedures that are in place to manage an incident. Once the incident is over, it is time to review the processes and evaluate corrective measures. Security incidents impact a wide variety of departments and processes. All of the processes that were involved with the security incident should be reviewed and any that need improvement based on this incident should be fixed accordingly.

Emergency Response Program

Emergency response procedures include all of the aspects that are invoked because of the security incident. This includes the response team's ability to react to the situation, contact the appropriate people, including infrastructure providers and partners, and handle any situation that may develop.

Emergency response teams have to coordinate with other emergency response teams when the incident is caused by a physical disaster. Disaster response teams will control and manage physically damaged sites. In a physical disaster scenario, information becomes just one aspect of the disaster. Personal safety and those things that jeopardize physical safety have higher priority.

Incident Management Program

Incident management is the process of controlling the incident. It defines the incident declaration criteria and the recovery escalation sequence. It includes coordinating all of the teams (e.g., Damage Assessment Team, Site Security Team), facilitating communications, and reporting. It handles issues of allocation of resources and personnel management.

Business Recovery Program

A business recovery program is an ongoing program that ensures the prudent reduction of risks and the resumption of key business operations following a major disruption. The recovery process is based on the mitigation of the impact of the incident. It encompasses disaster planning and recovery for production, information, sales, and services in both the short term and the long term. The key goal is the restoration of productive capacity and capability.

Improve the Safeguards

If the incident could have been prevented by implementing safeguards, then those safeguards should be implemented, if they are financially justifiable, even if the vulnerability is repaired. Once a vulnerability is discovered, it is probable that other similar vulnerabilities will also be discovered. Implementing a safeguard may prevent incidents based on similar vulnerabilities that have not yet been reported.

Improving safeguards includes changes to existing safeguards and adding new ones. Safeguards can be either technical or procedural.

Review Safeguards

All safeguards should be reviewed and their configurations adjusted based on the information gained from the incident. Evaluate whether there needs to be an adjustment to security procedures to maintain the configurations of these safeguards as new vulnerabilities are discovered or new services are added.

Add Safeguards

Evaluate if there is a need for additional safeguards in locations that were not anticipated, but which the incident brought to light. Determine if there is a need for new safeguards to protect new services or new locations.

Update Detection

If additional detection or changes in existing detection would have reduced the impact of the incident, then those changes should be made. Detection is the last line of defense. If vulnerabilities are exploited and safeguards are bypassed, rapid detection of the incident is the only hope of minimizing the impact of the incident.

Configuration Changes

Make the changes to the intrusion detection systems to better detect intrusions similar to that of the current incident. Review current vulnerabilities and determine if there are changes to the intrusion detection systems that will help account for these. The alerting methods and contacts should be reviewed to be sure that they are the most effective available.

Add Detection

Evaluate the system to determine if additional detection mechanisms are warranted. The addition of new products or plug-ins for the detection system may assist in the rapid detection of incidents. These steps should be made proactively, not just in response to an incident.

Process Improvement

In all cases, when the crisis is over, it is critical that the incident be reviewed so something can be learned from the experience. This analysis must focus on the process. How was the incident discovered? How was it handled? How was it resolved? Were procedures followed? Were the procedures sufficient? What should be added/removed/changed? Who was notified? When? Were business objectives met? What were the major obstacles? How can the process be improved? If the incident happened today, what would you do differently?

As in all things, it is most important that you learn and improve. You should strive to learn how the incident happened and thereby how to prevent another similar incident from occurring. You must analyze your processes and decide what worked and what did not, where and how your procedures can be improved, where there were gaps in your policies and procedures, and whether all contingencies were covered in this case.

Most businesses will want a financial analysis covering how much this incident cost the company in physical losses, the cost to restore data, and the losses of revenue due to downtime. In some cases, this will be a complete business impact analysis.

Implement Changes

The last step to take in this process is to make the changes to your security policy. Be sure to inform members of your organization as to the changes that have been made and how that may affect them.

Postmortem Documentation

Possibly the most important step following a security incident (and certainly one of the least done) is the process of writing the security incident postmortem. Postmortem follow-up requires documentation of the incident as well as reports for specific audiences, such as management and emergency response teams. These reports will be used to adjust the level of security that is implemented.

This report is crucial for bringing all the issues together. It is a chance to review the incident calmly, after the crisis has subsided, bringing together the views and insights from all parties involved to create a single, consistent description of the incident for all those who have a need to know.

This report is needed if any follow-up actions are going to be taken against the perpetrator. If the actions are warranted, this report will serve as the foundation of the prosecution. If the actions are disciplinary, management will need this report to determine the severity of the punishment. The report has three parts: the time line, the technical summary, and the managerial summary.

- The **time line** provides a details summary of the events as they occured. It illustrates the relationship in time of the attack and the response to the attack.

- The **technical summary** is fundamental to improving processes and creating best practices. This summary can be shared with other technical groups within the organization to educate them and increase the awareness of security issues throughout the company.

- The **managerial summary** gives management the insight needed to understand the size and scope of the incident and its impact. This knowledge is crucial to the process of making sound business decisions about the need for security, especially as it relates to budgets and personnel.

Follow-up Communication

Follow-up communication is as critical to the perception of the incident as any other aspect. Follow-ups should be handled by those individuals who have been identified to coordinate with outside organizations. These may include affected partners, emergency response personnel, the news media, and law enforcement.

News Media

If the incident is made public, the channel of communication to the news media is paramount to the public perception of the incident. Only a designated spokesperson with experience in handling the media should speak to reporters — preferably the chief public relations officer of the organization.

Glossary

acceptable use policy

A policy that describes the appropriate and inappropriate behavior of users on a system, spelling out the rights and responsibilities of all parties involved.

access

The method by which a user is able to utilize an information resource.

access control

The physical or logical safeguards that prevent unauthorized access to information resources

access control list (ACL)

A method of discretionary access that utilizes a list of users and permissions to determine access rights to a resource.

accountability

The ability to associate users with their actions.

accuracy

The quality of information which is dependent on the quality of the source of the information and the quality of the handling of the information.

administration

The process of managing and maintaining the information systems.

ARP — address resolution protocol

A protocol for translating between IP addresses and MAC-layer addresses in an Ethernet. It was defined in RFC 826.

ArpaNet — Advanced Research Project Administration Network.

A U.S. Department of Defense project designed as a redundant wide area network (WAN) capable of surviving a nuclear war. It was a precursor of the Internet.

attacker

A person who attempts to penetrate a computer system's security controls.

authentication

The process of correctly identifying a user as the person he presents himself to be.

authorization

A capability assigned to a user account by administrators that allows the user certain privileges. A privilege allows you to perform an action; an authorization gives you privileges.

availability

The ability of a resource to be utilized..

awareness

The process of educating users on the use of information security features, their importance, and how to spot and report misuse.

back door

An undocumented software feature that allows a user to gain access or privileges through its use. These features may be a software bug or something that was added by a programmer during development that was not removed when it was put into production. Generally back doors are put into the system by hackers to help facilitate their hacking.

BSD — Berkeley Software Distribution

The major UNIX variant created at the University of California at Berkeley.

business impact analysis
An evaluation of the business ramifications to the organization caused by a security incident.

business resumption program
A plan designed to minimize the unavailability of business processes.

cache
A small area of memory or disk holding recently accessed data, designed to speed up further access.

Caller ID
A method of identifying the source of incoming telephone communications.

change management
The process of controlling and tracking the modifications made to a system.

checksum
A mathematical algorithm that creates a unique numerical value for a unique input, used to validate the contents of a file.

client
A process that uses the resources of a server.

client / server
A computing model that divides the processing requirements between both the user's computer (the client) and the host (the server system.)

Computer Fraud and Abuse Act
The first comprehensive federal anti-hacking law, passed in 1986. It primarily protects the computers of the U.S. government.

confidentiality
The requirement to preserve the secrecy or privacy of information, so that only those authorized to have knowledge of it actually do so.

connection hiding
A process that removes evidence of a user's access to a system.

connection laundering

A process of connecting into and then out of a system so that the actual origin of the connection is unavailable from the target system.

data diddling

False data entry, changing data before or during their input into a system.

daemon

A process running in the background performing some service for other programs.

denial of services

A type of hacker attack which makes it difficult for valid users to access the computer.

dialback

A method by which a system is set up to call back the number from which an incoming call was placed.

dial-up security

A UNIX security feature which asks the user for two passwords: first, the user's password and second, a password based on the user's default shell. Although referred to as dial-up, it can be applied to any terminal or modem port on a port-by-port basis.

digital signature

A cryptographic means of uniquely identifying the sender of a message that can be used by the recipient to confirm the authenticity of the message. It is often implemented as a variation of public key cryptography.

discretionary access control

An access control in which an "owner" of a resource can define who else can access the resource. Usually, there are no restrictions on to whom the owner can grant access or the kind of access granted. The traditional UNIX mode bits and the access control lists are examples of discretionary access control.

DNS — Domain Name Services

A hierarchical naming system that allows each domain or subdomain to be divided into smaller subdomains, thereby requiring that a system name be unique only within its specific subdomain.

due care

The assurance that all reasonable and prudent precautions have been taken in the handling of a company's resources.

dumpster diving

The process of scavenging through materials that have been thrown away in order to find information.

e-mail

A means of exchanging messages through a network. E-mail can include attachments which can contain images, sounds, and programs — any electronic data.

encryption

The process of mathematically converting information into a form such that the original information cannot be restored without the use of a specific unique key.

fail over system

A secondary system which will assume the roles of the primary system in the event of a failure.

finger

A UNIX command that provides information about users, and can also be used to retrieve the .plan and .project files from a user's home directory.

firewall

A firewall is used on some networks to provide added security by blocking access to certain services in the private network from the public network.

FTP — File Transfer Protocol

A protocol used to transfer files between systems over a network.

GECOS

The personal information field in the UNIX password file. Originally added to the password file to facilitate print spooling from some early UNIX systems at Bell Labs to Honeywell GCOS machines.

group

A collection of users to which common authorizations can be assigned.

hackers

People who exploit known vulnerabilities in security systems. Hackers can range from students hacking for fun and intellectual challenge to professionals paid to break into systems for a specific reason.

identification

The process of presenting an identifier to an information system.

identifier

That which is used to uniquely represent a specific user.

IETF — Internet Engineering Task Force

The protocol engineering and development arm of the Internet.

in-band configuration

The use of the same connection to manage a device as the connection that the device controls.

information resource

Any of the processes or systems that contain, process, or utilize information and the information itself.

info-terrorism

An act of terrorism that is carried out through the use of computer systems.

integrity

The assurance of accuracy, completeness, and performance according to specifications.

internet

A group of interconnected networks. These networks can be private or public networks and need not be connected to the Internet.

Internet

A loose confederation of networks around the world that grew out of the U.S. Government ARPAnet project, and is specifically designed to have no central governing authority. The networks that make up the Internet are connected through several backbone networks. The primary domains of the Internet are com, net, mil, edu, gov, and org (which refer to commercial, network, military, education, government, and organization) and all of the 2-character country identifiers.

internet daemon

The primary daemon that controls communication over the network.

Internet time

An expression that reflects that time moves faster on the Internet. Due to the limited costs of entry, business can rapidly appear on the Internet and can rapidly change their tactics, so survival depends on the ability to react and change.

IP — internet protocol

A network protocol that uses internet addressing to route packets.

IP addressing

A hierarchical methodology of assigning unique addresses to all the systems attached to an internet. The first part of the address is a network address, the last part is the system address.

IP routing

The process of deciding where to send a message based on the IP address.

IP spoofing

The process of falsifying address information in a network packet to cause it to be misrouted, e.g., a hacker sends messages to a computer with an IP address indicating that the message is coming from a trusted source.

Kerberos

A process of providing secure authentication by use of a trusted third party.

LAN — Local Area Network

A network usually contained within one or more buildings, as opposed to a WAN.

least privilege

The security philosophy of granting the minimum privileges for the minimum amount of time to allow the user to complete the required task.

logic bomb

Code hidden in an application that causes it to perform some destructive activity when specific criteria are met.

login spoof

A program that pretends to be the login program so that it can capture login IDs and passwords.

MAC Address

The low-level address assigned to a device on an ethernet. MAC addresses are translated to IP addresses via ARP.

magic cookie

A piece of information passed between programs which serves as an identifier to allow the user to perform a given operation.

mandatory access control

An access control in which access is based on criteria defined by system administrators, and not generally definable by the users of a data object.

masquerading

One person uses the identity of another to gain access to a computer.

MIME — Multipurpose Internet Mail Extensions

A protocol for sending sound, graphics, and other binary data as attachments to mail messages.

mirrored disks

The complete replication of information onto multiple disks to increase availability in case of a hardware failure.

modem

Shorthand for MODulator/DEModulator. A modem allows the transmission of digital information over an analog phone line.

NTP — Network Time Protocol

A network protocol used to synchronize computer system clocks.

newsgroup

A message area in Usenet News. Each newsgroup can be either "moderated," with only postings approved by a moderator publicly posted, or "unmoderated," where all messages are distributed to the newsgroup immediately.

NFS — Network File System

One method of sharing files across a LAN or through the Internet.

NNTP — Network News Transfer Protocol

A system for reading and writing Usenet News articles across a network. This service is defined by RFC number 977.

Orange Book (TCSEC)

A U.S. Department of Defense standard that has become the principal criterion for the design of highly secure computer operating systems. The TCSEC is not a software specification, but rather a criterion intended to guide a team of evaluators in affixing a "security grade" to a particular computer system. In the order of increasing complexity, these grades are: C1, C2, B1, B2, B3, and A1. It is often called the "Orange Book" because its cover is orange. The National Computer Security Center performs evaluations under TCSEC and issues companion books that apply to other security areas, such as networking.

out-of-band configuration

The use of a communication path to configure a network device which is not the communication path that the network device controls.

parasite

Software that attaches itself to a program to utilize the resources of the host program.

password sniffing

The process of monitoring a network to obtain identification and authentication information.

permissions

Authorization attributes assigned to a resource that indicate what privileges are granted to which users.

phone phreak

A person who utilizes technology to illegally access the telephone system.

piggybacking

Following an authorized person through a locked door, either a physical one or a computer's security firewall.

PIN — Personal Identification Number

A password that is used with a physical card, together producing stronger authentication.

policy

A written definition of a security standard.

practice

A specific performed activity that supports a security procedure.

privileges

The rights granted to a user that define what the user can do with the resource.

procedure

A specific activity that supports a security policy.

public key encryption

An cryptographic method that uses two keys so that whatever is encrypted with one key can be decrypted only with the other. It can be used for both security and digital signatures.

race condition

The condition where two or more processes require the same unique resource.

RAID disks

A method of distributing information across multiple disk drives to eliminate data loss from a single disk drive failure.

rainbow series

A group of government publications that detail processes and standards in computer security whose colorful covers have inspired this name.

redundancy

The use of multiple systems to minimize unavailability.

RFC (Request for Comments)

A broad range of notes covering a variety of topics related to the Internet. RFCs are handled by the IETF and are archived at several sites.

salami slicing

The process of accumulating partial cents, which are the result of rounding to a whole cent, into an account.

security by obscurity

The theory that if no one knows about a security flaw, then no one will abuse it, and if no one is told about the flaw, he will not find it on his own.

security perimeter

A border that defines what is, and what is not, controlled by a specific security policy.

set-user-on-exec (setUID)

A UNIX file permission that indicates that the program will run as if it were run by the defined user.

set-group-on-exec (setGID)

A UNIX file permission that indicates that the program will run with as if it were run by the defined group.

server

A process which provides information or other services to its clients. Most network protocols are client / server based.

shell

One of several command line interfaces available on UNIX machines. Some common shells include Bourne shell, ksh, and tcsh.

SLIP — Serial Line Internet Protocol

A serial packet protocol used to connect a remote computer to the Internet using modems or direct serial lines. SLIP requires an Internet provider with special SLIP accounts.

smart card

A physical authentication device used in conjunction with a password to give greater assurance of authentication.

smart terminal

A terminal that has some local memory and processing that can be accessed programmatically.

SMTP — Simple Mail Transport Protocol

A protocol which defines a common mechanism for exchanging mail across a network. This protocol is described in RFC number 821. Usually SMTP is incorporated in a mail transport agent.

snooper

A program that listens to a network to gather information.

social engineering

The process of gathering information from people by use of deception and obfuscation. Someone manipulates others into revealing information that can be used to steal data, such as telling a help desk to reset the password of a stolen ID.

software piracy

Duplicating computer programs in violation of copyright law.

spamming

Mass mailing of unsolicited e-mail messages.

spoof

A program that impersonates another program to gather information.

sticky bit

The UNIX permission bit set on a directory used to keep the program in memory after it completes, so that it will be ready for its next invocation. It is also used on directories to limit the ability to delete a file in the directory to the owner of the file.

superhacker

The possibly mythical hacker whose skill allows him to move freely from system to system and network to network without detection.

superuser

A user who is granted all authorizations. On UNIX systems, this user is generally called "root."

SYSV — System V

A commercial version of UNIX from AT&T.

TCP — Transmission Control Protocol

The networking protocol that controls packet synchronization.

TCP/IP — Transmission Control Protocol/Internet Protocol

The networking standard commonly used on the Internet.

TFTP — Trivial File Transfer Protocol

A network protocol that allows unauthenticated transfer of files.

threat

That which if unchecked will cause a loss to the organization.

trap doors

A quick way into a program, bypassing security.

Trojan horse

A program that appears to be a useful program, but in reality performs malicious acts.

trusted advisor

A hacker who used his position and knowledge to his advantage by appearing to be trustworthy.

trusted hosts

A process by which a group of hosts can share a single authentication, so that once a user is authenticated onto one host in the trusted group, he can access all the hosts without having to authenticate himself again.

Usenet News

A network of systems that exchange articles using the Internet, UUCP, and other methods to establish public message conferences on some or all of over 6,000 topics or "news groups."

user

Any entity that utilizes information resources. A user can be an individual, a software program, a computer system, a network, etc.

UUCP

An acronym for UNIX to UNIX CoPy, UUCP is a protocol used for the store-and-forward exchange of mail, Usenet News, and other files, usually over a modem.

virus

A program that replicates itself by embedding a copy of itself in other programs.

vulnerability

A weakness that can be utilized to gain an inappropriate level of access or privileges with an information resource.

WAN

Acronym for Wide Area Network, which is generally a network connecting several physically distant locations, as opposed to a LAN. The Internet is an example of a worldwide WAN.

Worm

A program that makes its way across a network, copying itself as it goes.

wrapper program

A program used to augment another program without requiring reconstruction of the original program.

Index

Files

free
subscription

Want to know about new products, services and solutions from Hewlett-Packard Company — as soon as they're invented?

Need information about new HP services to help you implement new or existing products?

Looking for HP's newest solution to a specific challenge in your business?

inview features the latest from HP!

inview

4 easy ways to subscribe, and it's FREE:

- **fax** complete and fax the form below to (651) 430-3388, or

- **online** sign up online at www.hp.com/go/inview, or

- **email** complete the information below and send to hporders@earthlink.net, or

- **mail** complete and mail the form below to:

Twin Cities Fulfillment Center
Hewlett-Packard Company
P.O. Box 408
Stillwater, MN 55082

reply now and don't miss an issue!

name	title
company	dept./mail stop
address	
city	state zip
email signature	date

please indicate your industry below:

- ☐ accounting
- ☐ education
- ☐ financial services
- ☐ government
- ☐ healthcare/medical
- ☐ legal
- ☐ manufacturing
- ☐ publishing/printing
- ☐ online services
- ☐ real estate
- ☐ retail/wholesale distrib
- ☐ technical
- ☐ telecommunications
- ☐ transport and travel
- ☐ utilities
- ☐ other: _____

HP's world-class education and training offers hands on education solutions including:

- Linux
- HP-UX System and Network Administration
- Advanced HP-UX System Administration
- IT Service Management using advanced Internet technologies
- Microsoft Windows NT/2000
- Internet/Intranet
- MPE/iX
- Database Administration
- Software Development

HP's new IT Professional Certification program provides rigorous technical qualification for specific IT job roles including HP-UX System Administration, Network Management, Unix/NT Servers and Applications Management, and IT Service Management.

become hp certified

http://education.hp.com

LICENSE AGREEMENT AND LIMITED WARRANTY

READ THE FOLLOWING TERMS AND CONDITIONS CAREFULLY BEFORE OPENING THIS SOFTWARE MEDIA PACKAGE. THIS LEGAL DOCUMENT IS AN AGREEMENT BETWEEN YOU AND PRENTICE-HALL, INC. (THE "COMPANY"). BY OPENING THIS SEALED SOFTWARE MEDIA PACKAGE, YOU ARE AGREEING TO BE BOUND BY THESE TERMS AND CONDITIONS. IF YOU DO NOT AGREE WITH THESE TERMS AND CONDITIONS, DO NOT OPEN THE SOFTWARE MEDIA PACKAGE. PROMPTLY RETURN THE UNOPENED SOFTWARE MEDIA PACKAGE AND ALL ACCOMPANYING ITEMS TO THE PLACE YOU OBTAINED THEM FOR A FULL REFUND OF ANY SUMS YOU HAVE PAID.

1.   **GRANT OF LICENSE:** In consideration of your payment of the license fee, which is part of the price you paid for this product, and your agreement to abide by the terms and conditions of this Agreement, the Company grants to you a nonexclusive right to use and display the copy of the enclosed software program (hereinafter the "SOFTWARE") on a single computer (i.e., with a single CPU) at a single location so long as you comply with the terms of this Agreement. The Company reserves all rights not expressly granted to you under this Agreement.

2.   **OWNERSHIP OF SOFTWARE:** You own only the magnetic or physical media (the enclosed software media) on which the SOFTWARE is recorded or fixed, but the Company retains all the rights, title, and ownership to the SOFTWARE recorded on the original software media copy(ies) and all subsequent copies of the SOFTWARE, regardless of the form or media on which the original or other copies may exist. This license is not a sale of the original SOFTWARE or any copy to you.

3.   **COPY RESTRICTIONS:** This SOFTWARE and the accompanying printed materials and user manual (the "Documentation") are the subject of copyright. You may not copy the Documentation or the SOFTWARE, except that you may make a single copy of the SOFTWARE for backup or archival purposes only. You may be held legally responsible for any copying or copyright infringement which is caused or encouraged by your failure to abide by the terms of this restriction.

4.   **USE RESTRICTIONS:** You may not network the SOFTWARE or otherwise use it on more than one computer or computer terminal at the same time. You may physically transfer the SOFTWARE from one computer to another provided that the SOFTWARE is used on only one computer at a time. You may not distribute copies of the SOFTWARE or Documentation to others. You may not reverse engineer, disassemble, decompile, modify, adapt, translate, or create derivative works based on the SOFTWARE or the Documentation without the prior written consent of the Company.

5.   **TRANSFER RESTRICTIONS:** The enclosed SOFTWARE is licensed only to you and may not be transferred to any one else without the prior written consent of the Company. Any unauthorized transfer of the SOFTWARE shall result in the immediate termination of this Agreement.

6.   **TERMINATION:** This license is effective until terminated. This license will terminate automatically without notice from the Company and become null and void if you fail to comply with any provisions or limitations of this license. Upon termination, you shall destroy the Documentation and all copies of the SOFTWARE. All provisions of this Agreement as to warranties, limitation of liability, remedies or damages, and our ownership rights shall survive termination.

7.   **MISCELLANEOUS:** This Agreement shall be construed in accordance with the laws of the United States of America and the State of New York and shall benefit the Company, its affiliates, and assignees.

8.   **LIMITED WARRANTY AND DISCLAIMER OF WARRANTY:** The Company warrants that the SOFTWARE, when properly used in accordance with the Documentation, will operate in substantial conformity with the description of the SOFTWARE set forth in the Documentation. The Company does not warrant that the SOFTWARE will meet your requirements or that the operation of the SOFTWARE will be uninterrupted or error-free. The Company warrants that the media on which the SOFTWARE is delivered shall be free from defects in materials and workmanship under normal use for a period of thirty (30) days from the date of your purchase. Your only remedy and the Company's only obligation under these limited warranties is, at the Company's option, return of the warranted item for a refund of any amounts paid by you or replacement of the item. Any replacement of SOFTWARE or media under the warranties shall not extend the original warranty period. The limited warranty set forth above shall not apply to any SOFTWARE which the Company determines in good faith has been subject to misuse, neglect, improper installation, repair, alteration, or damage by you. EXCEPT FOR THE EXPRESSED WARRANTIES SET FORTH ABOVE, THE COMPANY

DISCLAIMS ALL WARRANTIES, EXPRESS OR IMPLIED, INCLUDING WITHOUT LIMITATION, THE IMPLIED WARRANTIES OF MERCHANTABILITY AND FITNESS FOR A PARTICULAR PURPOSE. EXCEPT FOR THE EXPRESS WARRANTY SET FORTH ABOVE, THE COMPANY DOES NOT WARRANT, GUARANTEE, OR MAKE ANY REPRESENTATION REGARDING THE USE OR THE RESULTS OF THE USE OF THE SOFTWARE IN TERMS OF ITS CORRECTNESS, ACCURACY, RELIABILITY, CURRENTNESS, OR OTHERWISE.

IN NO EVENT, SHALL THE COMPANY OR ITS EMPLOYEES, AGENTS, SUPPLIERS, OR CONTRACTORS BE LIABLE FOR ANY INCIDENTAL, INDIRECT, SPECIAL, OR CONSEQUENTIAL DAMAGES ARISING OUT OF OR IN CONNECTION WITH THE LICENSE GRANTED UNDER THIS AGREEMENT, OR FOR LOSS OF USE, LOSS OF DATA, LOSS OF INCOME OR PROFIT, OR OTHER LOSSES, SUSTAINED AS A RESULT OF INJURY TO ANY PERSON, OR LOSS OF OR DAMAGE TO PROPERTY, OR CLAIMS OF THIRD PARTIES, EVEN IF THE COMPANY OR AN AUTHORIZED REPRESENTATIVE OF THE COMPANY HAS BEEN ADVISED OF THE POSSIBILITY OF SUCH DAMAGES. IN NO EVENT SHALL LIABILITY OF THE COMPANY FOR DAMAGES WITH RESPECT TO THE SOFTWARE EXCEED THE AMOUNTS ACTUALLY PAID BY YOU, IF ANY, FOR THE SOFTWARE.

SOME JURISDICTIONS DO NOT ALLOW THE LIMITATION OF IMPLIED WARRANTIES OR LIABILITY FOR INCIDENTAL, INDIRECT, SPECIAL, OR CONSEQUENTIAL DAMAGES, SO THE ABOVE LIMITATIONS MAY NOT ALWAYS APPLY. THE WARRANTIES IN THIS AGREEMENT GIVE YOU SPECIFIC LEGAL RIGHTS AND YOU MAY ALSO HAVE OTHER RIGHTS WHICH VARY IN ACCORDANCE WITH LOCAL LAW.

ACKNOWLEDGMENT

YOU ACKNOWLEDGE THAT YOU HAVE READ THIS AGREEMENT, UNDERSTAND IT, AND AGREE TO BE BOUND BY ITS TERMS AND CONDITIONS. YOU ALSO AGREE THAT THIS AGREEMENT IS THE COMPLETE AND EXCLUSIVE STATEMENT OF THE AGREEMENT BETWEEN YOU AND THE COMPANY AND SUPERSEDES ALL PROPOSALS OR PRIOR AGREEMENTS, ORAL, OR WRITTEN, AND ANY OTHER COMMUNICATIONS BETWEEN YOU AND THE COMPANY OR ANY REPRESENTATIVE OF THE COMPANY RELATING TO THE SUBJECT MATTER OF THIS AGREEMENT.

Should you have any questions concerning this Agreement or if you wish to contact the Company for any reason, please contact in writing at the address below.

Robin Short
Prentice Hall PTR
One Lake Street
Upper Saddle River, New Jersey 07458

About the CD-ROM

The information on the CD-ROM is presented in hypertext format and should be viewed with a Web browser that supports HTML 4. It contains a variety of software packages and information archives which assists in securing a system and keeping it secure, as well as monitoring the actions of a hacker.

Accessing the CD-ROM

The CD-ROM is an ISO9660-XA format which enables Jouliet-style descriptive long file names. The CD-ROM will be automounted and autostarted on systems which support this. If your Linux system is not configured to automount the CD-ROM, then you will have to mount the CD-ROM. Depending on configuration this may be available to all users or it may require the superuser to issue the mount command. HP-UX requires that only the superuser can mount disk volumes. The "cdcase" option is *required* on HP-UX. The user will need to execute the following command, substituting the correct device file and mount point directory, to mount the CD-ROM:

```
mount -r -o cdcase [device file] [mount point]
```

For example:

```
mount -r -o cdcase /dev/cdrom /mnt/cdrom
```

You will then need to invoke a web browser to read the index.html file. The following command will display the index.

```
netscape /mnt/cdrom/index.html
```

Using the CD-ROM

The CD-ROM presents a trail guide to security resources including tools, information, and organizations which can help you secure your systems. When used on an Internet connected system it enables you to access all the online sites which contain security information as well as accessing the information and tools stored on the CD-ROM.

Tools

A variety of tools have been made available on the CD-ROM. These software tools include programs that check the quality of security on the system, or proactively attempt to keep the system secure, or are logging tools that monitor the system, as well as those that test a security problem by trying to exploit a security issue.

The tools are provided as-is and are for use at your own risk. No effort has been taken to verify that the software performs as the authors claim.

Much of the included code is copyrighted and can only be used within the bounds of the copyright. Be sure to read the respective files in each of the archives to understand these limitations before using any of the software included on this CD-ROM.

Information

The CD-ROM contains a variety of information which is useful in creating and maintaining a secure system. These include government publications, such as *The Rainbow Series,* public standards, such as *The Common Criteria,* the IETF's Request for Comments, and some mailing list archives.

In addition to the information which is included on the CD-ROM, the CD-ROM provides a number of links to websites of organizations which focus on computer security and law enforcement, UNIX and Linux system vendors, and security portals. There are links to newsgroups, mailing lists and both printed and online security magazines.

Permission

Be sure to have authorization to run any security tool on a system before doing so. Not doing so may put you in violation of security policies or in some cases in violation of the law. The information and software on the CD-ROM is for educational purposes. While the information presented is believed to be accurate, please verify it and test it in a controlled environment.